NEW EUROPE, NEW GERMANY, OLD FOREIGN POLICY?

BOOKS OF RELATED INTEREST

NEW EUROPE, NEW GERMANY, OLD FOREIGN POLICY?

German Foreign Policy Since Unification

Editor

Douglas Webber

FRANK CASS
LONDON • PORTLAND, OR

First published in 2001 in Great Britain by
FRANK CASS AND COMPANY LIMITED
Crown House,
47 Chase Side, Southgate,
London N14 5BP, England

and in the United States of America by
FRANK CASS
c/o ISBS
5824 N.E. Hassalo Street,
Portland, Oregon 927213-3640

Website: *www.frankcass.com*

British Library Cataloguing in Publication Data

New Europe, new Germany, old foreign policy? : German
  foreign policy since unification
  1.Germany – Foreign relations – 1990 –
  I.Webber, Douglas
  327.4'3

ISBN 0 7146 5172 9 (hb)
ISBN 0 7146 8185 7 (pb)

Library of Congress Cataloging-in-Publication Data

New Europe, new Germany, old foreign policy? : German foreign policy
since unification / editor, Douglas Webber.
    p. cm
  Includes bibliographical references and index.
  ISBN 0-7146-5172-9 – ISBN 0-7146-8185-7
  1. Germany–Foreign relations–1990- . 2. National
security–Germany. 3. Germany–Military policy. 4. Germany–Foreign
relations–Europe. 5. Europe–Foreign relations–Germany. I.
Webber, Douglas.
  DD290.3 .N48 2001
  327.43–dc21   2001028388

This group of studies first appeared in a Special Issue of *German Politics*,
(ISSN 0964-4008), Vol.10, No.1 (April 2001), [New Europe, New Germany, Old
Foreign Policy? German Foreign Policy Since Unification].

Printed in Great Britain by Antony Rowe Ltd., Chippenham, Wilts.

Contents

Introduction: German European and Foreign Policy Before and After Unification

DOUGLAS WEBBER

In early 1990, not long after the fall of the Berlin Wall, the well-known American political scientist, David Calleo, author of a standard work on the 'German problem' before the Second World War, came out strongly against the prospect of German reunification. He wrote:

> A resurrected Bismarckian Empire would have the same effect as the return of the monster Frankenstein. Anything which even looked like it would simply revive the old pattern of continental rivalry: the Russian–French alliance from the time before the First World War or the Anglo-French alliance of the inter-war years. German unity, so constructed, would be incompatible with European unity. It would be as if nobody had drawn the lessons from a century-long European tragedy.[1]

At the time he was writing, Calleo did not know that German unity would be achieved only ten months later and therefore could not take into account the conditions under which unification took place. It is impossible to say whether the pessimistic and sombre thrust of his analysis would have been different if he had foreseen the external terms of reunification. In any event, however, the second united Germany was not saddled with the same 'birth defects' as the first:

- It was not forged by 'blood and iron', but rather by a peaceful, democratic revolution;
- It was not a *fait accompli*, but rather was negotiated and agreed with the four Second World War allies (the US, the Soviet Union, France and Britain);
- It was not built on territorial conquest & acquisition, such that peaceful and stable relations with an important neighbouring state – namely France – were precluded, but rather renounced territorial claims on other states;
- It was not an authoritarian monarchy, but a democratic republic;
- It was not an unconstrained, autonomous actor in international affairs, but was tightly integrated into numerous alliances and regional and

Douglas Webber, INSEAD, Singapore/Fontainebleau

international organisations, such as the European Union (EU) and the NATO (North Atlantic Treaty Organisation).

The fears expressed by Calleo concerning the implications of German unity were nonetheless widely shared by political leaders in Europe in late 1989 and 1990. A good indicator of the coolness, if not indeed iciness, with which most member states of the EU viewed this prospect was the atmosphere and tone of discussion at the two meetings of the European Council (comprising the heads of government of the member states) held in Paris and in Strasbourg in November and December 1989. Kohl described the atmosphere at the Strasbourg summit as the most hostile he had ever encountered in this setting.[2]

Only the Spanish and Irish prime ministers, Felipe Gonzalez and Charles Haughey respectively, supported the idea of German unification without any 'ifs and buts'.[3] According to Kohl, Belgium and Luxembourg posed 'no problems',[4] but several other leaders, including the Dutch and Italian prime ministers and most notably the British Prime Minister Margaret Thatcher, openly stated their worries and misgivings, not to say hostility.[5] Her worries about the emergence of a united Germany and the demise of the Cold War order in Europe seem also to have been shared to a large extent by the French President, Francois Mitterrand. According to Thatcher, he was 'still more concerned than I was'.[6] The French President's spontaneous reaction, in the tradition of pre-Second World War French diplomacy, seems to have been to co-operate with Britain and the Soviet Union to try, if possible, to avert German unification. At the end of November 1989, he warned the German Foreign Minister Genscher darkly of the possible re-emergence of the pre-First World War state system in Europe, that is to say, of the revival of a Franco-Russian coalition against Germany, and the recurrence of war.[7]

Numerous reactions to the prospect of German reunification thus seemed to bear out Calleo's expectation that German unity would precipitate a revival of pre-Second World War balance-of-power politics, with other European powers banding together to 'balance' and contain the actual or prospective power of a single German state.

MAIN TRAITS OF GERMAN EUROPEAN AND FOREIGN POLICY, 1949–90

Clearly, most other European political leaders at the time expected – and were fearful – that a united Germany would pursue different, even very different European and foreign policies to those pursued between 1949 and 1990 by the governments of the old Federal Republic.

What were the principal traits of Bonn's European and foreign policies during the Cold War? First, Bonn's foreign policy was distinguished by its emphatically *Western orientation*. This policy trait was fixed by the first post-Second World War Chancellor and Rhinelander, Konrad Adenauer, in the 1950s. It represented a revolutionary change compared with pre-Second World War German foreign policy, which, exploiting the country's location at the geographical centre of Europe, frequently aimed to maximise German autonomy and influence by oscillating or 'see-sawing', as the occasion required, between East and West (*Schaukelpolitik*).

The principal manifestation of Adenauer's policy of Western integration was Germany's entry and participation in all the major West European and North Atlantic alliances and regional organisations, first and foremost the European Community and NATO. It may be argued that Adenauer simply made a virtue of a necessity, in as far as the Western allies (US, France and Britain) would not have permitted the new West German state to pursue any other kind of foreign policy. However, this would be to overlook the strength of resistance to Adenauer's Western policy in Germany in the 1950s, when the idea that Germany could play a bridging role between East and West was still popular and it was widely feared that the Federal Republic's ever closer integration into the West would diminish the prospects of German reunification.

Adenauer's Western integration policy was complemented later, of course, by Willy Brandt's *Ostpolitik* in the first half of the 1970s. However, Brandt's *Ostpolitik* was pursued from a firm anchorage in the West: rather than being an alternative to or rival of Western integration policy, *Ostpolitik* built on this policy and was facilitated by it, to the extent that *Ostpolitik* would have aroused much greater distrust, suspicion and opposition among its allies if the Federal Republic had not already been tightly integrated into the West. Also fiercely contested domestically at the time it was launched, *Ostpolitik* became a component of the foreign policy consensus in the Federal Republic just like the Western integration policy, but it did not replace, rather it was subordinated to, this policy.

Second, Bonn's foreign policy was distinguished by its *strong multilateral orientation*, which was the 'other side of the coin' of its *Westpolitik*. This policy trait had two aspects: first, it entailed a high level of preparedness to concede national decision-making competences to international or supranational organisations, such as the European Community; second, it involved renouncing independent initiatives on important foreign policy issues in favour of joint action with other, allied states. This strand runs right through the history of Federal German foreign policy from Adenauer's support for the Schuman Plan for a European Coal and Steel Community in 1950 to Kohl's for a single European currency in the 1990s. To the extent that, as an occupied country, the Federal Republic was transferring 'sovereignty' that it did not possess at the time, the choice in favour of ceding important powers to regional or international organisations was easier for Bonn than for other large European states. Likewise, acting jointly rather than alone on important foreign policy issues avoided the risk of provoking a revival of collective efforts to contain Germany and of isolating Germany diplomatically.

Indeed, one might argue that Bonn's multilateralist foreign policy orientation, by increasing other states' trust in the Federal Republic, ultimately – and paradoxically – facilitated German reunification in two senses. First, it reduced fears among other European states that the united Germany would strive to become a hegemonic power on the continent. Second, it contributed to the evolution of strong European regional organisations, first and foremost the European Community, which was strengthened at the moment of unification so as to make German unity more acceptable to other European states than it otherwise would have been.

This is not to say, however, that Bonn's foreign policy was conceived primarily with a view to achieving German reunification via a multilateralist deviation. For this, other motives were more important. First, in the context of the Cold War, given its geographic location and its incapacity to defend itself against the Communist bloc in the event of war, the Federal Republic had a powerful interest, more powerful arguably than that of any other state, in any policies that enhanced the economic, political and military unity of the West. Second, in Adenauer's era at least, multilateralism was an indispensable adjunct of the policy of Western integration, as the more strongly the Federal Republic was anchored in the West through its membership in all manner of regional organisations, the more difficult it would be for any government to the future to reverse this choice.

Bonn's multilateralist foreign policy orientation was complemented by the formation of two fundamental bilateral relationships, the one with the United States and the other with France, the pre-eminent member states of NATO and the European Community respectively. The German–American relationship was forged in the crucible of the Cold War, beginning with the Berlin Blockade, and was motivated on the German side by the knowledge that the United States – and only the United States – could guarantee the Federal Republic's military security *vis-à-vis* the Communist bloc. The Franco-German relationship, for its part, was initiallly conceived by both sides as a vehicle for preventing the other from taking the 'road to Moscow', as both France and Germany had done occasionally in the past. The Bonn–Paris 'tandem' or 'axis', as it became known, also provided the European integration process with a momentum that would have been difficult to generate otherwise, given the difficulties of co-ordinating and reconciling the positions of six and later nine, 12, and now 15 member states.[8] Given the importance of these two key bilateral relationships, not to have to choose between Washington and Paris became an axiom of Bonn's foreign policy.[9]

The third principal trait of the old Federal Republic's foreign policy was its *civilian* character. Bonn renounced the use of military force as an instrument of foreign policy or at least of its *own* foreign policy. This orientation was facilitated by the fact that Bonn basically imported its security from the United States. It was symbolised by and anchored in articles of the Basic Law banning wars of aggression and, at least according to the dominant interpretation before unification, also banning German participation in military interventions beyond the NATO area. It is underlined by the fact that, between the foundation of the Federal Republic in 1949 and German unification, not a single soldier of the German Bundeswehr fired a shot in action. Like its Western and multilateral orientation, the civilian character of German foreign policy also represented an important source of reassurance for other (West) European states concerning the benevolence of Bonn's foreign policy intentions.

The fourth and final important trait of Bonn's pre-unification foreign policy was its *Euro-centrism*. Again, in contrast to traditional Great Powers, the Federal Republic did not really have a global strategy or conception of its interests, except in as far as, given its high level of trade dependence, it had an interest, which it pursued in and via the European Community, in the maintenance and promotion of free international trade. Given the Cold War, the division of Germany, and Germany's location at the front line of the East–West conflict in Europe, and unencumbered as it was by overseas territories and colonies or former colonies, the overwhelming focus of German foreign policy was on issues very 'close to home', much according to the Bismarck's (1888) motto: 'My map of Africa lies in Europe. Here is Russia and here … is France, and we are in the middle; this is my map of Africa.'[10]

POST-UNIFICATION GERMAN EUROPEAN AND FOREIGN POLICY: RIVAL THEORETICAL PERSPECTIVES

German unification, the end of the Cold War, and the disintegration of the Communist bloc as well as of the Soviet Union itself raised questions concerning all four of these traits of pre-1990 Bonn European and foreign policies:

1. With the end of the Cold War, the principal rationale for the Western orientation of pre-1990 German foreign policy arguably disappeared.

Would the united Germany succumb afresh to the *Drang nach Osten* ('compulsion to go eastwards') sometimes identified as a centuries-old tradition in German history, with all that this implies for the future of the EU, NATO, and so on?

2. With the end of the Cold War and the restoration of German unity *and* sovereignty, would not the 'new' Germany (like France and Britain) be less enthusiastic about ceding decision-making competences to international organisations and less reluctant to act unilaterally in international affairs, as it appeared to be when recognising Slovenia and Croatia as independent states in 1991?

3. The disintegration of the Warsaw Pact and the security threat posed by the armed forces of the Communist bloc cast a question mark over the future of NATO. If it too disintegrated and Germany were affected by instability and violence in Central and Eastern Europe, would it not be tempted to assume the role of the guarantor of regional order, thereby shedding its Cold War identity as a 'civilian power'?[11] In the event of a possible US military withdrawal from Europe, might it not even want to develop its own nuclear weapons to protect itself against the possibility of nuclear 'blackmail', for example, by Russia?

4. With arguably less need for it to be concerned about threats to its security from its immediate environment, would not the united Germany aspire to play a more active worldwide political role – a role that would be more commensurate with its importance in the world economic and monetary affairs and that could be expressed, for example, by its assumption of a seat in the UN Security Council?

It is worth emphasising that all of the above observations rest on the assumption that changes in a country's foreign policy are brought about first and foremost by changes in its external environment. However, of the major international relations theories, only one or two identify the external environment as being the primary determinant of states' foreign policies. What predictions or insights can we derive from these theories for the likely future direction of German European and foreign policy and the prospective impact of German reunification on international relations in Europe?[12]

The oldest international relations paradigm, the *realist* one, posits, in its neo-realist guise, that a state's foreign policy behaviour is indeed shaped primarily by the structure of the international system. As this structure is essentially anarchic, in the sense that there is no world government, every state is constrained by its interest in self-preservation to maximise its own power. For realist theorists, such as the American John Mearsheimer, the Cold War, with its bipolar distribution of power, rough equality of military power between the two blocs, and mutual nuclear deterrence, was the best of all possible worlds for Europe. The end of the Cold War, by contrast, was likely to lead – via an American military withdrawal from Europe and the dissolution of the NATO – to a multipolar distribution of power, to greater unpredictability in the balance of power between competing poles, and either to a dangerous de-nuclearisation of the greater part of the Europe or to an equally dangerous process of nuclear proliferation – essentially to a restoration of the European state system of the pre-Second World War era in which 'without a common Soviet threat and without the American night watchman, West European states will begin viewing each other with greater fear and suspicion, as they did for centuries before the onset of the Cold War'.[13] In this new/old European state system, the united Germany would be much more powerful than almost all other states, other states would be bound to try to coalesce to balance German power, Germany would feel insecure and could fall prey to hyper-nationalist ideologies, and German aggression against neighbouring states such as Poland, Czechoslovakia and 'even Austria' could not be excluded.[14] In post-Cold War Europe, the united Germany, from this realist perspective, would be neither West-oriented, nor multilateralist, nor civilian, nor indeed 'civil', but rather, owing to the structure of the European state system, would behave more like pre-Second World War German governments than the old Federal Republic. The 'Frankenstein Monster' referred to by Calleo would become a reality.

In contrast to realism, the *liberal* paradigm of international relations identifies domestic politics as the primary factor determining a country's foreign policy. *Republican liberals*, for example, argue – on the basis of very strong historical evidence – that democracies do not fight each other. In their analysis, the origins of the world wars lay not in the structure of the international relations system in Europe, but in the fact that Germany was not yet a democracy in 1914 and no longer a democracy after 1933. From their perspective, the critical issue is what kind of constitution will prevail in the united Germany – as well as in other European states, for example, Russia (since the paradigm does not exclude the possibility of a democratic Germany participating in wars against non-democratic states). That is to say, will the new Federal Republic prove to be a stable democracy – and will the states of Central and Eastern Europe become stable democracies? 'Republican liberals' would be less concerned by the emergence of a multipolar distribution of power in Europe than by the growth of anti-democratic movements in Germany or the rise of authoritarian political regimes in post-Communist Central and Eastern Europe.

Some other liberal scholars of international relations – I shall call them *institutional liberals*[15] – take the survival of democracy in the Western world at least for granted and focus on the impact of domestic political decision-making structures on foreign policy patterns. In the case of the Federal Republic, they stress the implications of the pronounced fragmentation of power – between different ministries, between different parties in the federal government, between the federation and states, between the federal government and a host of para-public institutions, such as the Bundesbank, the Federal Constitutional Court, and so on. They argue that, other things being equal, the extreme dispersion of political power in the particular democratic system that developed in the old Federal Republic made it more or less impossible for Germany to formulate and implement a consistent and coherent European or foreign policy and that this constitutes a formidable obstacle to any German attempt to acquire or exercise a hegemonic role in organisations such as the EU. From this perspective, the relevant question to pose following German reunification is not whether the united Germany will be a stable democracy – this is assumed – but rather whether there will be any changes in the domestic balance of political power and structures of decision-making that will make it easier (or, for that matter, harder) for the federal government to conceive and implement a coherent, long-term-oriented foreign policy *strategy*.

A further strand of thinking in the liberal paradigm, that of *commercial liberalism*, emphasises the benevolent impact on international relations of the spread of commerce. From this perspective, ever greater mutual economic interdependence as a consequence of the expansion of international trade makes serious conflicts, including wars, between states increasingly improbable, because it would be economically counter-productive and therefore irrational for states to engage in military conflict with each other and because the growing prosperity engendered by international trade is in any case conducive to political stability. 'Commercial liberals', like institutionalist theorists of international relations, as we shall see in a moment, may attribute an important role in the promotion of international trade and political stability to regional economic blocs, such as the EU, whose rules help to ensure that member states fulfil their commitments to liberalise trade and which thus contribute to growing economic interdependence.

Although the third international relations paradigm, the *institutionalist*, shares some of the fundamental tenets of realism, its proponents hold that international organisations are capable of mitigating the otherwise anarchic character of the international system. Institutionalists argue that organisations such as the EU may promote co-operation between states and the peaceful resolution of inter-state conflicts by, for example, reducing uncertainty and increasing trust, facilitating linkages between different issues and the implementation and monitoring of common decisions, and contributing to the emergence of new, pacific norms in international relations.

For institutionalists, the compatibility of a united Germany with stable and peaceful international relations in Europe is first and foremost a function of the strength of the EU and NATO, that is to say, of their capacity to integrate Germany. The erosion and/or dissolution of these organisations would precipitate a reversion to the European state system of the pre-Second World War era; their survival or strengthening – such that Germany could not break out of these multilateral structures without incurring unacceptable economic and political costs and other European states are reassured that the new Federal Republic does not and cannot threaten their security – would perpetuate the pattern of international relations that developed in Western Europe during the Cold War and conceivably permit its extension to the East.

By and large, institutionalists are optimistic as to the future of the EU because it permits other member states to influence Germany, Germany to exercise influence and pursue its interests without alarming other members, all the member states to enhance their influence *vis-à-vis* the rest of the world, especially the US, and many member governments to implement policies at home that would otherwise be politically unfeasible.[16] If the institutionalists' optimism is vindicated, so, too, incidentally, would be the strategy of Robert Schuman, with Jean Monnet the founding father of the EU, who, when he launched the plan for the European Coal and Steel Community in 1950, did so with the explicit objective of 'creating such strong "organic" ties between the European nations and West Germany that no German government would be able to break them in the future'.[17]

In the final and youngest international relations theory, the *constructivist*, states' foreign policies are moulded primarily neither by the structure of the international system, nor by the nature or organisation of domestic political systems, nor by the degree and nature of their integration into international institutions. For constructivist theorists, ideas and identities are what shapes foreign policies more than anything else. States' identities and interests are not fixed once and for all; they are rather the 'highly malleable product of specific historical processes'.[18] In trying to predict the united Germany's future foreign policy path, constructivists would focus on the sources of possible changes in Germany's identity compared with that of the old Federal Republic. They would pay particular attention to the direction of political discourse in Germany and be especially watchful for signs of the erosion of core elements of that identity, such as the repudiation of the use of force or support for European integration, which might be presaged, for example, by attempts to 'normalise' the Holocaust or growing Euro-scepticism among the public and political elites.[19]

THE CONTRIBUTIONS

What kind of changes could be predicted in German European and foreign policy after unification and the end of the Cold War depends on the kind of assumptions that you make about the forces that shape states' foreign policy choices. If changes in the structure of the international system are the main source of changes in foreign policy, reunification and the end of Cold War might be expected to bring about very important – and alarming – changes in the European and foreign policies of the Federal Republic, albeit such a prognosis presupposes a shift from a bipolar to a multi-polar distribution of power and implies probably an American military withdrawal from Europe and the dissolution of NATO: assumptions which have not been borne out by events since 1990. If changes in domestic politics – in the party system or in political decision-making structures – exercise the strongest influence on foreign policy choices, one would expect, given the lack of constitutional changes following reunification, the relative stability of the German party system, and the fairly wide-ranging consensus between the major political forces on external relations issues, a great deal less change in German European and foreign policy.

If Germany's European and foreign policy orientation and stable and peaceful international relations in Europe depend less on the structure of the international relations and domestic political variables than on the existence of strong multilateral European organisations with the capacity to integrate Germany tightly into the European community of states, whether and to what extent the second united Germany proves compatible with a stable and peaceful international order in Europe will be shaped primarily by the future development of the EU and the NATO. Alternatively, if the constructivists are right, change and continuity in German foreign policy will depend predominantly on the extent to which the dominant collective memories and identity in the old Federal Republic can be carried over into the united Germany and how resilient these will prove in the face of undoubted new challenges.

The contributions to this volume look back at and analyse the first decade of the united Germany's European and foreign policies.[20] Apart from Germany itself, their authors come from states – the US, France, Britain and Poland – that belong to Germany's most important partners. In his paper, Hyde Price assesses the motives and implications of German participation in the 1999 Kosovo War. Germany's participation in the war was all the more remarkable, he argues, because it took place under a Red–Green federal government and was not legitimised by a UN mandate. Events in Kosovo forced the new government to choose between two foreign policy articles of faith of the German Left: *Nie wieder Krieg* ('Never again war') and *Nie wieder Auschwitz* ('Never again Auschwitz!'). The government tried to ease this dilemma by flanking its participation in the war with intensive efforts to secure a diplomatic settlement of the crisis. In Hyde Price's view, Germany remains a civilian power, despite its involvement in the war, because a civilian power is not defined by its rejection of the use of force under all circumstances but rather by its commitment to deploy such force strictly multilaterally. Defining a 'civilian power' more broadly than is typically done, Hyde Price concludes that Germany has 'finally evolved into a "normal" civilian power, comparable to other mature democracies in the Euro-Atlantic community'.

In a secondary analysis of literature on a range of post-unification foreign policy issues, Harnisch, in his contribution, comes to broadly similar conclusions. The combination of change and continuity in post-unification German foreign policy can best be explained, he argues, by a 'role-theoretical approach based on the civilian power ideal-type'. Germany's role behaviour cannot be 'cast in iron once and for all'. According to Harnisch, 'domestic interest formation' primarily has brought about some changes in German foreign policy, notably in respect of distributive issues in the EU, but there has been no fundamental shift in Germany's underlying foreign policy role or identity.

German foreign policy in the 1990s has been characterised by 'modified continuity'. The most important force for continuity has been the confirmation of the 'old' Federal Republic's foreign policy conception by the republic's success, culminating in unification; the most important force for change has been the 'learning process', supported by strong pressures from Germany's allies, engendered by initial policy failure during the new Balkan wars. Like Hyde Price, Harnisch emphasises how the Red–Green coalition was forced to choose between the two ideals of *nie wieder Krieg* ('never again war') and *nie wieder Auschwitz* ('never again Auschwitz'). Despite its participation in the Kosovo War, the German government tried to adhere as much as possible to the 'key norms' of the civilian power ideal-type: 'What resulted was a "creative reconstruction" of the civilian power role under different circumstances'.

Baumann and Hellmann offer a quite different interpretation of what they describe as 'far-reaching changes' in German attitudes and behaviour in respect of the use of military force. For them, the former 'discrepancy in attitudes towards war and the actual practice of war between Germany and [otherwise] similar Western countries has been shrinking' since unification, 'with the pace of convergence accelerating since the mid-1990s'. 'Germany', they conclude, 'is finally joining ranks with other Western states in terms of its attitudes towards and practices of war'. Rejecting both culturalist or structure-centred analyses that play down the degree of change in German foreign policy and actor-centred ones that observe an elite-driven process of the 're-militarisation' of this policy, Baumann and Hellmann prefer an explanation that recognises the 'interplay' of structure and agency. Focusing on the interaction of foreign policy discourse, public opinion and governmental decisions and action, they argue that German foreign policy makers 'did not just respond to a changing structure of the international system and to conflicting international and societal explanations ... They also managed to shape the public discourse in Germany and to establish new facts by slowly raising the scope of German military deployments, repeatedly moving beyond the established domestic consensus'. In their view evidently, at least when it comes to the use of military force, post-unification Germany has made a clean break from the Federal Republic's pre-1990 past.

As Miskimmon points out, the Kosovo War not only constitutes a turning-point as regards post-Second World War German attitudes and practice as regards the use of military force, but has also provided a powerful impetus for greater European security and defence co-operation. He suggests that, given Germany's self-conception as a 'civilian power', there might be important divergences between Germany, on the one hand, and France and Britain, on the other, when it comes to efforts to forge a common European security and defence policy. Germany remains the most 'pro-integrationist' of the three states when it comes to security and defence policy, but also the least enthusiastic concerning the use of military force. Germany's capacity to contribute to a European military force will depend on the outcome of the debate over the reform of the Bundeswehr and the volume of resources that is committed for its modernisation. Like Britain, Germany's goal is to develop an enhanced European military capability within the NATO rather than a rival to NATO. Miskimmon argues that a stronger European military capability should not disturb the transatlantic relationship with the US – this strategic relationship will 'continue to exist, but in a revised form in which Europe will carry more of the burden in crisis management'.

The predominant focus of the other contributions is on Germany's post-unification European policy. Wessels argues that, overall, German foreign policy has changed little since 1989. It is still 'cautious rather than assertive'. Except in recognising Croatian and Slovenian independence in 1992, Germany has not been tempted to 'go it alone'. The continuity in German foreign policy, especially in respect of multilateralism, is attributable to what Wessels calls the '"1905" trauma of being encircled by a hostile coalition of neighbouring countries' and to the '"1945" nightmare of being a front-line state in the core of a disastrous conflict'. Since 1998,

Chancellor Schröder has 'rapidly learned to continue pursuing long-standing German strategies' in the EU. There is little danger, according to Wessels, that a new generation of political leaders 'with no personal experience of World War II' will turn its back on the European integration process. Although they may be more relaxed about Germany's past and less inclined to draw explicit lessons from it, these leaders will nonetheless retain the 'shadow of history' in their 'sunken memory'. Moreover, 'moving the capital to Berlin' has not changed the 'map' of German interests.

Le Gloannec begins her contribution by noting the paradox that unification gave rise to increased fears of a growth of German power, despite its taking place in a period when, as a consequence of economic globalisation, the power of states as such seems to be in decline. Le Gloannec argues that, prior to unification, the Federal Republic's economic dominance in the EU enabled it to exercise 'semi-hegemonic' power in European economic and monetary affairs, but that this did not translate into political leadership. Moreover, the creation of a single European currency (accelerated, if not initiated, in response to German unification – DW) has 'dramatically changed the system of power in Europe', diffusing Germany's economic and monetary power as well. Le Gloannec's analysis implies that, a decade after unification, Germany is less powerful in the EU than it was beforehand – and that other European states', including France's, enduring strategy of trying to 'tame' German power by integrating Germany into Europe has been extraordinarily successful. To exercise power in the EU, the German government will increasingly be forced to form coalitions with other member states – something which would be made more difficult if its European policy were to be dictated increasingly by 'short-term' goals, such as the reduction of the German contribution to the EU budget.

De Schoutheete analyses German European policy up to 1998 from the vantage point of a diplomat with ten years' experience of German European diplomacy as the Belgian permanent representative to the EU and a member of the COREPER (Committee of Permanent Representatives). Unification, de Schoutheete observes, has had 'little or no perceptible impact' on German European policy. He attributes the stability of this policy first and foremost to the 'lack of change' in the personnel of Germany's 'foreign policy establishment', including the major federal ministries as well as the political leadership. De Schoutheete does note, however, that the 'political climate' in Germany has become more hostile to further integration, attributing this trend to a combination of factors, including the depressed economic conjuncture for much of the 1990s, the financial burdens of unification, the enhanced role of the relatively Euro-sceptical Länder governments in the European policy-making process, and the east German citizens' lack of socialisation into the European integration project before 1990. Noting the contingent character of some of these factors, especially the economic conjuncture, de Schoutheete speculates that, following the 1998 federal elections, German European policy could demonstrate 'renewed dynamism' – which arguably it did between the Amsterdam and Nice treaty revision negotiations. In any event, there will not, in his view, be any substantive 'Britishisation' of German European policy.

The contribution by Kranz is the only one that examines Germany's post-unification foreign and European policy from the vantage point of a country to Germany's east. Although Kranz is critical of a tendency of German policy on Central and Eastern Europe to be too strongly oriented towards not antagonising Russia, he nonetheless describes the post-unification transformation of German–Polish relations as a 'success story'. The united Germany has supported the Eastern enlargement of the EU and, ultimately, also of NATO. It indeed wants 'Western neighbours' to its east. Kranz expects German foreign policy to continue to be characterised by continuity, with a strong emphasis on multilateralism. There is a danger, however, that its European engagement and support for closer integration will be weakened by its preoccupation with its domestic economic and social problems. Like Wessels, too, Kranz argues that the direction of German foreign policy will be determined partly by the attitudes taken by its principal allies – France, Britain and the US.

Like most other contributors, Denison detects more continuity than change in post-unification German foreign policy. The German government still supports a strong transatlantic relationship with the US and a strong EU; its commitment to foreign policy multilateralism is unshaken. Two things, however, have changed. First, Germany is increasingly willing to participate in the deployment of military force, albeit not alone. Denison regards this change as 'qualitatively significant' and as having been brought about by a concern not to alienate Germany's Western allies and not to permit a repetition of the massacre of Bosnian Muslims at Srebrenica. Second, owing to growing fiscal constraints and the growing role of the Länder in European policy-making, Germany has become more assertive *in* multilateral institutions such as the EU. Denison refers to this practice as 'assertive multilateralism'. But it remains multilateralist nonetheless, not only because it has learned the 'lessons of history', but also because of its awareness of the incapacity of single governments to address a growing number of contemporary issues effectively. If anything, the US would have liked German foreign policy to change further and faster and Germany to become more assertive than it has done.

Bulmer, Maurer and Paterson depart in their analysis from the position that any EU member state's European policy reflects a combination of interests, identity and institutions. Although Germany's interests may have changed since 1990, these have been insufficient, they argue, to bring about major changes in a European policy shaped also by identities and institutions. Their contribution deals with the institutions of German European policy. The changes made in Germany's European policy machinery since unification, such as the enhanced participation rights of the Länder, have had nothing to do with unification as such and have heightened rather than reduced its pluralistic character. To change this 'slow, decentralized and complex' machinery would have required 'domestic constitutional change' [such that not even unification managed to provoke – DW]. The authors conclude that the 'events of 1989–90 did not serve to trigger a fundamental shift in the institutional structure towards a more interest-driven policy', not least, they argue, because the very occurrence of unification legitimised the European policy of the 'old' Federal Republic. Some scope for policy change remains, however. Externally, the Franco-German alliance, a massive force for continuity, is showing signs of erosion. Internally, an alternative scenario based on the growing role of the Finance Ministry and a series of political pressures on Chancellor Schröder is identified as a possibility.

CONCLUSION

A decade after the second German unification, most of the distinctive traits of pre-1990 (federal) German foreign policy are still clearly discernible in the foreign policy of the so-called 'Berlin Republic'. This policy is still strongly Western-oriented, strongly 'multilateralist' and Euro-centric. The principal change undoubtedly consists in the curtailment, if not erosion, of the civilian character of pre-1990 policy. The contributors who analyse this dimension of post-unification German foreign policy agree on the 'fact' of change – after all, German troops were not deployed in any pre-1990 war or in the Gulf War, but did participate in the Kosovo conflict. But they disagree as to the scope of the change and how to interpret and evaluate it. Whereas Hyde Price and Harnisch argue that German behaviour in respect of the use of military force remains reconcilable with the 'civilian power' model, Baumann and Hellmann clearly think otherwise and see the Berlin Republic rapidly developing – in this regard at least – into a 'normal' big European power.

The principal pressures for change in this dimension of German policy have been external. They have emanated in the first instance from Germany's Western partners and allies, who want Germany to share the burden of military intervention in international crises. Indirectly, of course, they have been generated by the Gulf and Balkan wars. The events in former

Yugoslavia especially have brought home to the German Left in particular that massive and barbaric violations of basic human rights have not ceased with the end of the Cold War in Europe, but on the contrary have escalated, that ultimately it may not be possible to combat such acts other than by the use of military force and that a country of Germany's size and with its history can hardly stand aside and leave this task entirely to others.   I   f one were to sum up the principal agents of change in German policy towards the deployment of military force, then they could be abbreviated as the three S's: Saddam Hussein, Slobodan Milosevic and Srebrenica. Precisely because this change has been encouraged and welcomed by Germany's allies and partners, because it has taken place strictly within multilateral frameworks (albeit, in the case of the Kosovo War, not that provided by the UN) and because it has been deployed with a view to preventing massive human rights violations, it does not presage the return of a political 'Frankenstein monster' and the revival of pre-Second World War patterns of inter-state rivalry in Europe.

If the major post-unification change in one of the distinctive traits of pre-1990 (federal) German foreign policy is attributable primarily to external stimuli and thus tends to support neo-realist analyses about the future direction of this policy, the preponderance of continuity in the other, more numerous distinguishing traits of German foreign policy points to the overall greater predictive power of international relations paradigms that emphasise the role of domestic variables – the organisation of the European and foreign policy-making process (liberalism) or historical memories and collective identities (constructivism) – or the constraints imposed (or opportunities offered) by membership in international organisations (institutionalism). Collectively, these variables continue to represent extremely potent forces making for 'stickiness' and continuity in German foreign and European policy. They provide an additional, extraordinarily strong assurance that, overall, the foreign policy of the Berlin-based unified Germany will not deviate too radically from that of the 'old' Bonn republic and that the second German unification will not turn into a re-run of the first.

NOTES

1. David Calleo, 'Einheit ja, Frankenstein-Monster nein', *Die Zeit*, No.2, 5 Jan. 1990. Calleo's seminal work on the 'German Problem' is David Calleo, *The German Problem Reconsidered: Germany and the World Order, 1870 to the Present* (Cambridge: Cambridge University Press, 1978).
2. Helmut Kohl (as told to Kai Diekmann and Ralf Georg Reuth), *'Ich wollte Deutschlands Einheit'* (Berlin: Ullstein, 1996), p.195.
3. Ibid., p.197.

4. Ibid., p.197.
5. Ibid., pp.196–7 and 150.
6. Margaret Thatcher, *The Downing Street Years* (London: HarperCollins, 1993), p.796.
7. Jacques Attali, *Verbatim. Tome 3: Chronique des années 1988–1991* (Paris: Fayard, 1995).
8. For a survey of the Franco-German relationship in the EU, see Douglas Webber (ed.), *The Franco-German Relationship in the European Union* (London/New York: Routledge, 1999).
9. Peter J. Katzenstein, 'Die Fesselung der deutschen Macht im internationalen System', in Berhard Blanke and Hellmut Wollmann (eds.), *Die alte Bundesrepublik: Kontinuität und Wandel (Leviathan-*Sonderheft 12/1991) (Opladen: Westdeutscher Verlag, 1991), p.74.
10. As quoted in Manfred Görtemaker, *Deutschland im 19. Jahrhundert: Entwicklungslinien* (Bonn: Bundeszentrale für Politische Bildung, 1989), p.345.
11. In a notable passage in their 'multi-speed' proposals on European integration, the then chairman of the CDU/CSU parliamentary party, Wolfgang Schäuble, and the party's European affairs spokesman, Karl Lamers, pleaded for the Eastern enlargement of the EU, arguing that, in its absence, Germany 'could be called on, or, out of concern for its own security, be tempted to try to stabilise Eastern Europe by itself and in the traditional manner' (CDU/CSU-Fraktion des Deutschen Bundestages, *Überlegungen zur europäischen Politik*, press statement, 1 Sept. 1994, p.3).
12. For a concise overview of the theories themselves, see Stephen M. Walt, 'International Relations: One World, Many Theories', *Foreign Policy* (Spring 1998), pp.29–46. Walt, however, subsumes institutionalist theories within the liberal camp, which, in my view, has a quite different understanding of the primary determinants of foreign policy.
13. John Mearsheimer, 'Back to the Future: Instability in Europe After the Cold War', *International Security* 15/1 (Summer 1990), p.47.
14. Ibid., p.33.
15. See, for example, Simon Bulmer and William Paterson, *The Federal Republic of Germany and the European Community* (London: Allen and Unwin, 1987), and Peter J. Katzenstein (ed.), *Between Power and Plenty: Foreign Economic Policies of Advanced Industrial States* (Madison: University of Wisconsin Press, 1978).
16. See, for example, Robert O. Keohane, 'Institutional Theory and the T after the Cold War', chapter 11 in David A. Baldwin (ed.), *Neorealism and Neoliberalism: The Contemporary Debate* (New York: Columbia University Press, 1993); and Robert O. Keohane and Stanley Hoffmann, 'Conclusion: Structure, Strategy, and Institutional Roles', in Robert O. Keohane, Joseph S. Nye and Stanley Hoffmann (eds.), *After the Cold War: International Institutions and State Strategies in Europe, 1989–1991* (Cambridge, MA/London: Harvard University Press, 1993), pp.381–404.
17. As quoted in Ludolf Herbst, *Option für den Westen: Vom Marshall Plan bis zum deutsch-französischen Vertrag* (Munich: Deutscher Taschenbuch Verlag, 1989), p.82.
18. Walt, 'International Relations', p.40.
19. For an excellent, more or less constructivist analysis which deals with the relationship between collective memories and identity and foreign policy in Germany, see Andrei Markovits and Simon Reich, *The German Predicament: Memory and Power in the New Europe* (Ithaca/London: Cornell University Press, 1997), especially the concluding chapter. See also Peter J. Katzenstein, 'The Smaller European States, Germany and Europe', in Peter J. Katzenstein (ed.), *Tamed Power: Germany in Europe* (Ithaca/London: Cornell University Press, 1997), pp.296–300. The basic tenets of constructivist theory are expounded by Alexander Wendt in 'Anarchy is What States Make of it', *International Organization* 46/2 (Spring 1992), pp.391–425. The role of norms, identity and culture as determinants of foreign policy is discussed in the various contributions to Peter J. Katzenstein (ed.), *The Culture of National Security: Norms and Identity in World Politics* (New York: Columbia University Press, 1996).

20. Five of the contributions were first presented at the first Roger Godino Conference, 'Germany – Quo Vadis? German European and Foreign Policy after Reunification', staged at INSEAD (European Institute of Business Administration), Fontainebleau, France on 27 March 1998. The editor would like to thank both Roger Godino and INSEAD for the financial support without which this volume would not have been possible. He would like also to thank the other participants in the conference – Philip Gordon (then Senior Fellow at the International Institute for Strategic Studies, London), Roland Freudenstein (Office of the Konrad Adenauer Foundation, Warsaw), Robert Cooper (British Foreign and Commonwealth Office), Antonio Borges (then Dean of INSEAD), and Immo Stabreit (former German Ambassador to France) – for their respective contributions.

Germany and the Kosovo War: Still a Civilian Power?

ADRIAN HYDE-PRICE

On 24 March 1999, four German ECR-Tornados took off from their base in Piacenza to participate in NATO's bombing of targets in the rump Yugoslav Federation. This event constituted a significant landmark in the history of the Federal Republic of Germany. For the first time since 1945, German military forces took part in offensive combat missions against a sovereign state. This historic watershed is all the more remarkable because it took place under a 'Red–Green' coalition government, and without a clear UN mandate.

German participation in Operation Deliberate Force was a defining moment in the domestic politics of the new Germany, and raised a number of important questions about this large and influential country's future role in Europe. The Berlin Republic, as many commentators noted, was 'born in war'. In addition, the tragedy in Kosovo erupted mid-way through the German presidency of the EU and the WEU, and its chairmanship of the G8. This thrust the new Red–Green government to the forefront of international diplomacy. The fact that NATO was engaged in an intensive bombing campaign against a sovereign state at the moment when the Alliance was planning celebrations of its fiftieth anniversary also generated considerable reflection in Germany – given that post-war German national identity has been deeply marked by its multilateral *Einbindung* (integration). The Kosovo War thus raised fundamental questions about Germany's self-perception as a 'civilian power', and about the future role of the Berlin Republic in the reshaping of post-Cold War European order.

THE BACKGROUND: GERMAN SECURITY POLICY IN THE 1990s

German participation in 'Operation Allied Force' is even more striking given its stance during the Gulf War. The Bonn government refused to participate in Operation 'Desert Storm' against Iraq in 1991, a position strongly supported by public opinion. This reflected post-war Germany's response to German aggression in the Second World War. Post-war West

Adrain Hyde-Price, Institute for German Studies, University of Birmingham

Germany consciously pursued a policy that was multilateral and defensively orientated. The constitution (*Grundgesetz*), it was argued, limited the role of the Bundeswehr to collective territorial defence within the framework of Article V of the Washington Treaty. This gave rise to a strategic culture which was focused on deterrence not defence, and which reflected the prevalence of pacifist sentiments throughout the population. Not surprisingly, West Germany was often described as a 'civilian power',[1] consciously eschewing great power *Realpolitik* and military power projection in favour of political and economic goals.

The Gulf War represented the first major challenge to the comfortable domestic consensus surrounding German foreign and security policy. The peace movement enjoyed another lease of life, and proved itself a potent political force. White flags were often seen hanging out of windows, and the slogan 'No War for Oil' received a wide echo. The Kohl government distanced itself from these pacifist sentiments, but nonetheless argued that the *Grundgesetz* forbade German participation in operation 'Desert Storm'. Instead, Germany provided financial support to the tune of $17 billion. This led to snide comments about Bonn's 'cheque-book diplomacy', and very real policy dilemmas for Germany's political elite. On the one hand, Germany prided itself on its role as a loyal ally of the US and a committed advocate of multilateralism. On the other, it sought to play a role as a civilian power committed to further international peace and co-operation. However, it became increasingly apparent that membership of multilateral organisations involved commitments and responsibilities for maintaining international peace which were incompatible with a policy of eschewing 'out-of-area' military operations. It was also clear that Germany's campaign for a permanent seat on the UN Security Council would fail unless it was willing to deploy the Bundeswehr in a wider range of military operations than hitherto envisaged.

In response to these pressures, the Kohl government followed a cautious, long-term strategy designed to gradually build up public support for participation in 'out-of-area' operations. German troops participated in peace-keeping operations in Cambodia and Somalia; Germans participated in AWAC operations over Bosnia; and the Bundeswehr provided a contingent of troops for IFOR/SFOR. The constitutional obstacles to German military crisis management were cleared by the Constitutional Court decision of July 1994.

This carefully calibrated strategy of committing troops to morally defensible peace-keeping or peace-support operations proved to be remarkably successful in preparing the ground politically for the Kosovo operation. Of particular significance in this respect was the change in attitude on the political Left. Both Social Democrats and Greens started the

1990s as parties strongly marked by pacifist sentiments, and opposed to 'out-of-area' operations. Bosnia provided the learning-ground: confronted by mass murder and ethnic cleansing, traditional pacifist ideas proved inadequate. The leading Green 'Realo', Joschka Fischer, played a pivotal role in changing attitudes on the German Left, declaring in 1995 after a visit to Bosnia that military force was morally justified in order to stop genocide, and that German troops should participate in such humanitarian intervention.

THE DECISION TO PARTICIPATE IN THE AIR CAMPAIGN

The decision by the German government to participate in the NATO operation has effected a sea-change in German domestic politics. It underlined once again that 'the fate of a country is decided in foreign policy rather than, for example, constitutional or social policy'.[2] CDU Chairman Wolfgang Schäuble argued that it brought 'a new seriousness' to the political debate in Germany – not surprisingly, given that issues of war and peace raise fundamental questions for any country.[3]

The Kosovo War constituted a defining moment for the Red–Green coalition. After months of a 'false-start', characterised by policy incoherence, intra-coalition wrangling and bureaucratic rivalries – culminating in the dramatic resignation of Oskar Lafontaine – the government faced its first real test. The coalition has responded with a unity of purpose that many commentators found surprising, given their previous disarray. Indeed, *Newsweek* declared that the Kosovo War has turned the government 'from a bunch of bumbling amateurs to a bunch of determined hawks'[4]. The decision to participate in operation Allied Force took 15 minutes, from the time of Clinton's phone call to the final 'yes'[5]. The subsequent debate in the Bundestag was remarkable for its lack of controversy, with only the former East German Communist Party, the PDS (Party of Democratic Socialism) opposing the war. Indeed, some critics noted that more controversy surrounded a proposed law against graffiti-artists than the debate on German military action against Yugoslavia.

German motivations for participating in the bombing campaign were three-fold. First, a strong sense of responsibility towards its NATO allies. For the Red–Green government, the first lesson they learnt from Kosovo was how limited foreign policy options are. Particularly for a country like Germany, whose identity and national role conceptions are intimately bound up with multilateralism, foreign policy is constrained by international commitments to allies and partners. In the case of Kosovo, not to have participated in the NATO action would have fatally undermined the international position of the new government, precipitating a major domestic political crisis.

Second, a strong sense of moral and political responsibility towards the humanitarian suffering in Kosovo. Such normative considerations are often overlooked in foreign policy analysis, but they can have a very real political force. This is certainly true in the case of Germany, given the legacy of Hitlerism and the Holocaust. Post-war German identity has been constructed around a rejection of its totalitarian past. Confronted by pictures of appalling human suffering, ethnic cleansing and Serbian atrocities, many Germans felt that 'something must be done'. The brutality of Serbian military and police units was widely equated with the ruthlessness of German military and special policy units in the Second World War, and this time most Germans wanted to be on the 'right side'. Hence the broad support for the use of military force to stop ethnic cleansing and widespread human rights violations in Kosovo.

A third factor, less openly discussed, but no less important, was a worry about a new wave of asylum-seekers and refugees. This has been a sensitive political issue in Germany – as it has throughout Western Europe, and has exposed the less attractive side of German politics – not least because it has fuelled the rise of racist and neo-fascist groups. Serbian ethnic cleansing in Kosovo threatened to precipitate large-scale migration into Western Europe, which the German government wished to prevent. As Rudolf Scharping commented, the ghastly events in Kosovo pose a fundamental question: 'do we deal with force, murder and expulsion by tackling these problems at their source? Or do we watch passively and wait until their consequences come home to us?'[6]

THE MANDATE ISSUE

What is particularly remarkable about the German government's decision to commit the Bundeswehr to its first active combat missions is its dubious legal status under international law.[7] It had long been assumed that Bundestag approval for military crisis management would require a clear UN or OSCE (Organisation for Security and Co-operation in Europe) mandate. The lack of such a mandate was criticised by many on both the Left and the Right. For a peace researcher like Ernst-Otto Czempiel, the lack of a UN mandate was the rubicon which both Germany and NATO crossed in Kosovo. He argued that it represented an attempt by the US and NATO to brand certain states as *Schurkenstaat* ('rogue states'), and to establish NATO as the dominant element in the European security order, rather than the EU or the OSCE.[8] At the other end of the political spectrum, former Cold Warriors like Alfred Dreggar, or Realpolitikers like Helmut Schmidt were also critical of the lack of a UN mandate.

On the other hand, other opinion formers on both Left and Right took a different stance. Karl-Heinz Kamp of the Konrad Adenauer Foundation (which is close to the CDU) argued that the mandate issue needed to be placed in its historical and political context. If the UN Charter was taken in isolation, then NATO's military action was illegal, and the sufferings of the Kosovo Albanians a question of 'domestic affairs' of Yugoslavia. However, he argued that this question should be seen in the context of efforts to reform the UN system and to make international law more relevant to the contemporary international security agenda. A choice needed to be made between a strict interpretation of the UN Charter and the duty to prevent human suffering. When a state violates its fundamental duty towards its citizens, namely to defend the life and freedoms of its citizens, it loses its right to sovereignty. Military measures aimed at preventing severe human rights violations are therefore fully in accord with the humanitarian norms of the UN, even in the absence of a Security Council resolution. In addition, Kamp argued, the UN Charter is not the only source of international law. The 1951 UN Convention on Genocide provided a legal basis for the NATO action.[9] Similarly, the SPD Minister-President of Saarland, Reinhard Klimmt, argued that although NATO's intervention lacked clear legitimation under international law, it did accord to the 'spirit of international law'.[10]

Not surprisingly, Defence Minister Scharping also argued that it was wrong to assume that the UN Security Council was the only source of international law. Scharping argued that 'the UN Charter, the UN Security Council resolution on Kosovo last year, and the right to *Nothilfe* [emergency help] together provide a clear basis under international law'. At the same time, he argued, NATO had no desire to act as a world-wide intervention force. Rather, its concern was with security and stability in the Euro-Atlantic area.[11] Similarly, Karl-Heinz Kamp rejected suggestions that NATO's 'self-mandating' may be misused in order to provide NATO with a new role as self-appointed 'world policeman'. As an alliance of 19 democratic nations, based on consensual decision-making procedures, he argued, NATO was not politically able to act in this way. The evidence for this was 'three years wavering and 200,000 dead in Bosnia'.[12]

HUMANITARIAN INTERVENTION AND THE LESSONS OF ŠREBRENICA

Closely bound up with the Mandate issue was the question of humanitarian intervention. Does the international community have a right to humanitarian intervention? This question has proven particularly divisive for the German Left – particularly since the shocking events in Šrebrenica.[13]

The dilemma that Šrebrenica spot-lighted for the Left was whether the old rallying cry 'nie wieder' meant 'Nie wieder Krieg' ('Never again war') or 'Nie wieder Auschwitz' ('never again Auschwitz').[14] The problem for convinced pacifists like Christian Ströbele who rejected military intervention against aggression on principle is that 'they must in the end also reject and condemn the war against Hitler'.[15] Very few Germans have adopted this extreme pacifist position, and consequently the moral dilemmas posed by military crisis management have faced most politically engaged Germans. These dilemmas have split both Left and Right, and generated new coalitions between erstwhile opponents – for example, between Egon Bahr, one of the leading architects of *Ostpolitik*, and conservatives like Alfred Dreggar and Karl Lamers, all of whom opposed military intervention.[16]

DOMESTIC POLITICAL CONSEQUENCES

The Kosovo tragedy had a major impact on German domestic politics and constituted the first real *Bewährungsprobe* (test) of the new government.[17] It precipitated a reshaping of German domestic politics and provided the new generation of political leaders (the '68ers') with their first major crisis.[18] Unlike the older generation, the '68ers' have no direct experience of the Second World War or its immediate aftermath. They have grown up in a Euro-Atlantic 'security community' characterised by multilateral co-operation, welfare states and democracy. Not surprisingly, therefore, their response to the Kosovo War was markedly different from the generation of Helmut Kohl, Alfred Dreggar and Helmut Schmidt.

The first important domestic political consequence of the Kosovo War was to improve the political reputation of the Chancellor, Gerhard Schröder. During the election campaign, Schröder was admired for his Italian designer clothes and televisual skills. Critics, however, pointed to the lack of substance and content behind his sound-bites. The responsibility of leading his country into its first military campaign since 1945 demonstrated his leadership qualities and his ability to take tough decisions. Similarly, Kosovo boosted the political capital of Defence Minister Rudolf Scharping. Previously seen as a rather dull and uncharismatic figure, his competent and unruffled performance during the campaign won him growing respect from colleagues and former critics. Last, but not least, the Kosovo tragedy has witnessed the final transformation of the Green Foreign Minister, Joschka Fischer, from 1960s radical to a bulwark of *Westbindung* (Western integration) and continuity in German foreign policy. Before the September 1998 election, Schröder commented that Fischer would soon become the 'darling' of the international community. Fischer's energetic and constructive diplomacy during the course of the war certainly won him many plaudits and underlined his statesmanlike qualities.

While the Cabinet itself, by and large, remained united behind the bombing campaign, the war seemed at times to present a serious threat to the very survival of the Red–Green coalition. Both parties were closely associated with the 1980s peace movement, and contained sizeable pacifist elements. The SPD held a Special Party Conference (*Sonderparteitag*) on 12 April 1999 under the slogan of 'responsibility' (*Verantwortung*). Schröder give an impassioned speech, full of conviction and determination, in which he stressed Germany's *Verantwortung*, both to its NATO allies and towards the victims of ethnic cleansing in Kosovo. At the same time, he stressed that pacifists had a home in the SPD. By the end of the conference, the majority of the party had united behind the bombing campaign. Opinion polls also showed solid and continuing support among SPD voters for NATO's intervention. However, the issue of deploying ground troops in combat roles remained highly controversial within the party, and any decision to commit Bundeswehr troops to such an operation would undoubtedly have opened up deep fissures among Social Democrats.

The Greens found the Kosovo War much more problematic, and much more divisive – not surprisingly for a party whose election programme contained an unequivocal rejection of using military means to enforce peace.[19] Most Green Bundestag deputies and a majority of party members reluctantly supported the line of their Foreign Minister, but opponents of military intervention grew each week the bombing continued. Given their origins as an 'eco-pax' (ecological and peace) party, this is not surprising.[20] Despite the impassioned arguments of Fischer and other 'realos', the Greens have not found it easy to come to terms with the political and ethical dilemmas of military intervention. Opinion polls also showed a steady fall in support for the bombing campaign among Green voters as the war continued. While there was no major haemorrhage of party members, there were mounting criticisms of NATO's targeting of Yugoslavia's economic, communications and transport infrastructure outside Kosovo itself. The issue of a combat deployment of ground troops was even more divisive. If NATO had embarked on a ground campaign with German participation, the result might well have been a major split in the Greens and the collapse of the coalition. Although this crisis was avoided, the support of the Red–Green government for a NATO bombing campaign has left many Greens uncertain of their fundamental principles and values.

THE 'LOYAL' OPPOSITION: CDU, CSU AND FDP

With the exception of the PDS, all the opposition parties in the Bundestag gave their critical support to the NATO operation. The CDU, CSU and FDP all expressed broad support for the government's policy, although all three parties made clear their opposition to the combat deployment of ground-troops. CDU support for the government's policy was not surprising. As Wolfgang Schäuble noted, as a political party that had long accepted the inescapable need to use military force in the last instance, the CDU had had fewer problems with the Kosovo intervention than the SPD, Greens and parts of the FDP. However, Schäuble also warned against an exaggerated moralistic rhetoric, and stressed the need for new political and diplomatic initiatives involving the UN and Russia.[21] This approach was endorsed by the CDU Party Conference in Erfurt (26/27 April 1999), as was the party's opposition to sending ground troops to fight in Kosovo.

CSU Chairman Stoibler also supported the NATO bombing campaign but stressed his opposition to the use of ground troops, particularly given the severe implications of this for relations with Russia.[22] Some in the CSU and on the Right of the CDU sought to make political capital from Kosovo by drawing a parallel between the expulsion of Germans from the east after 1945 and ethnic cleansing in Kosovo. Such views were also common in the letters pages of the conservative press, but did not find expression in the statements of CSU or CDU leaders.

Finally, the FDP has underlined their opposition to the use of ground troops as 'militarily risky and politically dangerous'. They also called on the government actively to push for the implementation of the Rambouillet peace plan, and for the Green and SPD critics of the bombing campaign to keep quiet, rather than giving support to Milošević.[23]

THE PDS – BETWEEN PACIFISM AND ANTI-IMPERIALISM

The Kosovo crisis accelerated the reconstitution of the German Left, a process which had been under way since the entry of the Greens into the Bundestag in 1982, and which received a further impetus from the electoral successes of the PDS. As the Social Democrats under Gerhard Schröder have moved to the centre and the Greens have abandoned much of their past radicalism, the PDS has sought to position itself as the only 'Left opposition' in Germany.

The PDS was the only party in the Bundestag to oppose the NATO operation. It argued that the 'war' against Yugoslavia violated international law, and was an act of aggression by NATO, led by the USA, against a sovereign state. Given their early reticence to condemn Serbian ethnic cleansing, and their support for national liberation struggles, their pacifist stance was not entirely credible. Their aim, however, was to strengthen their profile on the radical Left of the party spectrum, and to establish a political basis in western Germany amongst anti-war activists. As part of the PDS effort to construct an international network of left-wing parties against NATO's 'aggression', the PDS Bundestag leader, Gregor Gysi, travelled to Belgrade on 13 April to meet Serbian political and religious leaders.[24] His handshake with Miloševic led to subsequent taunts by Chancellor Schröder that the PDS had become the 'fifth column' of Serbia.

However critical Bonn politicians may have been of the PDS's anti-war stance, it certainly received a positive echo in eastern Germany. Indeed, the Kosovo conflict has starkly exposed the deep divisions between the two parts of Germany. While 59 per cent of west Germans believed that NATO's bombs were serving humanitarian ends, only 38 per cent of Easterners were of this view. In the west, 70 per cent supported the participation of the Bundeswehr in the Kosovo operation. In the east, only 41 per cent were in favour, while 48 per cent were against.[25] Finally, as early as mid-April nearly two-thirds of east Germans wanted to see an immediate end to the air-strikes.[26] The differences between the two parts of Germany reflected the legacy of two different socialisation processes, and underlined what a long-term process it is to integrate east Germans into the political culture of the Bundesrepublik.

GERMAN DIPLOMACY – THE FISCHER PEACE PLAN

In their coalition agreement, the Greens and Social Democrats had declared that 'German foreign policy is peace policy' (*Friedenspolitik*). Yet when faced with ethnic cleansing and atrocities in Kosovo, this 'peace policy' had been redefined to include air-strikes. The dilemmas involved in this policy shift were reflected in the twin-track strategy adopted by the Red–Green government. On the one hand, participation in the bombing campaign; on the other, intensive diplomatic efforts to find a solution to the crisis. A high-profile diplomatic role for the government also served a vital domestic political purpose, because only by demonstrating an active commitment to finding a political solution to the Kosovo tragedy could the government hope to contain opposition to the bombing campaign among sceptical Greens and Social Democrats.

Given its presidency of the EU, Germany played a pivotal role in negotiations to find a solution to the Kosovo War and to bring peace to the wider region. In early April, Foreign Minister Fischer announced a peace plan, which, it was hoped, would provide the basis for a new international diplomatic consensus. The German EU presidency also took the initiative in developing a 'Stability Pact for Southeast Europe', along with more focused economic and financial aid for Albania and Macedonia.

Throughout the bombing campaign, a key concern of German diplomacy was to involve both the United Nations and the Russians in the search for an end to the war. In his capacity as President of the European Council, Chancellor Schröder invited the UN Secretary-General Kofi Annan to attend the informal EU Summit in Brussels on 14 April. The future role of the EU in a peace settlement for the Balkans was also extensively discussed during Annan's three-day visit to Germany. As regards Russia, the German government recognised that UN involvement in Kosovo would only be possible if the Russians could be brought 'back in the boat'. Moreover, they did not want the Kosovo War to undermine a co-operative security relationship with Moscow, which remained a key aim of German foreign policy. Consequently, a key theme of German diplomacy was to engage Russia in the search for a peace settlement. All through April and May, a steady stream of German diplomats and political leaders travelled to Moscow to encourage the Russian government to play a positive role in the conflict. The German government also encouraged the Americans to intensify their dialogue with Moscow. Finally, the German government sought to use the G8 as a forum for building a political agreement with Russia. The success of this strategy was evident from the positive outcome of the G8 Summit in Bonn on 5 May, at which a set of 'principles' were agreed for ending the conflict.

In the medium to long term, the Kosovo War is likely to have a significant impact on Germany's relations with its key Western allies. Bundeswehr participation in the Kosovo operation demonstrates that united Germany has overcome its earlier reservations and is now politically willing and constitutionally able to join its allies in military crisis management. This will certainly make Germany an even more important partner for the USA, particularly in the context of NATO's New Strategic Concept. Yet at the same time, West European unease with the quality and direction of US 'leadership', coupled with a belief that the Europeans must do more for their own defence, has given renewed impetus to European defence and security co-operation. During the German EU presidency, historic decisions were reached at the Cologne European Council meeting (3–4 June 1999) concerning the building of a European Security and Defence Policy (ESDP) within the framework of the EU's Common Foreign and Security Policy (CFSP). This initiative was followed up at the Helsinki EU summit (10–11 December 1999) which set a 'headline goal' whereby EU member states would, by 2003, generate military forces capable of carrying out the full range of Petersberg tasks, 'including the most demanding', in operations up to corps level.[27]

If the EU succeeds it meeting its ambitious targets and forges an effective instrument for collective military crisis management, this will transform the face of the European security order. It will also have implications for transatlantic relations, the future of NATO, and EU–Russian relations.[28] At the heart of these interlocking processes of change will be Germany, a country that plays a key role in both NATO and the EU, and which enjoys a close alliance with the USA and a strategic partnership with Russia. Thus the lessons that German policy-makers draw from the experience of the Kosovo War will have an important influence on the reshaping of European order.[29]

WAR AND THE BERLIN REPUBLIC

On 19 April 1999, the Bundestag held its first plenary session in the redesigned and newly renovated Reichstag building in Berlin. The event marked another historical moment in the history of the Federal Republic, as the seat of government moved from provincial Bonn to the metropolitan city of Berlin.[30] The start of a new era in German history was an event heavy with symbolism, given Berlin's troubled history, and lingering concerns that the Berlin Republic might be more assertive and less Western-orientated than the Bonn Republic. In this context, it was particularly significant that that inauguration of the Reichstag building as the official seat of the Bundestag took place at a time when German troops were, for the first time since 1945, engaged in offensive military actions against a sovereign state. As the headline in the *Tageszeitung* from 20 April ominously declared, 'Im Krieg beginnt die "Berliner Republik"' ('In war begins the "Berlin Republic"').

Bundeswehr participation in NATO's military intervention has raised serious questions about the role of the Germany in the reshaping of European order and the future direction of German foreign policy. In particular, it poses a question mark over Germany's status as a 'civilian power'. In his book *Risiko Deutschland*, published in 1995, Joschka Fischer argued that it was certainly not in Germany's national interest to give up the dominant civilian character of its politics and adopt a more assertive foreign policy.[31] Today, however, Joschka Fischer is Foreign Minister in a coalition government that has deployed German military forces in combat missions abroad.

This demonstrates the ambiguities and dilemmas at the heart of post-war German foreign policy. On the one hand, the Federal Republic has been committed to shaping a European peace order in which military force and traditional *Realpolitik* have no part. On the other, it is aware of the international responsibilities that membership of the Euro-Atlantic community entails. Similarly, Germany, as a democratic *Rechtsstaat*, has striven to strengthen international law. On the other hand, it has argued that human rights cannot be seen as a matter of the internal affairs of sovereign states – notably in the context of the OSCE.

The dilemmas facing contemporary Germany reflect broader changes in the international system since the end of the Cold War. As Wilfred von Bredow, Professor of Politics at the University of Marburg, has argued, 'international politics has suddenly become considerably more ambivalent'.[32] New conflicts have emerged which are not amenable to simple solutions or black-and-white analyses. These dilemmas resulted in a hybrid war in Kosovo, which was a partisan-type war on the ground, fuelled by ethnic nationalism, and a high-tech war fought from the air by an Alliance committed to post-national normative values. Faced with a complex and ambiguous international system, von Bredow notes, the danger exists of a political paralysis. Consequently, he argues, the changed international context places greater demands on the judgement and negotiating skills of political leaders, who have to operate in a context in which legal and moral dilemmas abound.

The ambivalences of post-Cold War Europe are embodied in the distinctive character of the Kosovo War. Wars have traditionally been fought for, or in defence of, territory, population or resources. The Gulf War was motivated by concerns for oil and international law. The Kosovo War was different. In his speech to the opening session in the Reichstag building, Chancellor Schroder quoted the Albanian writer Ismail Kandaré: 'With its intervention in the Balkans, atlantic Europe has opened a new page in world history. It is not about material interests, but about principles: the defence of legality and of the poorest people on the continent. This is a founding act.' Kandaré's words may be somewhat of a rhetorical exaggeration, and overlook German and Western concerns about refugees, NATO's credibility and instability in Europe's 'back-yard'. But there was certainly a new factor present in this war. Kosovo was an example of military intervention for humanitarian purposes – for which there are few historical parallels. In this sense, the Kosovo war – and the moral and political dilemmas it poses – may be the prototype for future conflicts facing the international community in the twenty-first century.

CONCLUSION

The Kosovo tragedy has forced Germany to confront two distinct, but closely inter-linked questions that lie at the very heart of the reshaping of post-Cold War European order. The first concerns the role and utility of military force. One of the most difficult questions to answer is 'whether military power will be readied or employed to influence political developments in or near Europe, especially where the interests of the great powers are not fully engaged'.[33] The second is whether European order can continue to rest on the traditional principle of the Westphalian states system, namely sovereignty and non-intervention in the domestic affairs of states.[34] Does the 'international community' (however defined) have the moral and legal right to intervene in the case of large-scale human rights violations? These two questions have been obscured by endless debates on institutional architecture and NATO enlargement, but they are the key questions facing the reshaping of European order.

Given their traumatic history and their post-war identity as a civilian power, the Germans have been confronted with the moral and political dilemmas these two questions pose more starkly than many of their NATO allies. Most importantly, the German debate on Kosovo should reassure those who fear that Germany is seeking to escape from its past and emerge as a 'normal' great power. The German debate demonstrated a maturity and seriousness found in very few other countries – and certainly contrasted favourably with the public debate in the USA or the UK. This reflects a learning process over many decades during which Germans have sought to address the moral and political questions raised by the use of military force. German post-war history has witnessed intense debates about rearmament, Wehrmacht war-crimes, 'out-of-area' missions, missile deployments and humanitarian intervention. The cumulative impact of these debates has been to shape a German public discourse and political identity which is deeply conscious of the need to avoid simple answers to complex moral and political dilemmas. The number of convinced pacifists in Germany is small, but virtually all German politicians are aware of the complexities and moral dilemmas raised by Kosovo. As *Die Zeit* noted, 'traumas, scepticism and the political lessons of the last decades are certainly present in the collective consciousness'.[35]

The arguments for and against military intervention are not simply between opposed camps, but can be seen within parties, and to some extent within individuals themselves. As the writer Peter Schneider has argued, both those for and those against intervention 'find themselves in the same inner struggle' (*Seelenstreit*). 'This war is not suited for drawing sharp moral distinctions between "defenders of peace" and "good guys" on the one hand, and on the other, the power-hungry military, using any pretext to test their new weapons.'[36] For most Germans, Kosovo presents complex moral and political dilemmas which defy simple solutions.

Finally, is Germany still a 'civilian power', even after Kosovo? The concept of 'civilian power' is somewhat vague and loosely defined. Perhaps this partly accounts for its attractiveness to politicians and its frequent use in public discourse in Germany. Hans Maull defined a civilian power as a state that sought to pursue its foreign and domestic objectives primarily through political and economic means, and which was committed to multilateral co-operation and strengthening international law.[37] He did not, however, equate it with a pacifist renunciation of the use of military force under any circumstances. Rather, a 'civilian power' was expected to use military force only as a last resort, after the political and economic instruments of statecraft have failed. Even then, civilian powers are expected only to use military force multilaterally, on the basis of international law, and in a manner proportionate to the political goals. The Kosovo War demonstrated that the concept of civilian power needs further elaboration if it is to be analytically useful in exploring the moral and political dilemmas of military intervention for humanitarian purposes. In the case of Kosovo, both the status of the NATO operation under international law and the appropriateness of its targeting strategy raise difficult questions for civilian powers.

Nevertheless, the German public's response to the Kosovo War suggests that united Germany remains, at heart, a civilian power. This is evident from the overriding concern to stop human suffering; the desire to avoid collateral civilian casualties; the emphasis placed on using the Bundeswehr to build and run refugee camps in Macedonia and Albania; and the efforts of the government to reach a negotiated settlement. Not only is the identity of the Berlin Republic still deeply marked by a civilian power mentality, in contrast to the Bonn Republic, it is now a 'normal' civilian power. The reservations which the Bonn Republic had towards the use of military force for anything other than territorial defence under Article V of the NATO Treaty gave its 'civilian power' character a decidedly stunted and one-dimensional quality. The Berlin Republic is now willing to use military force for humanitarian goals within a multilateral framework. It has therefore finally evolved into a 'normal' civilian power, comparable to other mature democracies in the Euro-Atlantic community. Kosovo has underlined this fact, not changed it.

NOTES

1. Hans Maull, 'Zivilmacht Bundesrepublik Deutschland', *Europa Archiv*, 10 (1992).
2. *Frankfurter Allgemeine Zeitung*, 28 March 1999, p.3.
3. Interview in *Die Zeit*, No.17, 22 April 1999, p.9.
4. 'Spoiling for a Fight', *Newsweek*, 26 April 1999, p.28.
5. Gunter Hofmann, 'Ist die Nation erwachsen?', *Die Zeit*, 31 April 1999, p.6.
6. Scharping interview, *Der Spiegel*, No.13, 31 March 1999, p.218.
7. The legal basis of the NATO operation in international law was widely regarded in Germany as highly ambiguous, and the bombing of Yugoslavia was certainly not regarded as a traditional example of humanitarian intervention. See Ulrich Fastenrath, 'Intervention ohne UN-Mandate?' *Frankfurter Allgemeine Zeitung*, 22 April 1999.

8. Czempiel argued that the motives of NATO's political elite were 'to establish the NATO as a credible intervention force, to make it the dominant factor in preserving order in Europe, over and above the EU and the OSCE'. Interview in *Die Zeit*, 31 March 1999, p.7. At a discussion meeting in the Frankfurt Peace Research Institute on 21 April 1999, the lack of a UN mandate was widely condemned, and NATO likened to a 'vigilante group'. 'Gefahr der Willkür', *Frankfurter Allgemeine Zeitung*, 22 April 1999, p.4.

9. Karl-Heinz Kamp, 'UN-Charta nicht alleinige Richtschnur', *Focus*, 14 (1999), p.30.

10. *Frankfurter Allgemeine Zeitung*, 26 April 1999, p.6.

11. Scharping interview, *Der Spiegel*, No.13, 31 March 1999, pp.219.

12. Kamp, 'UN-Charta nicht alleinige Richtschnur'.

13. Cora Stephen, 'Die Friedensbewegung und die neue deutsche Aussenpolitik', in Thomas Schmid (ed.), *Krieg im Kosovo* (Hamburg: Rowohlt Taschenbuch Verlag, 1999), pp.269–78.

14. Jan Ross, 'Die Deutschen und der Krieg', *Die Zeit*, 31 March 1999, p.1.

15. Peter Schneider, 'Eiserne Mienen', *Frankfurter Allgemeine Zeitung*, Feuilleton, 23 April 1999, p.43.

16. Egon Bahr entered into a fierce debate with his former ally from the peace movement on the left Erhard Eppler, who supported intervention. Their open letters have been published in *Die Zeit*, No.16, 15 April 1999, p.7, and No.17, 22 April 1999, p.4.

17. 'The first deployment of German soldiers in a war since 1945, for which he [Schröder] is responsible, ends the trial phase for his government', *Frankfurter Allgemeine Zeitung*, 13 April 1999, p.1.

18. Günter Bannas, 'Bewährungsprobe einer Generation', *Frankfurter Allgemeine Zeitung*, 3 April 1999, p.1.

19. 'Militärische Friedenserzwingung und Kampfeinsätze lehnen wir ab', Election Programme, Bündnis 90/Die Grünen, 1998.

20. For a critical history of the Greens and foreign policy written from an 'insider' perspective, see Ludger Volmer, *Die Grünen und die Aussenpolitik – Ein Schwieriges Verhältnis* (Münster: Westfälisches Dampfboot, 1998).

21. Interview in *Die Zeit*, No.17, 22 April 1999, p.9.

22. 'Bodentruppeneinsatz könnte zu drittem Weltkrieg führen', *Frankfurter Allgemeine Zeitung*, 13 April 1999, p.7.

23. 'Opposition weiter zurückhaltend', *Frankfurter Allgemeine Zeitung*, 13 April 1999, p.6.

24. 'PDS will Aktion der europäischen Linken', *Frankfurter Allgemeine Zeitung*, 13 April 1999, p.6.

25. 'Stimmungsgefälle', *Frankfurter Allgemeine Zeitung*, 14 April 1999, p.16.

26. *Stern*, No.16, 15 April 1999, p.34.

27. For details see Francois Heisbourg, *European Defence: Making It Work*, Chaillot Paper 42 (Paris: WEU Institute for Security Studies, 2000), pp.6–7.

28. See Peter van Ham, *Europe's New Defence Ambitions: Implications for NATO, the US, and Russia*, Marshall Center Papers no.1 (Garmisch-Partenkirchen: George C. Marshall European Centre for Security Studies, 2000).

29. These questions are discussed at greater length in Adrian Hyde-Price, *Germany and European Order: Enlarging NATO and the EU* (Manchester: Manchester University Press, 2000).

30. Former Chancellor Kohl declared that this was comparable in historical significance to 3 October 1990 (the day of German reunification). *Die Zeit*, No.17, 22 April 1999, p.7.

31. Joschka Fischer, *Risiko Deutschland: Krise und Kukunft der deutschen Politik* (Cologne: Kiepenheuer und Witsch), pp.228–9.

32. Wilfred von Bredow, 'Der krieg im Kosovo und die Ambivalenz der Eindeutigkeit', *Frankfurter Allgemeine Zeitung*, 26 April 1999, p.16.

33. Philip Zelikow, 'The Masque of Institutions', *Survival*, 38/1 (1996), pp.6–18 (p.7).

34. See Rudolf Scharping, *Wir Dürfen Nicht Wegsehen: Der Kosovo-Krieg und Europa* (Berlin: Ullstein, 1999), pp.221–2.

35. 'Aber in kollektiven Bewußtsein sein Traumata, skepsis und die politischen Lehren der letzten Jahrzente präsent', *Die Zeit*, 31 April 1999, p.6.
36. Peter Schneider, 'Eiserne Mienen', *Frankfurter Allgemeine Zeitung*, Feuilleton, 23 April 1999, p.43.
37. See, for example, Hanns Maull, 'Germany and Japan: The New Civilian Powers', *Foreign Affairs*, 69/5 (Winter 1990/91), pp.91–106; and Hanns Maull, 'Civilian Power: The Concept and its Relevance for Security Issues', in Lidija Babic and Bo Huldt (eds.), *Mapping the Unknown: Towards a New World Order* (Stockholm: The Swedish Institute of International Affairs, 1993), pp.115–31.

Change and Continuity in Post-Unification German Foreign Policy

SEBASTIAN HARNISCH

In 1990, John Mearsheimer predicted all kinds of things that would happen in world politics after the demise of the bipolar Cold War system: the disintegration of NATO, the dismemberment of the EU and a powerful and assertive Germany that might go nuclear.[1] Ten years after, it is about time to replace this prognosis with empirical analysis. As several recent books on the topic reveal, continuity dominates change when it comes to Germany's foreign policy in the 1990s.[2] To begin with, Germany has been (among others) a key player in the process of deepening and widening the European Union (EU) and the North Atlantic Treaty Organisation (NATO). It has promoted major regulation in the field of arms control, non-proliferation and international criminal law, that is, the CFE treaty, the deepening and extension of the NPT (Non-Proliferation Treaty) and the creation of the International Criminal Court. It has also pushed for deregulation in agriculture within the context of the World Trade Organisation (WTO). Thus, Germany has come close to resembling a civilian power – a state that is willing to take the initiative and influence international politics through strategies that include (among others) the monopolisation of force within systems of collective security (such as the UN), the preference for non-violent resolution of disputes and the strengthening of the rule of law.[3]

Germany has by no means been the only civilian power in world politics. In Asia, Japan has pursued co-operative security through the deepening of the ASEAN Regional Forum (ARF) process since the early 1990s. During the North Korean nuclear crisis, both the United States and Japan helped to dissolve the crisis by insisting on peaceful means and supporting a co-operative institution, the Korean Peninsula Energy Development Organisation.[4] Yet there is no reason to assume that civilian powers are always successful or that they regularly promote 'good causes' abroad. In 1991 Germany failed miserably when it tried to 'internationalise' the conflict between Serbia, Croatia and Slovenia through the early recognition of the latter two. Several observers then suggested that

Sebastian Harnisch, University of Trier

Germany had worsened the crisis rather than mitigated it. In the 1999 Kosovo War, for the first time since joining NATO in 1955, Germany participated in a major combat operation without a proper UN Security Council mandate – thereby breaking a long-held tradition in German security policy. Thus a strong pacifist minority within the Alliance 90/Green Party accused the Red–Green coalition of succumbing to US pressure and participating in an aggressive war. Again in 2000, when German Foreign Minister Joschka Fischer proposed a moderate federalist model for the future constitution of the EU, several European neighbours suggested that Germany was trying to impose its own (hegemonic) design on its European partners. Some observers even argued that Germany's recent push for further integration is increasingly perceived as a serious threat to their (foreign policy) identity by some of its European partners, such as Denmark, which recently rejected the Euro.[5]

Although almost nobody denies that a distinct German foreign policy style existed during the East–West conflict, a controversy ensued after unification as to whether Germany still followed the foreign policy course of the 'Bonn Republic' or if it was normalising its external behaviour along the lines of other major power players such as France and Great Britain.[6] In this debate, three main schools can be identified. In short, they argue that Germany's foreign policy trajectory in the 1990s has varied according to:

1. *Shifts in international power structures* – the demise of the Soviet Union and the unification of the two Germanies. Thus realists posited that a more powerful Germany would seek both maximum autonomy outside transatlantic institutions or maximum influence in European institutions.[7]
2. *The degree of international embeddedness* – the integration of Germany in the regulative frameworks of NATO, EU and the Organisation for Security and Cooperation in Europe (OSCE). Thus, the (rationalist) institutionalists surmise that a thoroughly integrated Germany will follow the course prescribed by the norms and rules of these institutions.[8]
3. *The stability of its socially constructed foreign policy culture* – the endurance of its self-conception (identity) or role conception (stressing both ego- and alter-expectation of proper behaviour).[9]

The following summarises the basic assumptions and key features of the civilian power approach, discusses the empirical record of Germany's foreign policy behaviour from a civilian power perspective, presents evidence suggesting that Germany has departed from its traditional civilian power role conception and concludes by laying out two causal pathways that account for recent change and continuity in Germany's foreign policy in the 1990s.

THE CIVILIAN POWER ROLE APPROACH

The ideal-type civilian power role concept starts with the assumption that interdependence between states as well as between states and societies has left foreign policy-makers incapable of achieving 'power and plenty' through unilateral means. Systemic interdependence therefore favours certain administrative designs which translate these systemic pressures into a viable policy of securing a stable international environment for the 'politics of interdependence', that is, division of labour, lowering of transaction costs through liberalisation, institutionalisation to avoid free riding and so on. In this context, ideal-type civilian powers are states which actively promote the 'civilising' of international relations. Taking the domestication of the use of force in democratic communities as a matrix for international behaviour, civilian powers try to achieve six intertwined objectives:

1. Constraining the use of force in settling political conflicts, both within and between states, by initiating and lending support to co-operative and collective security arrangements (monopolisation of force);
2. Strengthening the rule of law through the development of international regimes and international organisations via multilateral co-operation, integration, and partial transfers of sovereignty (rule of law);
3. Promoting participatory forms of decision-making both within and between states (democratic participation);
4. Promoting non-violent forms of conflict management and conflict resolution (restraints on violence);
5. Promoting social equity and sustainable development to enhance the legitimacy of international order (social justice); and
6. Promoting interdependence and division of labour (interdependence).[10]

The role-theoretical dimension of the civilian power approach is based on a moderate constructivist perspective: actors are neither envisaged as pursuing single-mindedly fixed material interests (as in rational-choice theories) induced by systemic forces, nor are they expected to hold fixed normative preferences which they acquired in the past and which will determine their behaviour in the future. Rather, the approach has an (implicit) structurationist understanding of foreign policy interest formation, in which agency and structure are mutually constitutive.[11]

As the following empirical findings suggest, German interests and its foreign policy role were up for discussion in the 1990s, within Germany and between Germany and its neighbours and partners. Employing a role theoretical approach, these processes of interest formation are conceptualised as transnational and societal '(re)socialisation' and as 'foreign policy learning'.[12]

GERMANY'S FOREIGN POLICY IN THE 1990s: EMPIRICAL FINDINGS FROM A CP PERSPECTIVE

The premise of the civilian power approach is that recent realist and institutionalist studies of German foreign policy have failed to explain the 'modified continuity' in Germany's external behaviour because they limited their argument to either power considerations or material interests.[13] Instead it is argued here that Germany's foreign policy role concept as a civilian power determined German foreign and security policy after 1989. The findings do not suggest that power or material interests have been absent from Germany's post-Cold War foreign policies. Instead, it is argued that these factors were perceived through the distinct set of norms and values embodied in the civilian power role. However, the empirical record also shows that civilian power norms were not simply 'downloaded' and applied to political problems. In some cases, changes within the civilian power role concept accompanied policy changes. These (re)constructions of Germany's civilian power role are addressed below.

Deepening and Widening European and Transatlantic Institutions

Henning Tewes argues in his analysis of Germany's NATO enlargement policy that German behaviour fitted the ideal-type civilian power rather well. German Defence Minister Volker Rühe launched the enlargement debate in a speech at the International Institute for Strategic Studies (IISS) and German Chancellor Helmut Kohl, initially reluctant, also came round to pushing for NATO expansion just before the NATO summit in Brussels in January 1994. The analysis shows that German policy was guided by two somewhat contradictory principles: the principle of extending democracy towards its Eastern neighbours (upheld primarily by Rühe) and the principle of peaceful and close relations with Russia (which explains why Kohl and the Foreign Ministry initially hesitated on NATO enlargement). The change of emphasis between these two goals reflects shifting priorities in Germany's stance on enlargement. Furthermore, Tewes shows how the desire to follow, as far as possible, both principles simultaneously led to intensified co-operation with Russia, bilaterally and multilaterally. Germany's leading role as an initiator of the NATO–Russia Act and the institutionalisation of the Conference for Security and Cooperation in Europe (CSCE) process is explained by its contradictory role which called for both, peace with Russia and democracy in East-Central Europe. Thus, Tewes takes issue with the realist explanation of Germany's behaviour which interprets NATO expansion as a means to 'kick the Russians while they are down'.

Tewes also stresses that the institutionalist hypothesis which holds that Germany's pro-enlargement policy derives from the norms and values prescribed by EU and NATO does not account properly for the empirical record. If Germany had pushed for an enlargement due to institutional pressures, it should have done so from the beginning and without hesitation. But, according to Tewes, Germany waffled in the early 1990s, due to tension between two values central to its civilian power role (deepening integration and widening integration). As Tewes stresses, appeals to NATO's self-conception as a 'community of values' by East-Central European politicians were instrumental in turning the tide in the German enlargement debate. Democracies just could not leave democracies before closed doors.[14] Hence, NATO's self-conception began to change from being a *Schicksalsgemeinschaft* (community of destiny) and a *Zweckgemeinschaft* (community of purpose) to a *Wertegemeinschaft* (community of values) because of changed role expectations of others. With its self-conception, the institution itself changed as well. Therefore, the role theory of the civilian power approach provides a 'track record' of institutional change and foreign policy behaviour in this case of 'transnational socialisation'.

Similarly, Ulf Frenkler finds in his study of Germany's policy in two EU treaty negotiations (Maastricht 1990/91 and Amsterdam 1996/97) that Germany's foreign policy role indeed shaped the evolution of Germany's pro-integrationist stance.[15] The study emphasises that Germany basically held a consistent course despite French sensitivities about transferring sovereignty to the European level. As Frenkler points out, a role conflict between deepening European integration in the political area (Common Foreign and Security Policy and Home and Justice Affairs) and Germany's basic predisposition in European affairs to side with France when push comes to shove can be identified as being at the core of Germany's foreign policy behaviour. This finding supports the general thesis of civilian power research that Germany's defined material interests are deeply influenced by Germany's foreign policy role concept as a civilian power. While the institutionalist argument would suggest that norms are adopted equally by members of the same institution, the constructivist perspective of role theory makes it possible to explain differences in the internalisation of norms and values between different members in the institution.

This argument is taken up by Carsten Triphaus in his study of Germany's policy in the institutionalisation process of the CSCE.[16] He presents conclusive data that Germany was one of the key supporters of the institutionalisation of the OSCE even after the Kohl government had secured the acceptance of German unification at the CSCE summit in Paris (November 1990). As Triphaus stresses, from 1991 to 1993 Bonn pushed for both the broadening (in terms of geography and issue areas) and deepening of the OSCE (limitation of veto-power through consensus minus one procedure and so on), despite the scepticism of its main European and transatlantic partners – France, Great Britain and the United States. Hence, while Germany failed to position the OSCE as an equal player among the 'interlocking institutions' of the new European security architecture, Germany's strong push for a beefed-up OSCE is another example of its willingness to forfeit autonomy and its effort to strengthen democratic participation/legitimacy in international institutions.

Security at Home and Abroad: Non-proliferation, Human Rights and Out-of-Area Interventions

Oliver Meier demonstrates the strength of the constructivist civilian power analysis by dissecting Germany's non-proliferation policy in the 1990s.[17] He takes issue with the neo-realist expectation that a unified Germany will and should reassess its non-nuclear weapon state status in order to maximise its autonomy *vis-à-vis* its nuclear-armed allies. After the breakdown of the bipolar alliance structure in the early 1990s, neo-realists expected Germany and other states to reconstruct a new balance of power.[18] Meier provides rich evidence to prove this prediction wrong. He goes on to argue that Germany will stick to the non-nuclear path even if the nuclear umbrella from the US should falter. Hence, he refutes the institutionalist argument that Germany's nuclear weapons policy is solely interest-based and that Germany will remain a non-nuclear state only as long as it 'enjoys' the nuclear protection of the United States and its European nuclear-armed allies, France and the United Kingdom. At least rhetorically, Germany tried to roll back the nuclearisation of international politics and the militarisation in the non-proliferation field throughout the 1990s. However, solidarity with its nuclear allies in NATO was at least as important to Germany. Germany abandoned a major non-proliferation initiative in 1993 after it had received hefty criticism from its nuclear allies. It supported the positions of friendly nuclear-armed states in 1996, in the context of a ruling of the International Court of Justice on the legality of the use of nuclear weapons, and in 1998, when the US attacked presumed terrorist targets in Sudan and Afghanistan.

Two more of Meier's findings deserve mentioning in this context. First, as has been argued before, domestic interests are shaped through, but not determined by, the civilian power role. In defiance of its multilateralist inclinations, the German government still insists on the use of highly enriched uranium in a nuclear research reactor in Garching, due to pressure from the CSU-led state government of Bavaria. In a similar move, the Kohl government showed reluctance to support a more intrusive nuclear verification regime, when the International Atomic Energy Association (IAEA) launched the '93+2' reform of the IAEA safeguards system. Second, Meier presents some tentative indications that the new German government might not be as prone to domestic pressure in its non-proliferation policy as its predecessor but even more normatively biased. The Schröder government has committed itself to the eventual termination of the commercial use of nuclear energy, although the specifics still have to be hammered out. In addition, German Foreign Minister Joschka Fischer acted upon the coalition agreement's provision that the first use of nuclear weapons be renounced when he initiated a debate on this issue within NATO.

Florian Pfeil provides a very similar analysis of German human rights policies.[19] Those policies clearly reflect the importance of norms and values as factors shaping German foreign policy behaviour. Pfeil shows, for example, how Germany performed the important role of an initiator and facilitator in the process of establishing the International Criminal Court. However, he also discusses the limited congruence between convictions and role behaviour in the case of Myanmar and Nigeria.

In two recent studies, Nina Philippi and Hanns Maull offer persuasive interpretations of the changing German position on out-of-area missions of the Bundeswehr.[20] They demonstrate how the changing attitudes of the Kohl and Schröder governments towards out-of-area-missions in the 1990s have been driven by peer pressure, especially from the United States.[21] In the German out-of-area debate, this role expectation of others was translated into a call for *Bündnisfähigkeit* ('capacity to participate in alliances'), into a strong political emphasis on being a reliable partner both in NATO and the future European Common Foreign and Security Policy.

As both Philippi and Maull stress, Germany's abhorrence of military action outside its borders did not change easily. In 1992–94, although the fighting in former Yugoslavia intensified rapidly, the German coalition government was split on the question of constitutionality of out-of-area missions. Only after the Constitutional Court settled the matter in March 1994 were German troops deployed (with the consent of the parliament) in robust peacekeeping and then in peace enforcement missions, even without a mandate from the UN Security Council.

In the case of the changing German policy towards out-of-area missions of the Bundeswehr, the evidence for a transnational socialisation in German foreign policy is most obvious. The discontinuities in this policy area are obvious too. In the Gulf War Germany showed the utmost reluctance to commit military force and tens of thousands of Germans demonstrated against the allied intervention, while in the Kosovo War there were almost no demonstrations, but rather broad public support for sending the Bundeswehr to participate in combat operations.[22] If Germany had acted out of balance-of-power concerns, it might have intervened in the Balkans in order to preserve a regional balance of power. But it should have done so unilaterally to maximise its autonomy,[23] and it should have tried to create viable entities to foster credible conventional deterrence. Germany's Yugoslavia policy fails on both accounts. German policy in the former Yugoslavia has been multilateral, as it has been based on the notion of multi-ethnic states and democratic institutions to pacify their societies in contrast to a strategy of creating ethnic states and a stable military deterrence among those states.[24]

The evidence in this case suggests that changing external circumstances, which are reflected in changing role expectations of others in Germany – transnational socialisation processes in the institutional contexts of NATO and EU – had a determining effect on Germany's gradual policy change. This supports the institutionalist claim that institutions indeed matter and that norms and values shared in institutions may change preferences of member states. But again, as in the case of NATO enlargement, institutionalists face the challenge to explain why these institutions, such as NATO, EU and the UN changed their common set of rules and norms, prescribing military intervention in an ever expanding class of cases. This gap in rational choice and historical institutionalist explanations of NATO member countries calls for an explanation. Even more so since NATO countries changed a long-standing tradition that NATO acts only in accordance with the UN Security Council.

The empirical findings of the Kosovo case show that neither domestic nor transnational socialisation can fully explain why and how Germany changed its deeply embedded position on UN Security Council mandates in the Kosovo War. While the case illustrates that Germany's peculiarities in military affairs remain, the record of the public debate suggests that learning processes account for the policy shift in the Kosovo case.

Table 1 summarises the main empirical findings of the civilian power research concerning the policy trajectory in the cases presented here as well as the socialisation mechanisms within the civilian power approach which account for the change.

TABLE 1
CONTINUITY AND CHANGE IN GERMANY'S FOREIGN POLICY

Policy Area	Policy trajectory	Socialisation
Eastern enlargement	Continuity, few changes	Transnational socialisation
Non-proliferation	Continuity	- -
Out-of-area response	Continuity, some changes	Transnational socialisation, learning in to changing context/expectations
Human rights	Continuity	Domestic and transnational socialisation
EU treaty negotiations	Continuity, few changes	Domestic and transnational socialisation
OSCE institutionalisation and negotiations	Continuity, few changes	- -

In sum, three conclusions can be drawn from this empirical record. First, Germany has, by and large, kept its traditional role concept which resembles closely the civilian power ideal-type. Thereby, the role concept has shaped the foreign policy goals, the strategies and the instruments used by Germany in the 1990s. Second, those cases where Germany departed from its expected policy trajectory can be reconciled with and explained through the role-theoretical approach. This does not imply that 'power', 'national interests' or 'institutional pressures' were absent. Rather, these factors were perceived through, and weighed according to, the degree of their correspondence with the role concept. Third, alter- and ego-expectations as constituting parts of the role concept were not simply down- or up-loaded by policy-makers. These expectations were ripe for change as the end of the Cold War presented new challenges. Hence, key norms and the choice between them became the subject of intense debate both domestically and internationally.

HAS GERMANY DEPARTED FROM ITS TRADITIONAL FOREIGN POLICY ROLE?

The starting point of this paper was that other theoretical approaches to German foreign policy, namely realism and institutionalism, failed because they paid no attention to the influence of norms and values in foreign policy interest formation processes. In contrast, the studies presented above started by assuming that Germany's role concept as a civilian power shaped its foreign policy behaviour. Thereby, although this analysis started from a different, normative angle, it replicated the rationalist methodology when assuming that interests were fixed or relatively stable.[25] However, the civilian power studies discussed here share the constructivist conviction that roles – as part of a larger foreign policy culture – can be 'reconstructed'.[26] Indeed, as Philippi, Maull and Frenkler suggest in their case studies, Germany as a civilian power has already been reconstructed to some degree (though they would not necessarily agree as to whether the new German foreign policy role concept could still be seen as being in line with the civilian power ideal-type).

Theoretical Challenges: Conflicting Role Concepts and Domestic Interest Formation Processes

When we look at the strengths and weaknesses of the civilian power approach two conceptual problems come to mind: conflicting role concepts and domestic interest formation processes. First, as several case studies show, the role concept of civilian power is inherently complex and multi-dimensional, bundling several specific and distinctive role concept elements into a whole. For example, German foreign policy tries to behave as a 'good partner' *vis-à-vis* the United States and France, and thus to promote the deepening and widening of European integration and the Atlantic community. But these specific role concepts may not always be perfectly compatible. They may be inherently difficult to reconcile (such as efforts to both deepen and widen European integration) or they may be brought into contradiction under certain external circumstances.

Two main arguments are derived from this observation: (1) If Germany has been driven by its traditional role conception in the 1990s, this conception is dramatically changing, due to increasingly diverging role expectations from others, such as the United States. Thus, even if Germany wanted to stick to its civilian power role in the future, it could not due to external pressures;[27] and (2) If the role concept allows diverging expectations and thus different hypotheses as to likely behaviour, how could one tell which expectation will determine Germany's behaviour?

The role concept of civilian power is anchored in the normative notion that it may be possible to 'civilise', that is to transform, international relations. In such a context, it is also based on the constructivist notion that norms and prescribed patterns of behaviour can change too, albeit along a clearly definable trajectory. In our case this trajectory is defined by the ideal-type civilian power. In practice, the manifestation of civilian power behaviour will always deviate to some extent from the ideal-type. We cannot therefore expect the role behaviour of Germany to be cast in iron once and for all. There will be change (think about the change from *bourgeois* to *citoyen* in Elias' work). But this raises the issue of which changes are compatible with the essence of civilian power and which are not.

Conceptually, we have tried to tackle this challenge through two means. First, we have tried to identify patterns of rhetoric and behaviour falling into 'counter-categories' – that is, categories which are qualitatively different or even the opposite of what an ideal-type civilian power would be expected to say and do. One example would be the expressed willingness to use force unilaterally and without international legitimation. Second, we have simplified the originally rather complex ideal-type role concept to three core role segments: (a) the ability and willingness to act (*Gestaltungswille*); (b) the willingness to give up autonomy (*Autonomieverzicht*); (c) the willingness to accept short-term losses (in national utility maximisation) for long-term institutional interests (*interessenunabhängige Normdurchsetzung*).[28]

But these conceptual measures come at a cost. As the empirical record shows, Germany did not simply follow norms to re-enact and reproduce its traditional role concept. Instead, policy makers on several occasions (out-of-area, Eastern enlargement) contested the validity and legitimacy of key civilian power norms and principles.[29] In those instances, the issue what 'appropriate behaviour' means to a civilian power itself was contested.

In such a situation two policy trajectories are possible: (1) 'adjustment' of the policy instruments takes place while the key norms and goals of the role concept remain in place; or (2) 'learning', that is, change in foreign policy orientation (norms/goals)[30] takes place, learning which includes changes in strategies and instruments. In this case, however, civilian powers could 'learn' one of two things: (a) to diverge from the former role concept or (b) to 'learn' to reproduce it in modified form.

How could we tell the difference? We would expect, in both cases, a serious soul-searching, a prolonged political process of evaluation and innovation. The results would be compatible with civilian power only if:

- all key norms remained intact in principle;
- efforts were undertaken to ensure that behaviour as much as possible does justice to all principles under question; and
- the state concerned actively sought ways to reconcile the tensions (for example, by mediating between France and America, or by trying to bring in additional actors to forge compromises and even new institutional solutions).

Domestic Interest Formation

A second criticism is concerned with the assumption by many civilian power researchers of a highly coherent foreign policy consensus. In other words, either a political system is assumed to have a certain degree of autonomy from society or an overwhelming consensus exists between society at large and foreign policy-makers.[31] Neither scenario is very likely, but it is perhaps particularly problematic, given the explicitly democratic bent of this role concept, which in many ways reflects the transposition of democratic intra-state patterns of politics onto the level of inter-state relations. The reality is, of course, that foreign policy behaviour in democratic polities will generally be the result of pluralistic decision-making processes, putting the state – and hence also its foreign policies – (ultimately) at the disposal of the democratic sovereign, the people. How can we then expect foreign policies to be consistent over time and between issue areas, as seems required by the civilian power role concept?

To begin with, the civilian power approach works with the assumption that Germany's domestic setting is conducive to its 'civilised' foreign policy role concept. The Basic Law not only binds German foreign policy to certain fundamental values and opens the state to supranational integration,[32] it also establishes a constitutional environment for a strong civil society against the state in the form of basic rights (*Grundrechte*).[33] In the past, there has been a strong permissive domestic consensus allowing for an ever-closer European integration as well as a strong preference for non-military means of conflict management.[34] But several of the case studies presented here might be interpreted as challenging the underlying assumption that there still is a domestic consensus on a civilian power foreign policy in Germany.[35] Two examples stand out: first, in June 1997 during the Amsterdam EU treaty renegotiations, the Kohl government blocked further integration in the field of Home and Justice Affairs due to pressure from the Länder. Second, in contrast to the profound opposition of large parts of the German public during the Gulf War, no major protest erupted when the Schröder government sent combat troops to Kosovo without a UN Security Council mandate.[36]

How are these events to be interpreted? Assuming that there have been significant policy changes as a result of domestic political pressure, those changes could be *with* or *without* subsequent role concept change. In the first case, there would be a fundamental departure from the old role concept resulting from a process of domestic norm re-socialisation against the prevailing civilian power tradition. Such policy changes would indeed be profound and lasting, even if domestic pressure supporting a new set of norms diminished over time. In the latter case, we would have policy change without role change, and this would call for a different interpretation. If domestic pressures are able to produce policy outcomes which clearly deviate from continuing normative inclinations, then either domestic pressures on foreign policy decision-making must have increased significantly, or the relevance of norms and other identity factors for foreign policy must have declined. In this case, normative inclinations might again come to the fore once domestic pressures for alternative outcomes diminish.

The cases presented here contain convincing evidence that there is (some) policy change due to domestic interest (re)formation, but *without* role change. This is not to argue that role change could not happen in the future, but the evidence so far suggests that Germany will stick to its traditional role concept.[37] For example, as Maull suggests, the German participation in the Kosovo War can be reconciled with the role concept of an ideal-type civilian power if tensions between core values of the concept are taken seriously. In the Kosovo case, one has to take into consideration that German preferences were shaped by its role as a partner in NATO and a promoter of basic human rights that were in tension, if not contradiction, with its role as a promoter of the rule of law, that is, of the need to have a UN Security Council mandate.

In the cases where Germany obviously violated norms attached to its traditional role concept, one first has to ask whether policy change is omnipresent. If this is not the case – and this is the conclusion of the analysis here – one has to ask whether domestic pressure has increased in the specific policy field under study. The following cannot explain cross-policy variations, but a few suggestions for further study are in order.

Most cases where Germany was found to have failed to act as a civilian power relate to (re-)distributive policies in the European Union – the German Savings and Loan Associations, the German contribution to the EU budget, the reform of the Common Agricultural Policy, and so on. One could thus argue that the specific nature of the issue area is important in filtering the impact of identity factors on foreign policy outcomes. If so, Germany's willingness to go ahead with further integration was always dependent upon its ability to contain the negative side-effects of further integration through side payments in the domestic realm. The burden of unification and the recent deterioration of Germany's public finances have now undermined this possibility. Only when overriding national interests – such as the conclusion of German unity – overrule sector-specific interests, does integration proceed. If sector-specific interests are hurt by further integration and if they are able to mobilise domestic opposition behind their cause, integrationist policies might be diverted to the advantage of domestic interests. This interpretation implies that rule-governed behaviour in Germany's European policy hinges on traditional distributive bargaining.[38] Yet, while our cases and several other recent studies on Germany's European policy show that the key to understanding the domestication process lies with the changing role of the German Länder in Germany's European policy-making,[39] the record so far does not (yet) point to identity change in Germany's European policies.

In most cases under consideration, pressure by the Länder had a significant effect in pushing the federal government towards the 'pursuit of national interests'. At the Amsterdam summit meeting, the federal government rejected further integration in Home and Justice Affairs (HJA), due to pressure by some German Länder which feared losing the 'national veto' in asylum policies.[40] In the case of EU subsidies diverted to the benefit of Volkswagen, the federal government defended the inappropriate conduct of the Saxon government. Even in the case study on non-proliferation, Germany's development of nuclear weapons material in the research reactor Garching II can be traced back to the interests of Siemens and the Bavarian state government. Thus, deviations from the civilian power role model can be explained by a growing involvement of the German Länder in, and their growing scepticism towards, European integration or adherence to international non-proliferation norms.[41]

The studies presented here do not test this proposition. But their findings imply that after the introduction of the new article 23 of the Basic Law, the Länder not only hold a veto position on important issues of Germany's European policy-making, but that they also sometimes oppose foreign policy choices by the federal government. On the one hand, the German Länder increasingly acted as advocates within the political system for business or pressure groups. On the other, the Länder themselves pushed their own European political agenda, which focused on preserving state autonomy under the guise of the subsidiarity principle.[42]

Nonetheless, the proposition that the Länder might individually or collectively undermine the traditional foreign role concept should be taken with a grain of salt.[43] First, as the recent struggle and ultimate victory of Finance Minister Eichel on the issue of tax reform showed, the Länder are far from constituting a coherent and autonomous actor. In fact, their ability to speak with one voice has diminished since unification because of the growing gap between financially strong and weak states and the growing number of coalition governments that bridge traditional party cleavages and blur former party loyalties.[44]

In sum, the findings suggest that deviations from Germany's former role concept can be explained by incorporating domestic interest formation. In addition, the evidence presented here does not support the proposition that there is strong societal pressure to change Germany's role in Europe.[45] If this were the case, as has been argued recently,[46] the role-theoretical approach would suggest that Germany cannot in any case change its identity overnight. Moreover, if Germany were to start down the 'national road', it would immediately clash with the expectations of its partners and lose support among them for its policies.[47] This would very quickly impose severe constraints on Germany's foreign policy margins of manoeuvre.

CONCLUSION

The argument here is that Germany has held on to its previous foreign policy role concept and that its policy record in the 1990s can thus be described as one of 'modified continuity'. The end of the Cold War did not change the world power structure as realists claimed. States such as Germany had their own conception of what anarchy meant to them and they acted accordingly. This conception of the world and Germany's role within it did show considerable continuity and some change over the past ten years.

When we try to conceptualise the forces underlying change and continuity from a role-theoretical perspective, we come across two main causal pathways: the confirmation of Germany's role conception before, during, and after unification and the learning process ensuing from policy failure during the Balkan wars, especially the Kosovo conflict.

'Weiter so, Deutschland?!' The Confirmation of Germany's Foreign Policy Role Conception

The starting point of the continuity thesis is the empirical finding that the Kohl government's foreign policy rhetoric continued to stress central themes of the civilian power ideal-type. As Knut Kirste shows in a detailed content analysis of foreign policy speeches by various decision-makers, post-unification Germany stuck to its treasured 'policy of active integration and broad international cooperation', which included the proclivity to act multilaterally and the willingness to seize autonomy.[48] Equally, a strong influence of alter-expectations can be identified in central terms such as 'Germany's (grown) responsibilities' or new 'German duties' during the phase of unification.[49] This interpretation is supported by Bonn's foreign policy behaviour during unification, which resembled almost an ideal-type civilian power with Bonn's preference for the multilateral 2+4 process, its willingness to further integrate into the EU and NATO and its willingness to seize autonomy through the renunciation of nuclear weapons and the limitation on the troop strength of the German Armed Forces.

Through the successful 'closure' of the 'German Question', however, the mix of the constituting ego- and alter-part of Germany's role conception changed. Alter expectation still played an important part of Germany's role perception. First, the family of Western democracies – this *Wertegemeinschaft* (see above) – continued to figure prominently as the normative focal point of the German nation in the official rhetoric.[50] Second, as German decision-makers were never tired pointing out after the Gulf War, the unified Germany was facing 'larger responsibilities' in Europe and beyond.[51]

In a similar vein, the ego-part of Germany's foreign policy role concept underwent a significant change after unification. From 1989 on, we can identify increasingly positive self-images in the official rhetoric of the Kohl governments. These more positive self-images of Germany are/were held by a large majority of decision makers in all major parties. They are based on a 'sense of achievement and confirmation', because never before in history had Germany been at peace with its neighbours, unified, democratic and free. At last, as several key players pointed out, Germany had found its place in Europe.[52]

Thus, from an empirical perspective, a significant shift took place between the constituting ego- and alter-parts of Germany's foreign policy role conception during the 1990s.[53] But it would be misleading to attribute this 'new German self-assuredness' to a generational change or even worse to proclaim that there is a 'new German self-assertiveness' which (presumably) reflects Germany's increased power capabilities.[54] The

FIGURE I
ROLE SOCIALISATION PROCESS (1990–2000)

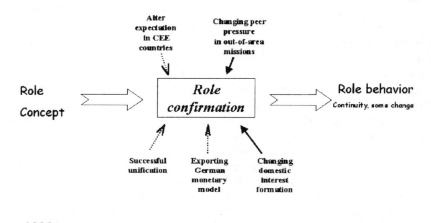

'Western security community of values' still represents the central point of reference for Germany's self-assured foreign policy role conception.

The most important example for this new German self-assuredness is the creation of the EMU through the Treaty of Maastricht. Again, it would be misleading to tie the creation of EMU and the Euro to German unification because, as its initiation in 1987 shows and the important decisions taken in Hanover in 1988 reveal, Germany's assertiveness in this case cannot be reduced to sovereignty gains during unification or generational change.[55] The empirical record fits nicely with the self-assuredness hypothesis. During the EMU negotiations the Kohl government strongly and successfully pushed for the 'German model' of an independent central bank, which was accepted by France and other key partners.[56] A self-assertive German policy cannot be reconciled with this record. Such a Germany should have wanted to keep the (presumed) hegemonic role of the Bundesbank in the DM zone instead of transferring autonomy in yet another important policy area.[57]

Moreover, the empirical record gives us ample evidence that Bonn's partners strengthened Germany's inclination to stick to its traditional foreign policy role concept. As Henning Tewes stressed in his case study on Germany, Central and Eastern European elites started to address the 'common democratic culture' of the EU and NATO member states and the new democracies in Central and Eastern Europe in the early 1990s. They appealed to a sense of community of East and West European democracies, which made an Eastern enlargement inevitable provided the EU did not change its identity as a 'community of democracies'.

In sum, three mechanisms can be identified to explain continuity in Germany's foreign policy role conception in the 1990s: first, the sense of achievement among Germany's elites to be able to close the 'German Question' through a democratic, peaceful and satisfied republic that is deeply embedded in an integrated Europe; second, through the successful export of the 'German model' of an independent central bank to the European level; and, third, through the strong alter expectations of its partners, especially the Central and Eastern European countries.

Foreign Policy Learning and Role Change

In general, two causal pathways for identity formation and (re)formation can be identified in role theory. First, a role concept can be challenged from within through social mobilisation of domestic interest groups.[58] In the case of Germany's approach to Europe, we find some policy change but no convincing evidence that Germany's ego-role conception for Europe has changed dramatically. Still, the situation is in flux. Second, a role concept can be challenged from abroad through transnational socialisation, as we have seen in the EU and NATO enlargement cases or during the Gulf War.

The case studies presented here do not systematically investigate socialisation, but we can still draw some tentative conclusions from their findings. First, we can interpret Germany's changing position on out-of-area missions of the Bundeswehr as a change in attitudes towards the utility and legitimacy of military action due to pressure from Germany's partners, based on experience with the need for military intervention in the Yugoslavian wars. Second, we can conceptualise change as a product of societal socialisation. But, as our critical review of the concept's explanatory power indicates, the role-theoretical approach still falls short of a theoretical mechanism to relate and integrate these two forms of socialisation. In particular, we might ask what explanation these two explanatory mechanisms give us, if and when the validity of norms (no matter where they come from) is contested and we observe changes in the role concept.

To illustrate this argument, we have chosen the out-of-area case study, and more specifically the German participation in the Balkan wars, as an example of the shortcomings of societal and transnational socialisation in explaining change in role behaviour. To begin with, it is clear that Germany broke with a central norm of its foreign policy identity as a civilian power when it acted in the NATO context without a clear UN Security Council mandate in Kosovo.[59] This breach was all the more significant because the new Schröder coalition government contained strong pacifist tendencies in both the Green and the Social Democratic parties.[60] Furthermore, support by the wider public for the intervention was weak. Domestic socialisation therefore does not persuasively explain the policy change.

On transnational socialisation, the findings of the Kosovo case seem ambiguous. Pressed by the United States in October 1998 to back military action (if needed), the newly elected Schröder government succumbed to peer expectations. This early decision could still be dismissed as a tactical move, or 'instrumental adaptation', to the NATO position, since the new government needed to present itself as a 'trusted ally' to a sceptical domestic and international audience. But when military action drew closer and questions about the legitimacy of a war without a UN mandate surfaced in earnest, decision-makers framed their argument in terms of the civilian power role concept, although they also emphasised the necessity to stick with Germany´s allies. The Kosovo War confronted the German foreign policy elite and the wider public with a conflict between key norms of its post-Second World War foreign policy role: multilateralism (never alone), observance of the law (never again), and human rights (never again concentration camps). The tension between these core values and between their protagonists in the German public debate was much more serious than in any of Germany's allies. The Balkan wars, and the Kosovo War in particular, struck right at the heart of Germany's post-Second World War role as a civilian (if not pacifist) power.

The incarnation of this struggle became Germany's first Green Foreign Minister, Joschka Fischer. Representing the pragmatic wing of the Green Party, Fischer had criticised German out-of-area missions in the early 1990s. But in 1995, as UN-protected 'safe havens' in Gorazde and Srebrenica fell to Serb forces during the Bosnian War, Fischer had changed his position on military intervention. Facing the dilemma that non-military means had not been sufficient to deter Serb forces from slaughtering civilians in UN-protected areas, Fischer argued that Germany's traditional pacifism could not mean that Germans would stand by idly when genocide happened.[61] In short, if Germans had to choose between 'never again war' and 'never again genocide', they would rather go to war than ignore genocide.

However, it cannot be denied that other motives also influenced Germany's behaviour in the Kosovo War. Maull has pointed out that policy-makers were concerned with flows of refugees and fears of a loss of influence within NATO if Germany should abstain.[62] Thus, a complex understanding of foreign policy outcomes is needed: while motives of self-interest and the 'logic of consequentiality' have certainly been part of the

Kosovo decision of the new Schröder government, it still seems true to say that the debate on the 'appropriateness' of foreign intervention without a UN Security Council mandate shaped German behaviour. It was a German initiative that led to the G8 peace proposal on 6 May 1999 which secured Russian participation and paved the way for a reintroduction of the Security Council as a legitimating body for the peace settlement. Germany, even as it deviated from the course expected by the civilian power role concept, strove to keep intact the key norms of the civilian power ideal-type as much as possible. What resulted was a 'creative reconstruction' of the civilian power role concept under difficult circumstances.[63]

It remains to be seen if the Kosovo case becomes a political and legal precedent for NATO to violate and thereby change international law. In this context, it is noteworthy that the Clinton administration wanted NATO to become an instrument of intervention independent of the UN. As the Deputy Secretary of State Strobe Talbott argued on 4 February 1999 in Bonn:

> We believe that NATO's missions and tasks must always be consistent with the purposes and principles of the UN and the OSCE. ... At the same time, we must be careful not to subordinate NATO to any other international body or compromise the integrity of its command structure. We will try to act in concert with the other organisations, and with respect for their principles and purposes. But the Alliance must reserve the right and the freedom to act when its members, by consensus, deem it necessary.[64]

Clearly, states might draw different lessons from the same event, due to different foreign policy roles. The civilian power role concept and the empirical findings in the Kosovo case suggest that Germany will not follow this suggested American course easily.

This study has argued that it is rewarding both to study the impact of a foreign policy role concept on foreign policy behaviour and to investigate the relationship between identities and social structures. The findings show that states do not simply follow one logic of social action. Foreign policy roles may include several, diverging as well as converging, modes of action. Yet it was Germany's role as a civilian power which guided its foreign policy behaviour during the 1990s.

NOTES

This study revises and expands Sebastian Harnisch and Hanns W. Maull, 'Conclusion: Learned its Lesson Well? Germany as a Civilian Power Ten Years After Unification', in Sebastian Harnisch and Hanns W. Maull (eds.), *Germany – Still A Civilian Power? The Foreign Policy of the Berlin Republic* (Manchester: Manchester University Press, forthcoming, 2001); Sebastian Harnisch, 'Deutsche Außenpolitik nach der Wende: Zivilmacht am Ende?'. Paper presented to the 21st conference of the *Deutsche Vereinigung für Politikwissenschaft* (DVPW), Halle, 1–5 Oct. 2000, http://www.uni-trier.de/uni/fb3 /politik/dtap/publications/conference/ harnisch.pdf [16.10. 2000]; Harnisch, '"Truth is what works", oder "Was nicht überzeugen kann, das wird sich auch nicht bewahrheiten". Eine Replik auf Gunther Hellmanns "Rekonstruktion der Hegemonie des Machtsstaates Deutschland unter modernen Bedingungen"?', University of Trier, http://www.uni-trier.de/uni/fb3/politik/dtap/publications/conference/Hellmann-Replik.pdf [06.12.2000b].

1. John Mearsheimer, 'Back to the Future: Instability in Europe After the Cold War', *International Security*, 15/1 (Summer 1990), pp.5–56.
2. Peter Katzenstein (ed.), *Tamed Power. Germany in Europe* (Ithaca: Cornell University Press, 1997); Thomas Berger, *Cultures of Anti-Militarism. National Security in Germany and Japan* (Baltimore: Johns Hopkins University Press, 1998); Thomas U. Berger, 'Norms, Identity and National Security in Germany and Japan', in Peter Katzenstein (ed.), *The Culture of National Security: Norms and Identity in World Politics* (New York: Columbia UP, 1996), pp.317–56; Knut Kirste, *Rollentheorie und Außenpolitikanalyse. Die USA und Deutschland als Zivilmächte* (Frankfurt/Main: Peter Lang, 1998); Carl Lankowski, *Break Out, Break Down or Break In? Germany and the European Union after Amsterdam* (Washington, DC: AICGS Research Report No. 8); John S. Duffield, *World Power Forsaken: Political Culture, International Institutions and German Security Policy After Unification* (Stanford: Stanford University Press, 1999); Thomas Banchoff, *The German Problem Transformed. Institutions, Politics and Foreign Policy, 1945–1995* (Ann Arbor: University of Michigan Press, 1999); Volker Rittberger, 'Deutschlands Außenpolitik nach der Vereinigung. Zur Anwendbarkeit theoretischer Modelle der Außenpolitik: Machtstaat, Handelsstaat oder Zivilstaat?', in Wolfgang Berger, Volker Ronge and Georg Weißeno (eds.), *Friedenspolitik in und für Europa* (Opladen, 1999), pp.83–107; Simon Bulmer, Charlie Jeffery and William Paterson, *Germany's European Diplomacy. Shaping the Regional Milieu* (Manchester: Manchester University Press, 2000).
3. The term 'civilian power' was originally coined by François Duchêne (1973) for the European Community. Hanns Maull has conceptualised it as a tool in comparative foreign policy analysis based on role theory, cf. Hanns Maull, 'Germany and Japan: The New Civilian Powers', *Foreign Affairs*, 69/5 (1990), pp.91–106; Hanns Maull, 'Zivilmacht Bundesrepublik Deutschland. Vierzehn Thesen für eine neue deutsche Außenpolitik', *Europa Archiv*, 47/10 (1992), pp.269–78; Hanns Maull, 'Civilian Power: The Concept and Its Relevance for Security Issues', in Lidija Babic and Bo Huldt (eds.), *Mapping the Unknown, Towards A New World Order* (Stockholm: The Swedish Institute of International Affairs, 1993), pp.115–31 (The Yearbook of the Swedish Institute of International Affairs 1992–93); Knut Kirste and Hanns Maull, 'Zivilmacht und Rollentheorie', *Zeitschrift für Internationale Beziehungen*, 3/2 (1996), pp.283–312.
4. Cf. Sebastian Harnisch and Hanns Maull, *Kernwaffen in Nordkorea. Regionale Stabilität und Krisenmanagement durch das Genfer Rahmenabkommen* (Forschungsinstitut der Deutschen Gesellschaft für Auswärtige Politik, DGAP) (Bonn: Europa-Union Verl., 2000).
5. Cf. 'In "No" Vote, Danes Show Doubt Over EU's Course', *International Herald Tribune*, 9 Sept. 2000.
6. Cf. Gunther Hellmann, 'The Sirens of Power and German Foreign Policy: Who Is Listening?', *German Politics*, 6/2 (1997), pp.29–57; Gunter Hellmann, 'Jenseits von "Normalisierung" und "Militarisierung": Zur Standortdebatte über die neue deutsche

Außenpolitik', *Aus Politik und Zeitgeschichte*, B 1–2 (1997a), pp.24–33; Ingo Peters, 'Vom "Scheinzwerg" zum "Scheinriesen" – deutsche Außenpolitik in der Analyse', *Zeitschrift für International Beziehungen*, 4/2 (1997), pp.361–88; A. James McAdams, 'Germany After Unification. Normal At Last?', *World Politics*, 49 (1997), pp.282–308.

7. Cf. Hans-Peter Schwarz, *Die Zentralmacht Europas. Deutschlands Rückkehr auf die Weltbühne* (Berlin: Siedler 1994); Arnulf Baring (ed.), *Germany's New Position in Europe: Problems and Perspectives* (Oxford: Berg 1994); Heinz Brill, *Geopolitik heute. Deutschlands Chance?* (Frankfurt a.M.: Ullstein, 1994); Gregor Schöllgen, *Die Außenpolitik der Bundesrepublik Deutschland: von den Anfängen bis zur Gegenwart* (Köln 1999: Bundeszentrale für politische Bildung 1999), pp.182–230; Geoffrey van Orden, 'The Bundeswehr in Transition', *Survival*, 33/4 (1991), pp.352–370; Werner Link, 'Alternativen deutscher Außenpolitik', *Zeitschrift für Politik*, 46/2 (1999), pp.125–43.

8. Cf. Banchoff, *The German Problem Transformed*; Peter Katzenstein, 'United Germany in an Integrationg Europe', in Katzenstein (ed.), *Tamed Power*, pp.1–48; Jeffrey J. Anderson and John B. Goodman, 'Mars or Minerva? A United Germany in a Post-Cold War Europe', in Robert O. Keohane, Joseph S. Nye and Stanley Hoffmann (eds.), *After the Cold War. International Institutions and State Strategies in Europe, 1989–1991* (Cambridge, MA: Harvard University Press, 1993), pp.23–62; Michael Staack, *Handelsstaat Deutschland. Deutsche Außenpolitik in einem neuen internationalen System* (Paderborn: Schöningh 2000); Harald Müller, 'Sicherheit für das vereinte Deutschland', in Monika Medick-Krakau (ed.), *Außenpolitischer Wandel in theoretischer und vergleichender Perspektive – die USA und die Bundesrepublik Deutschland. Festschrift zum 70. Geburtstag von Ernst-Otto Czempiel* (Baden-Baden: Nomos Verl., 1999), pp.145–98.

9. Cf. for an overview of different recent constructivist analysis of Germany's foreign and security policy, see Harnisch, 'Deutsche Außenpolitik nach der Wende', pp.2f.

10. Cf. Hanns W. Maull, 'Germany and the Use of Force: Still a Civilian Power' (Trier: Universität Trier, 1999), (Trierer Arbeitspapiere zur Internationalen Politik, Nr. 2), http://www.uni-trier.de/uni/fb3/politik/dtap/publications/tazip/tazip2/force.pdf [09/11/2000], p.27; Dieter Senghaas, *Wohin driftet die Welt?* (Frankfurt/Main: Suhrkamp Verl., 1994).

11. See Emanuel Adler, 'Seizing the Middle Ground: Constructivism in World Politics', *European Journal of International Relations*, 3/3 (1997), pp.319–63; Kirste and Maull, 'Zivilmacht und Rollentheorie', pp.293ff.; Henning Tewes, 'Das Zivilmachtskonzept in der Theorie der Internationalen Beziehungen. Anmerkungen zu Knut Kirste und Hanns Maull', *Zeitschrift für Internationale Beziehungen*, 4/2 (1997), pp.347–59 here p.354.

12. Cf. for a concise summary on transnational and societal socialisation, see Henning Boeckle, Volker Rittberger and Wolfgang Wagner, *Normen und Außenpolitik: Konstruktivistische Außenpolitiktheorie* (Universität Tübingen: Institut für Politikwissenschaft, 1999), pp.12–20 (Tübinger Arbeitspapiere zur Internationalen Politik und Friedensforschung, Nr. 34); on socialisation, see G. John Ikenberry and Charles A. Kupchan, 'Socialization and Hegemonic Power', *International Organization*, 44/3 (1990), pp.283–315; Frank Schimmelfennig, 'Internationale Sozialisation neuer Staaten. Heuristische Überlegungen zu einem Forschungsdesiderat', *Zeitschrift für Internationale Beziehungen*, 1/2 (1994), pp.335–55; Martha Finnemore and Kathryn Sikkink, 'International Norm Dynamics and Political Change', *International Organization*, 52/4 (1998), pp.887–917; on foreign policy learning, see Jack S. Levy, 'Learning and Foreign Policy: Sweeping an Conceptual Minefield', *International Organisation*, 48/2 (1994), pp.279–312; Dan Reiter, *Crucible of Beliefs. Learning, Alliances, and World Wars* (Ithaca: Cornell University Press, 1996); Sebastian Harnisch, *Außenpolitisches Lernen. Die US-Außenpolitik auf der koreanischen Halbinsel* (Opladen: Leske + Budrich 2000).

13. In this line of argument institutionalism explains the actors' compliance with the rules of an institution with the self-interest of the actor in lowering transaction costs through institutions. Compliance ends when institutions are unable to serve the self-interest of the actor or when those functions can be fulfilled through other means.

14. Tewes makes this point even more vigorously in his superb Ph.D. dissertation: Henning Tewes, 'Germany as a Civilian Power. The Western Integration of East Central Europe, 1989–1997' (Ph.D. thesis, University of Birmingham, 1998), pp.222–5; here p.234, citing Vaclav Havel saying in March 1991: 'An alliance of free and democratic states cannot close itself off from like-minded neighbouring states for ever'. Vaclav Havel, Speech at NATO Headquarter, 21 Jan. 1991, http://www.hrad.cz/president/Havel/speeches/1991/2103 uk.html [30.08. 2000].

15. Ulf Frenkler, 'Deutsche Politik in der Europäischen Union' (unpublished ms, University of Trier, 1997; http://www.uni-trier.de/uni/fb3/politik/workshop/depoineu.pdf, and 'Germany at Maastricht – Civilian Power or Power Politics?' in Harnisch and Maull (eds.), *Germany – Still a Civilian Power?*

16. Carsten Triphaus, 'Institutionalisierung und Konflifktprävention: Die deutsche KSZE/OSZE-Politik in den neunziger Jahren' (Studies in German and European Foreign Policy, No.1), University of Trier 2000, http://www.uni-trier.de/uni/fb3/politik/dtap/ publications/SGEFP/sgefp1.pdf [21.03.2001].

17. Oliver Meier, 'Eine vergleichende Untersuchung der deutschen und der japanischen Nichtverbreitungspolitik' (unpublished manuscript, University of Trier, 1997), and 'A Civilian Power Caught Between the Lines – Germany and Nuclear Non-Proliferation', in Harnisch and Maull (eds.), *Germany – Still a Civilian Power?*

18. As Volker Rittberger and his research team suggest, the striving to enhance its autonomy should have been a key feature of Germany's post-Cold War policy from a neo-realist perspective, cf. Rainer Baumann, Volker Rittberger and Wolfgang Wagner, 'Macht und Machtpolitik: Neorealistische Außenpolitiktheorie und Prognosen über die deutsche Außenpolitik nach der Vereinigung', *Zeitschrift für Internationale Beziehungen*, 6/2 (1999), pp.245–86.

19. Florian Pfeil, *Zivilmacht für die Menschenrechte? Menschenrechte in der deutschen Außenpolitik 1990–1998* (Hamburg: Verlag Dr. Kovac, 2000), and 'Civilian Power and Human Rights', in Harnisch and Maull (eds.), *Germany – Still a Civilian Power?*

20. Nina Philippi, 'Civilian Power and War – The German Debate about Out-of-Area Operations between 1990 and 1999', in Harnisch and Maull (eds.), *Germany – Still a Civilian Power?* Philippi's paper is based on a book-long analysis of Germany's out-of-area policy after unification: *Bundeswehr-Auslandseinsätze als außen- und sicherheits-politisches Problem des geeinten Deutschland* (Frankfurt/Main: Peter Lang Verl., 1996). See also Hanns Maull, 'Germany and the Use of Force: Still a "Civilian Power"?' *Survival*, 42/2 (2000), pp.56–80, and 'Germany's Foreign Policy, Post-Kosovo: Still a "Civilian Power"?' in Harnisch and Maull (eds.), *Germany – Still a Civilian Power?*

21. Consider statements like this from the then British Foreign Minister Douglas Hurd: 'Germany has to be willing to function on the same basis as everybody else, as regards the use of its armed forces and security matters. We cannot have the most powerful member of the community claiming that it cannot operate like everybody else', personal interview, December 1995, cited in Lisbeth Aggestam, 'Role Conceptions and the Politics of Identity in Foreign Policy' (ARENA Working Papers 99/8), http://www.sv.uio.no.arena /publications/wp99_8.htm [12.07.1999], here p.12.

22. Maull, 'German Foreign Policy, Post-Kosovo: Still a "Civilian Power"?' *German Politics*, 9/2 (2000), pp.8–10.

23. Some authors argue that Germany had been driven by these concerns when recognising Croatia and Slovenia unilaterally, cf. Beverly Crawford, 'Defection from International Cooperation: Germany's Unilateral Recognition of Croatia', *World Politics*, 48 (1995), pp.425–521; Thomas Jäger, Jens Paulus and Kathrin Winter, 'Macht Führung regeln? Die Koordinierung der Außenpolitiken der EG-Staaten im Konflikt um Jugoslawien', in Michéle Knodt and Beate Kohler-Koch, *Deutschland zwischen Europäisierung und Selbstbehauptung* (Mannheimer Jahrbuch für europäische Sozialforschung, Bd. 5), (Frankfurt/Main: Campus Verl., 2000), pp.110–34.

24. Cf. Kirste, *Rollentheorie*, pp.365–74, 397–415; Hanns W. Maull, 'Germany in the

Yugoslavia Crisis', *Survival*, 37/4 (Winter 1995–96), pp.99–130.

25. A static constructivist approach is the basis of the analysis of Germany's foreign policy in the 1990s presented in Boeckle *et al.*, *Normen und Außenpolitik*; Duffield, *World Power Forsaken*.

26. Cf. Thomas Risse, 'Identitäten und Kommunikationsprozesse in der internationalen Politik – Sozialkonstruktivistische Perspektiven zum Wandel in der Außenpolitik', in Medick-Krakau, *Außenpolitischer Wandel*, pp.33–57, here 43f.

27. Gunther Hellmann, '"Hegemonie des Machtstaates Deutschland unter modernen Bedingungen"? Zwischenbilanzen nach zehn Jahren neuer deutscher Außenpolitik'. Paper presented to the 21st Congress of the Deutsche Vereinung für Politikwissenschaft, Halle/Saale, 1–5 Oct. 2000, pp.80f.; http://www.uni-trier.de/uni/fb3/politik/dtap/publications/conference/hellmann-halle.pdf (16.10.2000).

28. Harnisch, 'Der Zivilmachtansatz ist keine Schönwettertheorie. Überlegungen zur methodischen und theoretischen Verortung' (unpublished ms, University of Trier, 15 May 1997), pp.6–8; Kirste, *Rollentheorie*, pp.460–62.

29. Whether these cases constituted processes of 'argumentative rationality' (Harald Müller, 'Internationale Beziehungen als kommunikatives Handeln. Zur Kritik der utilitaristischen Handlungstheorien', *Zeitschrift für Internationale Beziehungen*, 1/1 (1994), pp.15–44; Thomas Risse, '"Let's Argue!" Persuasion and Deliberation in International Relations', *International Organization*, 54/1 (2000), pp.1–39 is not the issue here. To answer that question one would have to differentiate between deliberate acts of persuasion and cases of individual learning as well as interaction between the two processes.

30. Foreign policy learning can be defined as: 'a change in central beliefs or instrumental beliefs on international politics, which is followed by policy change'. FP learning can be distinguished from foreign policy adaptation. Learning is a change of preferences while adaptation is a change of means to maximise gains with regard to a stable preference order, cf. Jack S. Levy, 'Learning and Foreign Policy: Sweeping a Conceptual Minefield', *International Organization*, 48/2 (1994), pp.279–312, and Harnisch, 'Deutsche Außenpolitik nach der Wende'.

31. Cf. on domestic interest formation processes in general: Andrew Moravcsik, 'Taking Preferences Seriously: A Liberal Theory of International Politics', *International Organization*, 51/4 (1997), pp.513–53; Derk Bienen, Corinna Freund and Volker Rittberger, 'Gesellschaftliche Interessen und Außenpolitik: Die Außenpolitiktheorie des utilitaristischen Liberalismus' (Tübinger Arbeitspapiere zur Internationalen Politik, Nr. 33, 1999), Universität Tübingen: Institut für Politikwissenschaft.

32. The institutional fit between Germany's federalism and European integration has been a major argument of recent institutionalist accounts as to why Germany is so prone to lead the integrationist drive, cf. Simon Bulmer, Charlie Jeffrey and William Paterson, 'Deutschlands europäische Diplomatie: die Entwicklung des regionalen Milieus', in Werner Weidenfeld (ed.), *Deutsche Europapolitik. Optionen wirksamer Interessenvertretung* (Münchner Beiträge zur Europäischen Einigung) (Bonn: Europa-Union Verl., 1998), pp.11–102; Simon Bulmer, 'Shaping the Rules? The Constitutive Politics of the European Union and German Power', in Katzenstein (ed.), *Tamed Power*, pp.49–79.

33. Cf. Ulf Frenkler, 'Germany at Maastricht – Civilian Power or Power Politics?', in Harnisch and Maull (eds.), *Germany – Still a Civilian Power?*; for the openness of the German Basic Law towards international law. The democratic underpinnings of civilian powers in the domestic realm are described in Hanns Maull, 'Zivilmacht Bundesrepublik Deutschland. Vierzehn Thesen für eine neue deutsche Außenpolitik', *Europa Archive*, 47/10 (1992), pp.781–3, and Tewes, *Germany as a Civilian Power*, pp.84–7.

34. Cf. for the permissive consensus on European Integration, Hans Rattinger, 'Einstellungen zur Europäischen Integration in der Bundesrepublik. Ein Kausalmodell', *Zeitschrift für Internationale Beziehungen*, 2/1 (1996), pp.45–78; Oskar Niedermayer, 'Die Entwicklung der öffentlichen Meinung zu Europa', in Matthias Jopp, Andreas Maurer and Heinrich Schneider (eds.), *Europapolitische Grundverständnisse im Wandel. Analysen und*

Konsequenzen für die politische Bildung (Bonn: Europa-Union Verl, 1998), pp.419–48. On recent changes in this attitude: Manuela Glaab *et al.*, 'Wertgrundlagen und Belastungsgrenzen deutscher Europapolitik', in Weidenfeld (ed.), *Deutsche Europapolitik*, pp.167–208

35. Cf. Frenkler, 'Germany at Maastricht'; Hanns W. Maull, 'Quo vadis, Germania? Außenpolitik in einer Welt des Wandels', *Blätter für deutsche und internationale Politik*, 42/10 (1997), pp.1245–56; Meier, 'A Civilian Power Caught Between the Lines'.

36. Maull, 'German Foreign Policy, Post-Kosovo', p.9.

37. For two recent interesting endorsements of this interpretation: Alvin Z. Rubinstein, 'Germans on their Future', *Orbis* (Winter 1999), pp.127–37, esp. p.129, and Rittberger, 'Deutschlands Außenpolitik nach der Vereinigung. Zur Anwendbarkeit theoretischer Modelle der Außenpolitik: Machtstaat, Handelsstaat oder Zivilstaat?' in Berger *et al.* (eds), *Friedenspolitik*.

38. As Geoffrey Garrett and Barry R. Weingast suggest in 'Ideas, Interests, and Institutions. Constructing the European Community's Internal Market', in Judith Goldstein and Robert O. Keohane (eds.), *Ideas and Foreign Policy. Beliefs, Institutions, and Political Change* (Ithaca, NY: Cornell University Press, 1993), pp.173–206, here p.186: '[ideational factors will be more important] the lesser the distributional asymmetries between contending equilibria and the smaller the disparities in the power resources of actors.'

39. Cf. Jeffrey Anderson, 'Hard Interests, Soft Power, and Germany's Changing Role in Europe', in Katzenstein (ed.), *Tamed Power*, pp.80–107; Jeffrey Anderson, *German Unification and the Union of Europe: The Domestic Politics of Integration Policy* (Cambridge, MA: Cambridge UP, 1999); Charlie Jeffery, *The Länder Strike Back: Structures and Procedures of European Integration Policy Making in the German Federal System* (University of Leicester, 1994), (Leicester University Discussion Papers in Federal Studies 94/4).

40. Christian Barth and Michael Mentler, 'Länderpositionen für Innen-und Rechtspolitik der Europäischen Union', in Franz Borkenhagen, *Europapolitik des deutschen Länder. Bilanz und Perspektiven nach dem Gipfel von Amsterdam* (Oplanden: Leske + Budrich, 1998), pp.86–102.

41. This trend is also supported by recent decisions of the Federal Constitutional Court, cf. Frenkler, 'Germany at Maastricht'; Joseph Weiler, *Der Staat 'über alles'. Demos, Telos and the German Maastricht-Decision* (Cambridge, MA: Harvard Law School, 1995), (Jean Monnet Working Papers 6/95) http://www.law.harvard.edu/programs/JeanMonnet/papers/95/9506ind.html [07.09. 2000].

42. Maull, 'Die deutsche Außenpolitik am Ende der Ära Kohl', in Erich Reiter (ed.), *Jahrbuch für Internationale Sicherheitspolitik 1999* (Hamburg: Mittler Verl., 1998), pp.274–95, and Michèle Knodt and Nicola Staeck, 'Shifting Paradigms: Reflecting Germany's European Policy' (European Integration Online Paper 3:3 (1999); http://eiop.or.at/eiop/texte/1999-003a.htm)

43. Bulmer *et al.*, *Germany's European Diplomacy*, p.83; Christian Engel, 'Kooperation und Konflikt zwischen den Ländern: zur Praxis innerstaatlichen Mitwirkung und der deutschen Europapolitik aus der Sicht Nordrhein-Westfalens', in Rudolph Hrbek (ed.), *Europapolitik und Bundesstaatsprinzip. Die 'Europafähigkeit' Deutschlands und seiner Länder im Vergleich mit anderen Föderalstaaten* (Baden-Baden: Nomos Verl., 2000), p.58; Charlie Jeffery and Stephen Collins, 'The German Länder and EU Enlargement: Between Apple Pie and Issue Linkage', *German Politics*, 7/2 (1998), pp.86–101.

44. Katrin Auel, 'Regieren im Mehrebenensystem. Deutschland zwischen nationaler und europäischer Politikverflechtungsfalle?' (Paper presented to the second conference of the project *Zukunft des Nationalstaates in der Europäischen Integration* of the Deutsch-französische Zukunftswerkstatt, Otzenhausen, 7–8 Sept. 2000).

45. Markus Jachtenfuchs, 'Deutsche Europapolitik: Vom abstrakten zum konkreten Föderalismus', in Michèle Knodt and Beate Kohler-Koch (eds.), *Deutschland zwischen Europäisierung und Selbstbehauptung: Mannheimer Jahrbuch für empirische*

Sozialforschung, Vol.5 (Frankfurt am Main: Campus Verl., 2000).

46. Cf. Glaab *et al.*, 'Wertgrundlagen'; Gunther Hellmann, 'Machtbalance und Vormachtdenken sind überholt: Zum außenpolitischen Diskurs im vereinigten Deutschland', in Medick-Krakau (ed.), *Außenpolitischer Wandel*, pp.97–126; Gunther Hellmann, '"Hegemonie des Machtsstaates Deutschland unter modernen Bedingungen"? Zwischenbilanzen nach zehn Jahren neuer deutscher Außenpolitik' (Beitrag für den 21. Wissenschaftlichen Kongress der Deutschen Vereinigung für Politische Wissenschaft in Halle/Saale, 1–5 Oct. 2000, http://www.uni-trier.de/uni/fb3/politik/dtap/publications/conference/hellmann-halle.pdf [09.11.2000]); Knodt and Staeck, 'Shifting Paradigms, http://eiop.or.at/eiop/texte/1999-003a.htm [02.07.1999]; Michéle Knodt, 'Europäisierung à la Sinatra: Deutsche Länder im europäischen Mehrebenesystem', in Knodt and Kohler-Koch (eds.), *Deutschland zwischen Europäisierung und Selbstbehauptung*, pp.237–64.

47. A telling example of how this could look is the rather sad story of the first German nomination for the IMF Director position, cf. Sebastian Harnisch, 'Germany's National IMF Policy: Lessons To Be Learned', *German Foreign Policy in Dialogue*, 1/1 (2000), http:/www.uni-trier.de/uni/fb3/politik/dtap/newsletter/archive/issue01.html [14.12.2000].

48. Knut Kirste, 'Das außenpolitische Rollenkonzept der Bundesrepublik Deutschland 1985–1995' (unpublished manuscript, University of Trier, 1998); trier/de/fb3/politik/workshop/usarolle.pdf.

49. Kirste, *Rollentheorie*, p.456.

50. Foreign Minister Hans-Dietrich Genscher, 'Erklärung zum 40. Gründungstag der NATO am 3. April 1989', *Bulletin* 31 (06.04.1989), S. 274: 'Our membership in the Western world's community of values, based on freedom and human dignity, is an absolute necessity for our self-image as a nation', cited after Paul Létourneau and Marie-Elisabeth Räkel, 'Germany: To Be or Not Be Normal?', in Philippe G. Le Prestre (ed.), *Role Quests in the Post-Cold War Era. Foreign Policies in Transition* (Montreal: McGill-Queen's University Press, 1997), pp.111–30, here p.123.

51. Kirste, *Rollentheorie*, pp.135 and 202ff.

52. Cf. Bundeskanzler Helmut Kohl, 'Regierungserklärung, 30 Jan. 1991', *Deutsche-Außenpolitik 1990/1991* (Munich: Moderne Verlagsgesellschaft), p.328; Bundespräsident Richard von Weizäcker, 'Ansprache am 30. April 1992', *Bulletin* 49 (09.05.1992), p.470.

53. Létourneau and Räkel, 'Germany: To Be or Not To Be Normal?'.

54. Cf. Hellmann, 'Hegemonie des Machtsstaates Deutschland ...?', and my critical response: Harnisch, 'Truth is What Works'.

55. See Joseph Grieco, 'State Interests and Institutional Rule Trajectories: A Neorealist Interpretation of the Maastricht Treaty and European Economic and Monetary Union', in Benjamin Frankel (ed.), *Realism: Restatements and Renewal* (London: Frank Cass, 1996), pp.261–306; Kenneth Dyson and Kevin Featherstone, 'EMU and Economic Governance in Germany', *German Politics*, 5/3 (1996), pp.325–55; and Eckart Gaddum, *Deutsche Europapolitik in den 1980er Jahren: Interessen, Konflikte und Entscheidungen der Regierung Kohl* (Paderborn, 1994).

56. Bulmer *et al.*, *Germany's European Diplomacy*, p.92.

57. Cedric Dupont and Dieter Wolf, 'Germany and EMU: A New Institution to Preserve an "Old Good"' (Working Paper, Center for German and European Studies, University of California at Berkeley, 1998); and Thomas Risse *et al.*, 'To Euro or not to Euro? The EMU and Identity Politicks in the European Union', *European Journal of International Relations*, 5/2 (1999), pp.147–87.

58. For a comparative analysis of social mobilisation in the case of changing domestic norms on citizenship in Germany, Ukraine and Russia, see Jeffrey T. Checkel, '(Regional) Norms and (Domestic) Social Mobilization: Citizenship Politics in Post Maastricht, Post-Cold War Germany' (ARENA Working Papers 99/3), http://www.sv.uio.no.arena/publications/wp99 3.htm [12.07.1999]; Jeffrey T. Checkel, 'International Institutions and Socialisation' (ARENA Working Papers 99/5), http://www.sv.uio.no.arena/publications/wp99 5.htm [12.07.1999]

59. Whether this breach already constitutes an identity change is debatable, since key decision-makers claim that this behaviour will be a one-time exception', e.g. Foreign Minister Klaus Kinkel before the Bundestag on 16 Oct. 1998: 'The decision of NATO [on air strikes against the FRY] must not become a precedent. As far as the Security Council monopoly on force [Gewaltmonopol] is concerned, we must avoid getting on a slippery slope', Deutscher Bundestag, Plenarprotokoll 13/248, 16 Oct. 1998, p.23129.

60. In fact, the coalition very nearly collapsed when a special congress of the Green Party in Bielefeld on 12 May 1999 decided by only a small margin to tolerate the government's course.

61. Consider the statement of Fischer before the Bundestag in 1995: 'We are in a real conflict between basic values. On the one hand, there is the renunciation of force as a vision of a world in which conflicts are resolved rationally, through recourse to laws and majority decisions, through the constitutional process and no longer through brute force; a world in which military means are rejected, and in which the aim is to create structures to replace them and make them redundant. On the other hand, there is the bloody dilemma that human beings may be able to survive only with the use of military force. Between solidarity for survival and our commitment to non-violence – that is our dilemma ...' Joschka Fischer, speech given in the Bundestag on 6 Dec. 1995, quoted in *Das Parlament*, 15 Dec. 1995.

62. Maull, 'German Foreign Policy, Post-Kosovo'.

63. As Bruno Simma points out Germany took pains to stress that NATO acted in conformity with the 'sense and logic' of the resolutions that the Security Council had managed to pass, Bruno Simma, 'NATO, the UN and the Use of Force: Legal Aspects', *European Journal of International Law*, 10 (1999), pp.1–21, here p.12

64. Cited in Simma, 'NATO', p.15.

Germany and the Use of Military Force: 'Total War', the 'Culture of Restraint' and the Quest for Normality

author block
RAINER BAUMANN AND
GUNTHER HELLMANN

For most of the past century, Germany's attitudes towards and practices of war have been special in two ways as compared to other 'Western' or 'developed' countries. First, in the German case the changes that took place during the last century were probably more dramatic than in the case of similar societies (or similarly positioned states). Second, the development in Germany often seemed to contravene the trends prevalent in such other societies. The so-called Bonn Republic appeared to be almost as much of an extreme in comparison to other Western countries as was the Third Reich. Where Hitler and his associates pushed war to new extremes in both theory and practice, post-war West Germans were, for the most part, willing recipients or even zealous proponents of the anti-militarist re-education favoured by the Western allies. Where Goebbels was declaring 'total war' to the world, West German 'Genscherists' were declaring 'total peace', as one German journalist put it at the time of unification.[1] Most observers could probably agree that both the Third Reich and the second German Republic were special in their attitudes towards war compared to other countries and societies during the same era. Whatever 'normal' may have meant in terms of defining Western attitudes during both periods, Germany diverged from this norm more than most. Since the late 1980s, however, this discrepancy in attitudes towards war and the actual practice of war between Germany and similar Western countries has been shrinking, with the pace of convergence accelerating since the mid-1990s. While Germans were still almost totally absent from the scene of military action during the Gulf War of 1990/91, they found themselves centre-stage only nine years later in NATO's war in Kosovo.

This study examines these changes, paying particular attention to public attitudes and political discourse as well as to concrete foreign policy behaviour. In order to understand the German case, it is necessary to study the developments in these three dimensions and their interplay, which we view as

Rainer Baumann and Gunther Hellmann, Johann Wolfgang Goethe University of Frankfurt a process of socialisation taking place within a changing international environment. In fact, this interplay can be presented in very different ways. In the second section, we discuss three different perspectives in this regard. Most observers concentrate on the impact that international structural factors (that is, Germany's international environment) as well as domestic structural factors (such as Germany's anti-militarist political culture, which can be witnessed in discourse and public attitudes) have on German participation in military interventions. These observers argue that Germany has remained exceptional in its behaviour, as domestic structural factors have prevented profound policy changes. In contrast to this structure-centred perspective, other observers have identified an ongoing re-militarisation in German foreign policy. According to this actor-centred position, political decision-makers have repeatedly pushed the limits for German participation in military interventions. Here, it is concrete political action that impacts on domestic structural factors such as public attitudes. Assuming a third perspective, we will position ourselves in the middle, stressing the co-constitutive effects of public and elite discourse, public attitudes and foreign policy behaviour. While the changes we observe have often been initiated deliberately, inspired by 'normalising' ambitions of German decision-makers, decision-makers are fully free neither from Germany's international environment nor from the expectations advanced and the limits set by German society.

The subsequent sections substantiate our argument by examining the development of public attitudes, foreign policy discourse and government action. Given the constraints of space we are not able to examine these processes in detail. However, in sketching the broad outlines of developments since the late 1980s (including a more detailed analysis of Germany's policy *vis-à-vis* the two most important conflicts of the 1990s, the Gulf War and the Kosovo War), we hope to show how domestic and international structural factors as well as the strategic ambitions of foreign policy decision-makers have produced the far-reaching changes in German attitudes and behaviour towards the use of force which we can observe today.

GERMAN PARTICIPATION IN MILITARY INTERVENTIONS: THREE PERSPECTIVES

The 'Culture of Restraint', or the Constraining Effects of Social Structures

Among the substantial number of scholars who have studied Germany's position on the use of military force, one view is most prominent. It holds that, in light of the disastrous consequences of German militarism during the Nazi period, a stable anti-militarist political culture has evolved in Germany. This culture, also known as the 'culture of restraint', is seen as responsible for Germany's exceptionalism on the use of force ever since the founding of the

Federal Republic and as bound to inhibit Germany's future 'normalisation' in this regard. This position is pronounced most clearly by proponents of culturalist approaches to the study of German foreign policy.[2] According to them, the formulation of a country's foreign policy is profoundly shaped by its political culture. The culturalists concede that such political culture may change in the light of dramatic political events. The transformation of German militarism into the post-Second World War 'culture of antimilitarism' of the Federal Republic provides a good example for this argument.[3] Yet, in general, political culture is perceived as very stable. Consequently, from this perspective, the German 'culture of restraint' that has evolved after Germany's loss of the Second World War and the breakdown of the Third Reich still has an enormous impact on Germany's readiness to take part in military interventions. Public attitudes and the political discourse in Germany on the participation in military interventions reflect Germany's political culture and shape the room for manoeuvre for political decision-makers. Thus, culturalists would draw arrows from political culture to public opinion and political discourse, and from there to foreign policy behaviour, paying little attention to the reverse effects German foreign policy behaviour may have on discourse and public opinion, and, finally, on the 'culture of restraint'.

A similar position has been developed by Hans Maull, who argues that Germany has adopted the role of a civilian power.[4] Similar to the culturalists, Maull views Germany's self-identification as a civilian power as an outgrowth of lessons learned after the Second World War.[5] While the role of a civilian power is basically an attribute of an actor rather than a component of a certain structure surrounding that actor (as is political culture), Maull in fact treats it as a stable and quasi-structural condition of Germany's foreign policy behaviour.

The consequence of this perspective on the development of the German position is that there is comparatively little change to be identified for the last decade as well as expected for the future. While Germany may be pressed by its partners to give up its exceptionalism on the use of force, Germany's domestic social structures slow down or even prevent substantial changes of the German position. Thus, the undeniable change of German policy from remaining absent in the Gulf War to fully participating in the Kosovo War is to be seen as a reluctant adaptation to a changing international environment, and there is little prospect (or danger) of Germany fully giving up its reservations about the use of force in the foreseeable future.

'Salami Tactics', or the Socialising Effects of Political Action

In contrast to this view, other observers have portrayed the development in quite a different way. Stressing that, within a decade, German decision-makers have almost completely turned around Germany's policy with regard to the use of military force, these authors view this policy change as a central element of a remilitarisation of German foreign policy.[6] They view the evolving German readiness to participate in military interventions not as a reluctant adaptation to a changing environment, but as the result of a deliberate strategy of German decision-makers who wanted the use of force to become an accepted means of German foreign policy right from the beginning. Yet such a redirection of foreign policy could not be accomplished at once, but only in steps. The German public had to get accustomed to Bundeswehr soldiers 'out of area'. Likewise, the idea of Germans taking part in military interventions had to gain acceptance in public and elite political discourse. Consequently, German decision-makers expanded the scope of Germany's contributions to out-of-area operations step by step, utilising what can be called 'salami tactics'.[7] Slice after slice, so to speak, the political discourse has been reshaped and the limits of legitimate German use of force set by public opinion have been removed. From this perspective, international crises and the pressure of Germany's Western partners are to be seen less as causes of German policy changes but more as welcome opportunities for the proponents of re-militarisation to legitimise their course. According to this argument, within a decade the parameters in Germany concerning the political use of military force have changed dramatically, and these changes were intended from early on. In the wake of the Gulf War, German participation in hostilities would have been unacceptable for the German public, but only eight years later, decision-makers could count on broad public support for Germany's participation in the Kosovo War.

This view implies that public opinion and political discourse to a great extent follow concrete political action. While the culturalists stress the restraining effect of public sentiments on foreign policy, proponents of the re-militarisation thesis would draw an arrow in the opposite direction. According to them, anti-militarist public sentiments in Germany may have had a restraining effect of German policy, but German policy-makers have managed to dominate the political discourse and to push public opinion in their desired direction.

Gradual Change and the Quest for Normality, or the Co-Constitutive Effects of Agency and Structure

While the *structuralists* emphasise the inhibiting effects of German political culture characterised mainly by a 'culture of restraint', and while the *actionalists* emphasise the intentionality of a German political elite bent on getting rid of former restrictions on the use of the Bundeswehr, our third (and preferred) *interactionist* perspective emphasises the co-constituting effects of structure and agency. In the abstract, our model presupposes that both structural factors (such as the distribution of power in the international system, international law, the domestic political system, decision-making structures or political culture), as well as actor-related (or 'actional') factors (such as intentionality, decision-making and decision-implementation) exercise causal power. Structure and agency shape and (re-)produce each other through complex processes, the causal paths of which are not easily identified. For example, we argue that German attitudes towards the use of force as well as the respective policy changes which have taken place between the 1980s (Iran–Iraq War) and 1999 (Kosovo War) are indeed far-reaching. Yet we would argue neither that this reflects the malicious designs of a trigger-happy foreign policy elite determined to implement a course of 're-militarisation' (or 'normalisation') of German foreign policy along traditionalist great power lines nor that Germany (and its elites) have been 'forced by events', by systemic forces or the pressures of the allies to shed previous restrictions. Rather, our argument is that structural as well as actional factors shape each other. Consequently, in order to understand adequately the development of the German position on the use of military force, these processes of agency–structure interplay need to be taken into account.

This discussion focuses primarily on three factors: foreign policy discourse, public opinion and governmental decisions and action. Obviously, the latter clearly falls on the agency side of the structure–agency dichotomy. Foreign policy discourse has both structural and actional features: it is structural in the sense that meaning generated through discourse has deep roots in social life, encompassing (relatively) stable basic concepts such as 'sovereignty', 'foreign policy' and 'military force' as well as combinations of these concepts in judgements which reflect (more or less) adequately relatively durable political realities. It also comprises, however, aspects of agency. Discourse always reflects the action-guiding beliefs of individual and/or collective actors which, in their ability to invent and express old as well as new ideas, are behaving routinely as well as creatively. Public opinion, finally, sheds light on the beliefs held among the German population. Thus, we use it here as an indicator of the cognitive-normative structures with which German decision-makers are confronted.[8] In consequence we interpret the evolution of the German position as a process of socialisation: the (constructions of) foreign policy problems to be tackled by Germany (that is, relevant individual as well as collective actors in Germany, such as foreign policy decision-makers, but also foreign policy experts participating in and shaping foreign policy discourse as well as public opinion more broadly) and its partners have to be seen against the menu of problems perceived and presented by other international actors – if only because Germany has always been (and continues to be) closely integrated in an intricate web of international institutions.

By implication this position leads us to expect significant change along the lines of those observers who interpret Germany's increasing readiness to use force either as a process of 'normalisation' or 'abnormalisation'.[9] In the terminology of the normalisation-sympathisers, Germany is in the process of 'coming of age', becoming more 'self-confident' and assertive, feeling less inhibited (*befangen*) by its pre-Second World War legacy.[10] In the eyes of the abnormalisation critics, in contrast, Germany is again 'militarising' its foreign policy, thereby returning to the dubious past of 'power politics' (*Machtpolitik*) and a 'security policy of re-confrontation'.[11] We agree with the advocates as well as the critics of 'normalisation' as to the significance of the dramatic departures from old foreign policy practices. However, in contrast to both, we prefer a more detached social science vocabulary in (primarily) describing and explaining (rather than politically evaluating) these changes.

GERMANY AND THE USE OF MILITARY FORCE: TRENDS IN GOVERNMENT BEHAVIOUR, POLITICAL DISCOURSE AND PUBLIC OPINION

It can be argued that nowhere has change in German foreign policy been more profound in the last decade than with respect to the willingness to take part in multilateral military operations. Table 1 summarises the development of German contributions to international military operations during the 1990s.

The change in German foreign policy behaviour becomes even more visible in a graphical illustration. Figure 1 shows that, in the 1990s, the scope of German contributions has grown gradually but, in the end, substantially. 'Scope' in this sense has both a quantitative and a qualitative dimension, as

FIGURE 1
DEVELOPMENT OF GERMANY'S PARTICIPATION IN MILITARY OPERATIONS

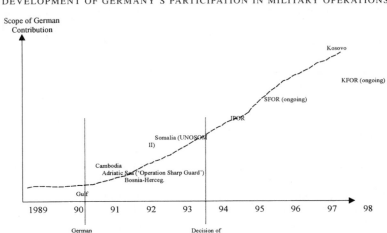

TABLE 1
GERMAN PARTICIPATION IN MILITARY OPERATIONS

Conflict/Military Operation	Scope of German Participation
Persian Gulf 1987 Escort of Kuwaiti ships; US skirmishes with Iran; minesweeping	Logistical support only; German ships to Mediterranean, but not to Gulf region
Namibia 1989 Peace-keeping operation (UNTAG)	Contribution to international police force
Gulf War 1990/91	Financial and logistical support only; Dispatch of 200 soldiers and 18 fighter jets to Turkey as part of a NATO contingent
Cambodia 1991-92 Peace-keeping operation (UNAMIC)	Medical troops
Adriatic 1992-96 Monitoring of embargo against FRY (Operation Sharp Guard)	Naval forces ('no combat operation')
Somalia 1993-94 (UNOSOM II)	Supply and transport units
Bosnia-Hercegovina 1993-95 (UNPROFOR)	Logistical support only (airlifts to Sarajevo etc)
Bosnia-Hercegovina 1993-95 monitoring of no-fly zone; NATO air strikes against FRY	Air-force personnel as part of AWACS unit; No participation in NATO air strikes
Georgia, since 1994 (UNOMIG)	10 German medical officers and military observers as part of UN peace- keeping force
Bosnia-Hercegovina 1995-96 (IFOR)	Some 3,000 non-combat ground troops, stationed in Croatia
Bosnia-Hercegovina since 1996 (SFOR)	Some 3,000 ground troops (including combat troops), stationed in Bosnia-Hercegovina
Iraq 1998 US-led air raids	Offer to grant US the use of military bases in Germany; no participation in attacks
Kosovo/FRY since 1998 (KVM; air strikes; KFOR)	Participation in unarmed OSCE-led Kosovo Verification Mission; Participation in NATO air strikes (no UN Security Council mandate); Contribution to KFOR with some 8,000 ground troops

German military contributions have become larger and, at the same time, the operations Germany is ready to take part in have become more 'militarised' and thus more dangerous.

While this development has been a gradual process, a few events can be identified that were crucial in driving this process. Thus, this section examines German behaviour as well as discourse and public opinion in the 1980s, during the Gulf War, the UN operation in Somalia, the decision of the German Constitutional Court in 1994, the conflict in Bosnia-Hercegovina, and the Kosovo War. We will pay special attention to the Gulf War and the Kosovo War, as the former was crucial in initiating the developments which are the focus of our analysis whereas the latter marks its culmination point, at least for the time being.

The German Position before Unification

The foreign policy discourse in the old Bonn Republic was shaped largely by the legacy of German militarism and the notion of a 'special (German) path' (*Sonderweg*). *Multilateralism* (never again going it alone), *European integration* (with an emphasis on regaining recognition, trust and economic wealth) and *anti-militarism* ('culture of restraint'; 'civilian power') were accordingly the defining concepts in Germany's foreign policy vocabulary during the time of the Bonn Republic. Within this discursive setting, the political use of force, even in concert with the allies, was not perceived to be an acceptable instrument of German foreign policy. Of course, in the 1980s, when the scope of UN peace-keeping was still limited and the problem of 'out-of-area' operations was rarely discussed in NATO,[12] the question of deploying troops abroad attracted only limited attention in West Germany anyway. In 1982, the federal government's security council (*Bundessicher-heitsrat*) stressed that, in accordance with a broad 'security-political consensus' in Germany, the Basic Law prohibited any deployments of Bundeswehr troops out of area.[13] Of course, legal experts differed on whether this was indeed the proper interpretation of the Basic Law, but it was widely shared among the political parties, if not least for political reasons.[14]

Yet, only a few years later, in 1987, some participants in the decision-making process started to question this consensus. In their effort to secure the passage of Kuwaiti oil tankers in the Persian Gulf, US forces engaged in a number of skirmishes with Iran. In July 1987, the US called upon its European allies, West Germany among them, to provide military assistance in this conflict. The US administration asked the German government to send several ships to the Persian Gulf to provide military protection for tankers as well as for mine sweeping.[15] In the end, the Germans, pointing to their constitutional restrictions, limited their support to sending a few ships to the Mediterranean (that is, remaining within NATO territory).[16] Still, there were first signs that the consensus on out-of-area operations was beginning to crumble among the West German foreign policy elite. In the process leading to the rejection of the US request, the German Ministry of Defence took a position that deviated from the decision of 1982. It maintained that it was constitutional to deploy Bundeswehr forces to protect German merchant ships on the high seas as well as for clearing mines in international shipping lanes. It also unsuccessfully proposed to base further decisions of the federal government on this interpretation, in order to enlarge the Bundeswehr's room for manoeuvre.[17] While the federal government did not take this position in 1987, we can nonetheless see that the beginnings of what later turned into the 'out-of-area debate' date back to the time before German unification.

Germany in the Gulf War

A much bigger challenge to the German insistence on military restraint came with the Gulf War of 1990/91. Iraq's invasion in Kuwait occurred at a time when the German foreign policy establishment was preoccupied with wrapping up the 'Two-plus-Four' negotiations leading to German unification. During that time, the political rhetoric was filled with 'Genscherist' terminology: the united Germany carried significantly more 'European' and 'global responsibility' and the conduct of a 'policy of the good example' (*Politik des guten Beispiels*) or, alternatively, a 'policy of responsibility' (*Verantwortungspolitik*) were imperative under the new conditions. Multilateralism and European integration continued to be the guiding concepts and the repeated emphasis on Germany's responsibility for building 'a new culture of international co-existence' made clear that 'responsibility' was the code word for sticking with the anti-militarist 'culture of restraint' of the old Bonn Republic.[18]

The course of the Gulf crisis, culminating in the war in January and February 1991, put many of the assumptions and positions that characterised this German discourse under immense pressure. Already in August 1990, the US administration had asked the Kohl government whether Germany could send troops to the Gulf.[19] CDU representatives within the government briefly considered responding positively, but eventually the government decided that it would be unwise to make such a departure from long-established foreign policy practice without broad domestic support and at a time when the Two-plus-Four Treaty, requiring Soviet approval, had not yet been ratified.[20] Like three years earlier, the government stressed that the German constitution would not allow for a deployment of Bundeswehr soldiers in the Gulf. The difference was that this time several politicians, notably from Chancellor Kohl's Christian Democrats, portrayed this 'constitutional limitation as an obstacle to be overcome rather than a fundamental constraint to be dealt with on its own terms'[21] by stressing that, after the federal elections in December

TABLE 2
PUBLIC OPINION ON CHANGE OF BASIC LAW TO ALLOW FOR GERMAN TROOPS
IN UN OPERATIONS (OCTOBER 1990, FEBRUARY 1991)

Question: 'Chancellor Kohl demanded that the Basic Law be changed after the parliamentary elections in order to allow for deployment of German troops for UN-activities. Do you agree?' (in %)

| | October 1990 | | February 1991 | |
	Old Länder	New Länder	Old Länder	New Länder
I agree	24	19	36	16
I disagree	55	53	49	66
Don't know	21	28	15	18

Source: Elisabeth Noelle-Neumann and Renate Köcher (eds.), *Allensbacher Jahrbuch der Demoskopie 1984–1992* (Munich: K.G. Saur, 1993), p.962.

1990, Germany should amend its Basic Law to allow for certain deployments of German soldiers abroad. According to public opinion polls taken during that time, the German people were rather sceptical about such prospects. Table 2 shows that vast majorities in both East and West opposed such a change of the Basic Law.

The overwhelming majority of Germans both among the elites as well as the broader public at this point still shared the view that only political means were justified to resolve international conflicts. Former Chancellor Willy Brandt best expressed these sentiments when he implored the Kohl government in November 1990 to stick to diplomatic means and economic sanctions 'in order to reach, in every conceivable way, a political solution' to the conflict in the Gulf. Germany 'must not lag behind anybody in its efforts for peace', Brandt said, because war, in his view, was 'the *ultima irratio* of politics'.[22]

Meanwhile, Germany supported its allies with substantial financial contributions totalling some DM 18 billion.[23] In December 1990, the Turkish government filed a request for assistance by its NATO allies against a possible Iraqi attack. As a result NATO's Defence Planning Committee decided in early January to send the Allied Mobile Force's air component to bases in south-eastern Turkey. Given the fact that a NATO ally was calling for help and since this rapid reaction unit was highly integrated and included some 200 Bundeswehr soldiers and 18 German fighter jets (besides similar Belgian and Italian contingents) the German government would have had a very hard time to justify not participating. On the first day of the new year the German government decided to send the Bundeswehr to Turkey in order to 'deter aggression', as the government spokesman said.[24] However, the opposition parties as well as some senior representatives of the governing coalition were arguing that an Iraqi attack on Turkey would *not* automatically lead to

German assistance to Turkey under Article 5 of the Washington Treaty because, as some critics argued, allied air strikes from Turkish soil under the mandate of the UN Security Council would in effect amount to *offensive*, not *defensive* operations. If Iraq were to retaliate, as one might expect, this could not be taken to trigger assistance obligations under Article 5 of the Washington Treaty.[25] Although this eventuality never materialised, the 'war automatism' (Genscher[26]) could not be stopped. Germany stood by, largely paralysed by what it was seeing and pondering what 'greater responsibility' might mean in the future. As the subsequent years showed, this experience had a lasting effect in that it initiated the 'normalising' nation to the sobering realities of a new world order which contrasted sharply with Hans-Dietrich Genscher's hopes for 'a new culture of international co-existence' and which also seemed to run counter to the expectations raised by the rhetoric of a 'policy of the good example'.

The Out-of-Area Debate and German Military Deployments in the Early 1990s

Against the background of the increasing pressures from Germany's allies to shoulder 'more responsibility', the German foreign policy debate during the early 1990s was marked by a polarisation between those charging that the Kohl government was pursuing a course of 'militarisation', on the one hand, and those calling for a process of 'normalisation' by shouldering the same burdens as the Western allies, on the other. This debate was instrumental in re-defining the boundaries for a legitimate German use of military force. Yet it not only set limits for government behaviour, but was also heavily influenced by government behaviour itself. This happened mainly in two ways.[27]

First, the government kept arguing for a constitutional amendment and took a leading role in reshaping the political discourse on German participation in out-of-area operations. Many representatives of the CDU/CSU held that an amendment of the Basic Law was not necessary, as it would already legitimise German participation in multilateral out-of-area operations covered by international law. Still, they supported the call for a change of the Basic Law, since partisan consensus was lacking and the coalition partner, the Free Democrats, thought that an amendment was necessary to clarify the issue. More important than the mere call for a constitutional amendment was the fact that proponents of German participation in out-of-area operations managed to introduce a new meaning of the term 'responsibility' (*Verantwortung*) to the political discourse. Representatives of the Kohl government repeatedly argued that the unified Germany was expected by its partners to 'take over more responsibility' by contributing to international military operations.[28] The word was no longer used to refer to a 'politics of responsibility' (*Verantwortungspolitik*) that stood

TABLE 3
PUBLIC OPINION ON PARTICIPATION IN UN MISSIONS (MARCH 1992)

Question: 'Two people are talking about whether Germany should participate in UN-peacekeeping forces. Which opinion would you agree with?' (in %)

	Old Länder	New Länder
'Germany has finally to participate in UN-peacekeeping troops, the so-called blue helmets. We cannot shirk our responsibilities and leave it to others to lose their heads.'	45	26
'Considering our history we should not take part in UN-peacekeeping troops. We should use our economic and political influence rather than soldiers.'	37	57
Undecided	18	17

Source: Noelle-Neumann and Köcher, *Allensbacher Jahrbuch*, p.1094.

in contrast to old-style 'power politics' (*Machtpolitik*). Instead, it was now used to indicate that responsible German foreign policy would be in contrast to the old Federal Republic's alleged privilege of standing by and leaving dangerous missions to its allies. In the end, the rhetoric of responsibility, which in itself conveyed the impression of continuity, was used to pave the way for significant change.

But, apart from such rhetorical efforts to gather support for a change in the role of the Bundeswehr, the federal government also followed a second path. It reached policy decisions to engage German troops abroad that stretched the legal limitations further and further. Although all these deployments have to be seen as low-scale deployments, there was a clear rise in the scope of the German contributions: from medical troops to the UN peace-keeping operation UNAMIC in Cambodia in 1991/92 through naval monitoring forces for the west European Union (WEU)'s 'Operation Sharp Guard' monitoring the embargo against Yugoslavia in the Adriatic from 1992 to 1996 to the dispatch of supply and transport units of the Bundeswehr to Somalia in 1993/94 as part of UNOSOM II (see Table 1).

We can see that, during these years, both German foreign policy behaviour and the concomitant political discourse were in flux, but this is also true for public opinion. As Table 3 shows, by spring 1992 the number of supporters of German participation in UN-led military operations had already grown significantly. There was still a considerable part of the German public that opposed such UN deployments, but, according to the Allensbach opinion poll, at least in West Germany the number of supporters had surpassed that of the opponents.

The development of foreign policy behaviour, foreign policy discourse and public opinion in the early 1990s substantiates our main argument. This development can only be understood if the interplay of structural and agency factors is taken into account. The structuralists are correct that the federal government was confronted with growing demands by its allies resulting from the structural changes after the end of the Cold War, on the one hand, and with existing domestic constraints created by an established anti-militarist political culture, on the other. Thus, the government certainly responded to structural incentives and constraints. This, however, is only one aspect of the foreign policy behaviour, since the government also had a strong impact at least on the domestic constraints. The efforts to re-frame the political discourse and the practice of accustoming the German public to out-of-area deployments of the Bundeswehr played a key role in bringing about the gradual change of these domestic constraints.

Although the proponents of a stronger participation in military operations increasingly dominated the political discourse, although public opinion was becoming more sympathetic towards such participation, and although the scope of the actual deployments of Bundeswehr troops grew, the controversy was still unsettled.[29] Yet, after another controversial engagement, the German political parties finally did what they have often done when unable to resolve a political dispute politically: they called up the Federal Constitutional Court to reach an authoritative decision.

Around the same time that the first non-medical Bundeswehr soldiers were sent 'out of area' to participate in UNOSOM II in Somalia, NATO for the first time took on a military task from the UN. On 12 April 1993, it agreed to monitor the no-fly zone over Bosnia-Hercegovina.[30] In the course of the next year, NATO deployed its airborne early-warning unit AWACS to the Mediterranean; in February 1994, NATO fighter jets shot down four Serbian fighters after repeated Serbian intrusions into the no-fly zone; and in April 1994 NATO planes even attacked Serbian ground forces in order to stop the onslaught on the UN-protected area of Gorazde.[31] In Germany, these NATO operations led to a heated debate on whether and to what extent Bundeswehr soldiers should and could participate. While Germany was not ready to take part in NATO's air strikes,[32] German air force personnel did participate in the surveillance and monitoring operations of AWACS, as they made up about one-third of this integrated multinational unit. Government officials stressed that AWACS would not be involved in NATO air strikes.[33] Still, the decision was preceded by disputes not only between government and opposition, but also between the CDU/CSU on the one side, and the FDP on the other.

Most leading Free Democrats, such as Foreign Minister Klaus Kinkel himself, politically approved of the AWACS deployment, but thought it was not covered by the Basic Law. The FDP pressurised its larger coalition partner to work for a constitutional amendment, which would have required the support of the SPD in order to reach the necessary two-thirds majority. When it became clear that no agreement could be found between the CDU/CSU and the SPD, the FDP took a rather unusual step: in April 1993, it gave its consent to the decision in favour of German participation in the AWACS deployment, but at the same time joined the SPD and the Greens in filing suit to the Constitutional Court against this decision.[34] So eventually the Constitutional Court was called upon to decide whether such deployments were in accordance with the Basic Law. On 12 July 1994, it decided the issue in the affirmative: the Bundeswehr may take part in an out-of-area operation if the Bundestag gives its authorisation and if this operation is conducted within the framework of a system of collective security. Also, the Constitutional Court supported the contention that NATO can be seen as such a system of collective security.[35] This ruling immediately put an end to the contentious debate, since all its participants now accepted the constitutional basis for German out-of-area deployments as indicated by the Constitutional Court.

German Troops in the Balkans: Participation in IFOR and SFOR

After the 1994 decision of the court and against the background of the deteriorating situation in the Balkans, new coalitions were forming. In the domestic context of Germany, Srebrenica served as a catalyst for the formation of a coalition in favour of allied intervention demands comprising traditionalist, pro-Western normalisers, on the one hand, and, on the other, increasing numbers of more left-leaning internationalists who were having ever more difficulties rejecting the analogies between the cruelties in the Balkans and Germany's historical legacy of Auschwitz. This provided the basis for another important step towards greater readiness to take part in military interventions. In the light of Srebrenica, it was now widely accepted in the German political elite that the legacy of German history should not only be to call for 'No more wars!' ('Nie wieder Krieg!') but also for 'No more Auschwitz!' ('Nie wieder Auschwitz!'). This became visible after a request by NATO in February 1995. At that time the NATO allies were considering sending a large NATO force to the Balkans to secure the retreat of the unsuccessful UNPROFOR. Like other NATO members, Germany was requested to indicate firmly which troops it would provide for such an operation.[36] Two weeks later, Bonn actually responded positively to that request, declaring its readiness to contribute a contingent of 1,800 soldiers.[37] This operation never materialised, but Germany was soon confronted with another – and still bigger – challenge.

In December 1995, the Balkans Contact Group, with strong US leadership, managed to broker the Dayton Peace Accord. The German government had already indicated in October that it would contribute several thousand Bundeswehr soldiers, mainly from logistics and transport units, to the NATO-led force that was to police the agreement.[38] When the Dayton

Accord was signed, the Bundestag authorised the German participation in IFOR with a broad majority, as most deputies of the SPD and almost half of those of the Green Party voted with the government.[39] Of course, the 3,000 German troops mainly provided medical and logistical assistance to those from France and other partner states, and they were stationed in Croatia, outside of Bosnia-Hercegovina. But this was nonetheless a major step. The next step was taken when SFOR took over the functions of IFOR in 1996. The fears of many in Germany that the German public would soon be confronted with casualties and that the presence of German soldiers in the Balkans would do more to aggravate rather than to solve the conflicts in the region had not come true. So there was hardly any opposition now against another removal of limitations on German deployment: Germany's SFOR contingent included combat forces and the Bundeswehr troops were regularly stationed in Bosnia-Hercegovina.[40]

Germany's full participation in SFOR demonstrated that the country had gone a long way since its military absence from the Gulf War coalition six years earlier. This was not only indicated by the mere fact of the German contribution to SFOR, but also by the fact that there was no controversial discussion about this contribution, with a large majority of the Bundestag faction of the SPD and even a majority of the Green faction supporting it.[41]

Using Force without UN Authorisation: German Participation in the Kosovo War

Germany's participation in NATO's Kosovo War was the culmination point of this realignment. The stunning result – unimaginable for most Germans only five years ago – was that this has been widely accepted both among foreign policy elites as well as the public more broadly. Perhaps the most stunning thing was that this development took place under a government formed by the two German parties with the highest internationalist as well as 'anti-militarist' credentials. For the first time in the history of the Federal Republic, German soldiers were deployed to use force deliberately in a military operation with an at least questionable legal basis.

One of the central questions of the debate surrounding the German government's decision has been to what extent the new government was forced to this particular course of action by decisions taken prior to the assumption of power in October 1998. According to the line of argument advanced by Schröder and Fischer, they were left with almost no choice by the Clinton administration.[42] But other reports from the second half of 1998 claim that not much pressure had to be applied to secure approval for a strategy of escalation. According to the minutes of a meeting between Schröder and Clinton which took place during the German election campaign, Clinton had told Schröder that his administration thought that NATO had to prepare for military action in case diplomacy failed. In this conversation in early August 1998, Schröder affirmed that he would support such a course if he were elected Chancellor, adding, however, that it would be desirable to secure a UN mandate. According to the minutes, Secretary of State Madeleine Albright rejected this condition outright because the UN was deemed incapable.[43] Both Schröder and Fischer publicly expressed an even harder line, attaching less importance to securing a UN mandate, prior to their first meeting with Clinton after their election victory, on 9 October 1998.[44] To be sure, given the presumed need for the Red–Green coalition government to prove its alliance loyalty, Schröder and Fischer had little choice. Yet there are few indications that, during the months leading up to the start of the air campaign against Serbia in March 1999, the key figures among German foreign policy decision-makers actually pushed an alternative course of action. Rather, in public statements as well as preparations for war (such as the mobilisation of troops for deployment in Macedonia in early February) the Schröder government tried to convey an image of determination to both Belgrade and its own allies.[45] During a prominent transatlantic conference in February 1999, Schröder himself was at pains to emphasise 'in all clarity' that Germany would 'remain a reliable partner'. Moreover, in contrast to past attitudes, according to which Germany's historical legacy 'prohibited any deployment of German troops out of area', the Chancellor emphasised that Germany's 'historical responsibility' made it 'imperative' to 'prevent mass-murder with all the necessary means'. In his view Germany had 'come of age' as a full member of NATO, now being ready 'without any reservations (*ohne jedes Wenn und Aber*), to assume responsibility as a 'normal ally'.[46]

None of this is meant to imply that Germany was keen on going to war against Milosevic, as some analyses imply.[47] But the responses of German decision-makers after the failure of final diplomatic efforts at Rambouillet were remarkable indeed, especially in comparison to the paralysis in the final days prior to the escalation of the Gulf War in early January 1991. The similarities in the failure of diplomacy in both cases were striking. Yet, whereas the Conservative Kohl government appeared to be helplessly clinching to a 'political solution' even in the face of a diplomatic stalemate, the left-leaning Schröder government appeared to be surprisingly resigned and determined to carry out the plans for military escalation it had jointly developed with its allies in spite of the fact that internal ministerial analyses were providing a much more differentiated picture of the situation on the ground in Kosovo itself. After the war had started on 24 March 1999, the key figures of the German government were constantly referring to unacceptable Serbian 'terror against the majority of the Albanian population', describing the overarching goal of the 'use of military means' to be 'a halt to continuing serious and systematic violations of human rights as well as the prevention of

TABLE 4
PUBLIC OPINION ON GERMAN PARTICIPATION IN THE KOSOVO WAR (MARCH 1999)

	Yes	No
'Do you believe that participation in the air strikes corresponds with the unified Germany's role in world politics?'	58	32
'Is Bundeswehr participation to be continued if German soldiers should die in combat?'	52	36

Source: Forsa poll on behalf of the magazine *Der Stern*, No.14, 31 March 1999, p.52.

a humanitarian catastrophe'.[48] However, according to internal documents from the Foreign Ministry analysing the situation on the ground in Kosovo immediately prior to the war, this was not the kind of picture which German intelligence was providing. According to an intelligence assessment dated 19 March 1999, the truce was violated not only by Serbian troops, but by the Kosovo Albanian UCK as well. Moreover, reports from Kosovo showed that, in contrast to 1998, Serbia could not be charged with systematic expulsions. Rather, available evidence showed that Albanians and Serbians were 'equally' affected by the war.[49]

It comes as little surprise that this dramatic change in German policy over the course of a decade has left its imprint on public opinion as well as on the political discourse. In a poll taken by Forsa during the Kosovo War, a majority of the interviewees both agreed that Germany's participation properly reflected its role in world politics and maintained that this participation should be continued even if German soldiers were to die in combat, as Table 4 shows.

Thus, in the German political discourse, 'taking over responsibility' today largely means playing the same role militarily as the big Western partners. 'Normalisation' has progressed to such an extent that it is no longer necessary to call for it. The current debate about the restructuring of the German armed forces is focusing on whether or not to give up yet another one of the celebrated institutions of the Bonn Republic, the conscription of 'citizens in uniform'. Apart from a small circle of experts, few are interested in the implications of increasing Germany's contribution to European or allied intervention (or 'rapid reaction') forces, and the German public tends to support both the establishment of such forces and German participation in them, as recent polls conducted by EMNID indicate.

There is little discussion on what such a European intervention force could or should be used for. Germans seem to view this project with a mixture of neglect and support that sharply contrasts with the anti-militarist attitudes that were so dominant a decade ago. So this is yet another sign of Germany's new normality as a European great power which is making rapid progress in shrinking the differences to Britain and France.

TABLE 5

PUBLIC OPINION ON THE ESTABLISHMENT OF A EUROPEAN INTERVENTION FORCE
(1999, 2000)

Question: 'Do you support or oppose the planning of the establishment of a rapid military intervention force (something like a EURO-Army) by the European Union?'

	November 1999	March 2000
Support	29	32
Tend to support	28	23
Tend to oppose	22	22
Oppose	17	18

Source: EMNID, *Meinungsbild zur sicherheitspolitischen Lage 2000* (Bielefeld: repräsentative Umfrage durch EMNID, 2000).

TABLE 6

PUBLIC OPINION ON GERMAN PARTICIPATION IN A EUROPEAN INTERVENTION
FORCE (2000)

Question: 'Should Germany participate in such a European intervention force?'
(only interviewees who answered the previous question affirmatively)

	March 2000
Yes, without restrictions, including soldiers	47
Yes, but on a case-by-case basis	47
Yes, but only with financial contributions	3
No, under no circumstances	1

Source: EMNID.

CONCLUSION

We can see that both the structuralist and actionalist perspectives are correct to some degree, but that both are incomplete on their own. Beginning with the Gulf War, the German government was certainly confronted with both new international demands to provide military contributions to international conflict management endeavours and societal scepticism about embracing such a new role. But the German policy-makers did not just respond to a changing structure of the international system and to conflicting international and societal expectations, as structuralists would maintain. They also managed to shape the public discourse in Germany and to establish new facts by slowly raising the scope of German military deployments, repeatedly moving beyond the established domestic consensus. Only by observing the continuous interaction of structural and actional factors can this change in German foreign policy be adequately understood.

The changes in Germany's readiness to participate in military interventions have been more than a mere adaptation to a changing international environment, as suggested by the culturalists and the proponents of the civilian-power thesis. In the last decade, Germany has changed significantly by giving up most of its exceptionalism concerning the use of military force. Yet by doing so Germany has also contributed to a change of the view of military interventions predominant in the societies of Western Europe (as witnessed by the plan to establish a European intervention force of 60,000 men).

Some may view it as a sign of maturity that Germany is finally joining ranks with other Western states in terms of its attitudes towards and practices of war. German world-views during the last decade certainly have been shaped and changed by the reappearance of war on the European horizon – although this is a very different kind of war in comparison with what Germans in East and West had been preparing for previously. However, our emphasis on the re-socialisation effects should not be interpreted in the sense that Germany is shedding all its 'civilian' traditions. What we are saying is rather that the German self-image of being a 'civilian power' different from other more 'traditional' Western powers is misleading. What is more, these 'civilian' inclinations may lead to military interventions which more 'hard-nosed' calculations of 'national interests' would refuse. It is in this sense also that Germany's change may make an ambivalent contribution to the transformation of war.

NOTES

An earlier version of this paper was presented at a conference 'La guerre entre le local et le global: sociétés, États, systèmes', staged by the Centre d'Etudes et des Recherches Internationales (CERI) at Paris, 29 and 30 May 2000. A slightly different version of this article will appear in French in a volume documenting the proceedings of this conference. We are grateful to Pierre Hassner and Roland Marchal for permitting us to publish this article here.

1. Jörg Bischoff, 'Oft die Mittel gewechselt, nie das Ziel. Der Antikommunist Hans-Dietrich Genscher, die Destabilisierung des Sowjetsystems und die kleine Rache für erlittenes Unrecht', *Der Tagesspiegel*, 21 March 1990.
2. Cf. Thomas U. Berger, 'Norms, Identity, and National Security in Germany and Japan', in Peter J. Katzenstein (ed.), *The Culture of National Security. Norms and Identity in World Politics* (New York: Columbia University Press, 1996), pp.317–56; Thomas U. Berger, *Cultures of Antimilitarism. National Security in Germany and Japan* (Baltimore, MD: Johns Hopkins University Press, 1998); John S. Duffield, *World Power Forsaken. Political Culture, International Institutions, and German Security Policy after Unification* (Stanford, CA: Stanford University Press, 1998); John S. Duffield, 'Political Culture and State Behavior. Why Germany Confounds Neorealism', *International Organization*, 53/4 (1999), pp.765–803.
3. Cf. Berger, *Cultures of Antimilitarism*, pp.22–32.
4. Cf. Hanns W. Maull, 'Germany and Japan. The New Civilian Powers', *Foreign Affairs*, 69/5 (1990), pp.91–106; Hanns W. Maull, 'Zivilmacht Bundesrepublik Deutschland. Vierzehn Thesen für eine neue deutsche Außenpolitik', *Europa Archiv*, 43/10 (1992), pp.269–78; Knut Kirste and Hanns W. Maull, 'Zivilmacht und Rollentheorie', *Zeitschrift für Internationale*

Beziehungen, 3/2 (1996), pp.283–312; Hanns W. Maull, 'Germany and the Use of Force. Still a Civilian Power?' *Survival*, 42/2 (2000), pp.56–80.

5. Maull, 'Germany and the Use of Force', p.56.

6. Cf. Reinhard Mutz, 'Schießen wie die anderen? Eine Armee sucht ihren Zweck', in Dieter S. Lutz (ed.), *Deutsche Soldaten weltweit? Blauhelme, Eingreiftruppen, 'out-of-area' – Der Streit um unsere sicherheitspolitische Zukunft* (Reinbek: Rowohlt, 1993), pp.11–26; Reinhard Mutz, 'Militärmacht Deutschland? Die Bundeswehr auf der Suche nach ihrer Zukunft', in Friedhelm Solms, Reinhard Mutz and Gert Krell (eds.), *Friedensgutachten 1994* (Münster: Lit Verlag, 1994); Peter Glotz, 'Im Zangengriff der Krieger', in Peter Glotz, *Die falsche Normalisierung. Essays* (Frankfurt am Main: Suhrkamp, 1994), pp.133–6; Michael Berndt, *Deutsche Militärpolitik in der neuen 'Weltunordnung'. Zwischen nationalen Interessen und globalen Entwicklungen* (Münster: Agenda, 1997).

7. Cf. Nina Philippi, *Bundeswehr-Auslandseinsätze als außen- und sicherheitspolitisches Problem des geeinten Deutschland* (Bern *et al.*: Lang, 1997). Despite her emphasis on 'salami tactics', though, Philippi stresses that her findings provide much support for the civilian-power hypothesis.

8. We are fully aware, of course, that this decision is not without problems, since the concept of political culture cannot be fully grasped by merely analysing public opinion polls. However, our decision should be seen as a pragmatic decision resulting from the limits of space allotted here.

9. 'Normalisers' as well as 'abnormalisers' fundamentally disagree on how to *judge* the observed processes of change in Germany's attitudes toward war. However, in contrast to the structuralists they tend to agree that Germany has come a rather long way in very short period of time. In general, the advocates of 'normalisation' welcome that Germany has 'finally' become a 'normal country' once again, taking over 'normal responsibility' as 'our Western allies had already requested during the Gulf War'; see Ruppert Scholz, 'Deutschland auf dem Weg zur internationalen Normalität', *Der Mittler-Brief*, 1 (1994), p.5. (In the late 1980s Scholz, a member of the CDU, served as German Defence Minister.) The critics say that Germany is 'again' becoming as 'abnormal' as other great powers – 'normality' here being defined as corresponding to a stringent *normative* standard; see Mutz, 'Militärmacht Deutschland?', p.221.

10. Cf. '"Weil wir Deutschlands Kraft vertrauen ..."', Regierungserklärung von Bundeskanzler Gerhard Schröder vor dem Deutschen Bundestag am 10.11.1998', *Bulletin*, No.74, 11 Nov. 1998, p.910; Patrick Bahners, 'Total Normal. Vorsicht Falle: Die unbefangene Nation', *Frankfurter Allgemeine Zeitung*, 3 Nov. 1998, p.43; Werner A. Perger, 'Wir Unbefangenen', *Die Zeit*, No.47, 12 Nov. 1998, p.7; 'Total normal?', *Der Spiegel*, No.49, 30 Nov. 1998, pp.40–48.

11. Cf. Mutz, 'Militärmacht Deutschland?', p.227; see also Jürgen Habermas, *Die Normalität einer Berliner Republik* (Frankfurt am Main: Suhrkamp, 1995), p.187.

12. Discussions of the 'out-of-area question' as perceived within NATO in the 1980s can be found in Marc Bentinck, *NATO's Out-of-Area Problem*. Adelphi Paper 211 (London: International Institute for Strategic Studies, 1986) and Douglas Stuart and William Tow, *The Limits of Alliance. NATO's Out-of-Area Problems since 1949* (Baltimore/London: Johns Hopkins University Press, 1990).

13. The decision is reprinted in *Militärpolitik Dokumentation*, 13/78–9 (1990), p.72.

14. As Harald Müller put it, before 1990 there existed 'an unequivocal interpretation of ambiguous legal language'. Harald Müller, 'German Foreign Policy after Unification', in Paul Stares (ed.), *The New Germany and the New Europe* (Washington, DC: The Brookings Institution, 1992), p.139.

15. Janice Gross Stein, 'The Wrong Strategy in the Right Place. The U.S. and the Gulf', *International Security*, 13/3 (1988/89), p.158.

16. Cf. Gerhard Krancke, 'Einsatz der Marine im Mittelmeer. Sichtbares Zeichen der Solidarität', *Marineforum*, 12 (1987), pp.424–5; Jochen Hippler, *Westliche Flottenpräsenz am Persischen Golf und die Diskussion um Out-of-Area-Einsatzmöglichkeiten der Bundeswehr* (Institut für Internationale Politik, Arbeitspapiere, Nr. 6, Wuppertal, 1988); Thomas Giegerich, 'The German Contribution to the Protection of Shipping in the Persian Gulf: Staying Out for Political or Constitutional Reasons?' *Zeitschrift für ausländisches Öffentliches Recht und*

Völkerrecht, 49 (1989), pp.1–40.

17. This position was expressed in an internal paper that was published three years later: Cf. Bundesminister der Verteidigung, 'Rechtliche Bewertung der Einsatzmöglichkeiten der Streitkräfte. Nicht-öffentliches Papier aus dem Bundesverteidigungsministerium, Herbst '87', reprinted in *Militärpolitik Dokumentation*, 13/78–9 (1990), pp.72–4.

18. Cf. Erklärung der Bundesregierung zum Vertrag über die abschließende Regelung in bezug auf Deutschland durch den Bundesminister des Auswärtigen, Hans-Dietrich Genscher, 20 Sept. 1990, Deutscher Bundestag, Stenographischer Bericht, 226. Sitzung (subsequently cited as DBT 11/226, 20.9.1990), pp.17803D and 17804C.

19. Cf. Michael J. Inacker, *Unter Ausschluß der Öffentlichkeit. Die Deutschen in der Golfallianz* (Bonn: Bouvier Verlag, 1991), p.84.

20. For a more detailed description, see Gunther Hellmann, 'Beyond Weltpolitik, Self-Containment and Civilian Power: United Germany's Normalizing Ambitions' (The University of Birmingham, Institute for German Studies, IGS Discussion Papers Series No. 99/10, 1999), pp.5–23.

21. Jonathan P.G. Bach, *Between Sovereignty and Integration. German Foreign Policy and National Identity after 1989* (Hamburg: LIT Verlag, 1999), p.122.

22. DBT, 11/235, 15 Nov. 1990, pp.18842B and 18843C. For a sample of views along these lines among the opposition parties see Antje Vollmer, DBT 11/220, 9 Aug. 1990, p.1740D; Ludger Volmer, *Die Grünen und die Außenpolitik – ein schwieriges Verhältnis* (Münster: Verlag Westfälisches Dampfboot, 1998), pp.383–90; Die Grünen, *Das Programm zur 1. gesamtdeutschen Bundestagswahl* (Bonn: Die Grünen, 1990), pp.18–21; SPD, *Regierungsprogramm 1990–94* (Bonn: SPD, 1990), pp.21–2; Oskar Lafontaine, DBT, 11/226, 20 Sept. 1990, pp.17809C–17810C.

23. For a detailed discussion of Germany's financial, military-technical and logistical contributions to the anti-Saddam coalition, see Gunther Hellmann, 'Absorbing Shocks and Mounting Checks: Germany and Alliance Burden-Sharing in the Gulf War', in Andrew J. Bennett, Joseph Lepgold and Danny Unger (eds.), *Friends in Need. Burden-Sharing in the Gulf War* (New York: St. Martin's Press, 1997), pp.165–94, here pp.167–72.

24. See DPA report from Bonn, 2 Jan. 1991, in FBIS-WEU-91-002, 3 Jan. 1991, p.12. For the background to the decision, see Inacker, *Unter Ausschluß der Öffentlichkeit*, pp.108–9.

25. For a sample of statements along these lines from representatives of the opposition as well as the governing coalition parties, see Claus Gennrich, 'Bonn will durch Entsendung von Alpha-Jets den Irak abschrecken', *Frankfurter Allgemeine Zeitung*, 4 Jan. 1991, p.2; 'Keine Mehrheit für Bundeswehr-Einsatz', *Süddeutsche Zeitung*, 23 Jan. 1991, p.2. Joschka Fischer, who at that time was heading the Greens in the state parliament of Hesse, criticised that the deployment of German troops to the front marked a 'qualitative change' in post-World War II history. For the first time German soldiers were called to 'war service' ('Kriegsdienst') rather than mere 'military service' ('Militärdienst'). In a prophetic tone he added: 'And I fear that this is only the beginning of a new development.' See 'Kaum ist die Einheit da, schickt man deutsche Soldaten zur Front. Interview mit Joschka Fischer', *Frankfurter Rundschau*, 9 Jan. 1991, p.6.

26. Genscher interview with Hessen Radio, cited in DPA report from Frankfurt, 10 Jan. 1991, in FBIS-WEU-91-007, 10 Jan. 1991, pp.14–15.

27. For a similar argument, see Bach, *Between Sovereignty and Integration*, pp.122–3.

28. The following passage from a speech of Defence Minister Volker Rühe is but one example: 'Unified Germany is endowed with a greater international responsibility. I am deeply convinced that the Bundeswehr must be given the means to make its contribution, within systems of collective security, to the stabilisation and reconstitution of peace and security in Europe but also beyond. Unified Germany has no interest in remaining different from its friends and partners in this respect', Volker Rühe, 'Sinn und Auftrag der Bundeswehr im vereinten Deutschland', *Bulletin* No.37, 7 April 1992, p.346 (our translation). For similar statements, see the speeches by Foreign Minister Klaus Kinkel, 'Die Rolle Deutschlands in der Weltpolitik', *Bulletin* No.18, 3 March 1993, p.141, and by Volker Rühe, 'Deutsche Sicherheitspolitik vor neuen Aufgaben', *Bulletin* No.83, 8 Oct. 1993, p.948.

29. For a good description of the positions taken by the political parties in this controversy, see Lothar Gutjahr, *German Foreign and Defense Policy after Unification* (London: Pinter, 1994).

30. The no-fly zone had been established by the UN Security Council on 9 Oct. 1992 (S/RES 781).

31. For more extensive information on NATO's role on the Balkans in 1993/94, see the yearbooks of the International Institute for Strategic Studies, *The Military Balance*, for 1994–95 (London: 1994, pp.273–6) and 1995–96 (London: 1995, pp.303–5).

32. Germany also did not participate in UNPROFOR, the UN peace-keeping operation in Bosnia-Hercegovina. For a good discussion of the background of the Bosnian conflict, see Marie-Janine Calic, *Krieg und Frieden in Bosnien-Herzegowina* (Frankfurt/Main: Suhrkamp, 1996).

33. 'Deutsche Soldaten werden an Luftschlägen nicht teilnehmen', *Frankfurter Allegmeine Zeitung*, 12 Feb. 1994.

34. Cf. Marc Fisher, 'Germans on Bosnia Patrol? Well, Sort of', *International Herald Tribune*, 3 and 4 April 1993, pp.1 and 5 and 'Kohl und Kinkel vor Gericht', *Der Spiegel*, 5 April 1993, pp.18–22.

35. The decision is published in *Entscheidungen des Bundesverfassungsgerichts*, Vol.90 (Tübingen: Verlag J.C.B. Mohr, 1994).

36. 'NATO-Anfrage an Bonn zum Bosnien-Abzugsplan. Forderung nach einer verbindlichen Zusage', *Neue Zürcher Zeitung*, 9 Feb. 1995.

37. 'Deutsche Pläne für einen UNO-Abzug aus Bosnien. Formelle Benennung des Bundeswehr-Kontingents durch Bonn', *Neue Zürcher Zeitung*, 24 Feb. 1995.

38. Cf. Alan Cowell, 'German Soldiers to Go to Balkans, Despite the Memories', *International Herald Tribune*, 12 Oct. 1995, p.8.

39. Cf. John S. Duffield, *World Power Forsaken*, pp.215–16; and Alice Holmes Cooper, 'When Just Causes Conflict with Accepted Means: The German Peace Movement and Military Intervention in Bosnia', *German Politics and Society*, 15/3 (Fall 1997), pp.99–118.

40. Cf. 'Deutsche Teilnahme an der Bosnien-Folgemission. Bonner Kabinettsbeschluß für ein SFOR-Kontingent', *Neue Zürcher Zeitung*, 12 Dec. 1996, p.3.

41. 'Deutsche Teilnahme an der Bosnien-Folgemission'.

42. See the history of German decision-making based on extensive interviews with government officials, Gunter Hofmann, 'Wie Deutschland in den Krieg geriet', *Die Zeit*, 12 May 1999, p.18.

43. Minutes of the meeting between Gerhard Schröder and President Clinton, 4 Aug. 1998, quoted according to Andreas Zumach, 'Rambouillet, ein Jahr danach', *Blätter für deutsche und internationale Politik* 45/3 (March 2000), p.274.

44. Cf. Joseph Fitchett, 'Politics Stalls Momentum for Attack', *International Herald Tribune*, 10 Oct. 1998.

45. Cf. '"Bonn rüstet sich zum Kosovo-Einsatz". Bundeskanzler Schröder sichert NATO-Generalsekretär Javier Solana volle Unterstützung zu', *Die Welt*, 2 Feb. 1999 (reprinted in *Stichworte zur Sicherheitspolitik*, Feb. 1999, pp.57–8); see also 'Bundesminister der Verteidigung Rudolf Scharping hat die Aufstellung von Verstärkungskräften der NATO-Notfallschutztruppe für die OSZE-Mission in Kosovo gebilligt', Pressemitteilung des Bundesministeriums für Verteidigung vom 5. Februar 1999', *Stichworte zur Sicherheitspolitik*, Feb. 1999, p.59.

46. 'Deutsche Sicherheitspolitik an der Schwelle des 21. Jahrhunderts', Rede von Bundeskanzler Schröder vor der 35. Münchener Konferenz zur Sicherheitspolitik, 6 February 1999', *Stichworte zur Sicherheitspolitik* (Feb. 1999), pp.25, 28.

47. Cf. Matthias Küntzel, *Der Weg in den Krieg. Deutschland, die NATO und das Kosovo* (Berlin: Elefanten Press, 2000), esp. pp.154–78.

48. 'Erklärung von Bundeskanzler Gerhard Schröder zur Lage im Kosovo', 24 March 1999, *Stichworte zur Sicherheitspolitik* (March 1999), p.41. In his statement Schröder was at pains to emphasise that 'we are not conducting a war'. Instead, he said, 'we are called upon to enforce a peaceful resolution (of the conflict) in Kosovo with military means'.

49. Lageanalyse des Auswärtigen Amtes, 19 March 1999, quoted according to Dieter S. Lutz, Frieden – Meisterwerk der Politik, oder: War der Kosovo-Krieg wirklich unvermeidbar? at http://www.rrz.uni-hamburg.de/ifsh/index.htm; see also Heinz Loquai, *Der Kosovo-Konflikt. Wege in einen vermeidbaren Krieg* (Baden-Baden: Nomos Verlagsgesellschaft, 2000).

Recasting the Security Bargains: Germany, European Security Policy and the Transatlantic Relationship

ALISTER JOHN MISKIMMON

Since 1998 and in particular since the moves made by Britain towards a more active role in the Common Foreign and Security Policy (CFSP), the European Union's capacity to act in the sphere of foreign and security policy has made rapid advances. The United States' growing reluctance to carry the main burden for security provision for its European allies means that Europe can no longer afford not to act as one in its security requirements. For Germany, as for France and the United Kingdom, this would entail taking over major responsibilities from the United States in crisis management and consequently being confronted with new challenges in security co-operation. The new demands placed on Germany in security provision may create more problems for the Red/Green coalition than for its major European partners. Where does Germany envisage the course of European security co-operation leading and what will Germany do to flesh out existing conceptions of the CFSP? In this connection, how is Germany translating its national interests in this field into EU policy through the process of co-ordination and bargaining with the other 14 member states? These are highly pertinent questions in German policy-making circles at present and must be considered in the light of the changing geopolitical dynamics on the European continent. This study begins by outlining the historical development of Germany's role in European security before going on to analyse Germany's relations with its major partners and recent events in Europe affecting transatlantic security relations.

HISTORICAL BACKGROUND TO GERMANY'S ROLE IN EUROPEAN SECURITY

The Post-War Security Bargain

The post-war security bargain which emerged in the years immediately after 1945 was based on material and ideational factors. The material factors

Alister John Miskimmon, University of Birmingham

enforcing the emergent transatlantic security bargain in the Federal Republic were plain to see, notably the stationing of Allied troops on German soil and, more importantly, the extension of American guarantees to provide a nuclear shield against the Soviet threat. The Washington Treaty signed in 1949 laid down the commitment of the Allied powers to safeguard the peace of Western Europe. The succession of West Germany to NATO in 1955 marked an acceptance of Adenauer's belief in the rationale of integration into the West, the welcoming of the Federal Republic back into the Western state system and the recognition by West Germany of the primacy of the United States in the security provision of Western Europe. Whilst military hardware was the visible sign of the commitment of West Germany and its major partners to a system of co-operative security, the clear visibility of the Soviet threat and the commitment to a democratic order were the cohesive forces which held NATO together.

German post-war foreign policy was based on a series of bargains struck by Germany in order to re-establish itself and insert itself into the international system. These were founded on Bonn's commitment to *Westbindung* (Western integration). Central to this bargain was NATO. This was a result of the mutual security need felt by both West Germany and the other allies in the face of the Warsaw Pact. This not only secured West Germany's security but also provided the basis for the post-war recovery of the German state. This post-war bargain was not, however, a one-way process. The multi-faceted bargain ensured German recovery, but also provided the allies with a strong defensive bulwark against the East. The central argument here, however, is that, with the end of the Cold War period, the security bargains are in the process of being recast. The bombing of Serbia and Kosovo marked a turning point in US–EU relations. The United States is now demanding greater Western European involvement in European regional security. This expectation has had major repercussions on Franco-German and British–German security co-operation within the European Union.

The development of norms and the ensuing socialisation of national elites into shared beliefs based on sustained mutual co-operation during the Cold War were instrumental in the longevity of the transatlantic security bargain.[1] West Germany's increasing reliance on multilateral security arrangements in the face of the huge military forces gathered on its borders presented West Germans with salient reasons for membership of co-operative security structures based on the presence on the USA. The hard security guarantees that could be offered only by the United States resulted in the predominance of the USA in NATO and placed limitations on Western Europe's ability to conduct a distinctive diplomatic policy.

As Hoffmann contends, Germany has not departed from its reliance on multilateralism, but this reliance is now founded on a more assertive Germany, less inhibited by its past and the international environment.[2] This shift has had a major impact on the development of EU security structures in which Germany seeks to play a leading role. The underlying security bargain which Germany struck with the United States – that of the nuclear shield and 'hard' security provisions – remains. However, a more assertive, self-confident Berlin has incrementally sought to influence the future course of European security policy according to its own ideals and tied to the goal of eventual Political Union with its European partners.

Germany and the Development of European Union Security Policy

There are or have been three main reasons for German policy-makers to consider the development of a European foreign policy to be in the best interests of Germany. First, Germany's support for the European Political Co-operation (EPC)/CFSP process was a means to counteract the deficiencies in German foreign policy.[3] Second, the growing confrontational aspect of the Cold War during the late 1970s and early 1980s necessitated the development of a distinctive European 'voice' in the international system. Subsequently, the post-Cold War European system has seen a 'collapse of illusions' regarding the future role and interests of the US in European regional security concerns. Finally, Germany has viewed the extension of co-operation in foreign and security policy among EU member states as a furtherance of the integration process. CFSP can be viewed as an area of the European integration process where Germany continues to play the role of *Musterknabe* (the 'best pupil in the class').

The function of NATO in the foreign and security policy of West Germany was limited in the field of diplomacy. Moreover, the 'inability of Europeans significantly to influence the course of events and the nakedness of its exposure to external aggression was nowhere more keenly felt than in the German Foreign Ministry'.[4] It was important for Bonn to develop channels for pursuing policies which did not impact directly on the East/West conflict. EPC provided an invaluable opportunity for the pursuit of Bonn's foreign policy objectives. Membership of EPC provided an outlet for German diplomacy while multilateralising it to prevent any suspicions of a German *Sonderweg* arising. Germany actively pursued the process of European integration, most notably in the Genscher–Colombo proposals of 12 November 1981 to deepen integration and bring EPC into the EC process, with the aim of developing a common defence. EPC provided Germany with the first tentative means for the expression of Bonn's diplomatic interests. In addition, German leaders and foreign policy officials were worried by what they diagnosed as a waning of the commitment of the German people to European integration, and the need – not just in Germany, but also in the rest of Europe – to raise European ambition and reconfirm the loyalty of the member states to the community ideal.[5] Most importantly, EPC provided West Germany with an important 'alibi function' which served as a 'means of deflecting external pressure, and cover for shifts in national policy'.[6] NATO could not be used as a forum for expressing Germany's singular foreign policy interests because of the sensitive nature of the Cold War and the intention not to upset the close transatlantic relationship.

West Germany's attempts to create a European security policy were very much reliant on the support of the United Kingdom and France, the major Western European military powers. The constraints on West Germany's military capacity, embodied in the modified Western European Union Treaty of 1954 with its restrictions on the development of ABC (atomic, biological and chemical) weapons, accounted for the notable modesty of German security policy. However, despite the Federal Republic's relative aversion to military security, beyond that of national defence, it scored a number of diplomatic successes through the Conference on Security and Co-operation in Europe (CSCE) and Chancellor Schmidt's successful efforts to include intermediate-range nuclear forces (INF) negotiations in the NATO agenda in the late 1970s.[7]

Chancellor Kohl pushed for foreign and security policy integration at Maastricht very much as a way of deepening Germany's commitment to the European integration process. The German government also viewed the closer ties between the West European Union (WEU) and the EU as a way of legitimising defence in the post-Cold War environment and as a way of influencing the debate concerning German participation in 'out-of-area operations'.[8] The development of the CFSP must be viewed in the context of the continued German commitment to European integration post-unification, at a time when Germany's future commitment to multilateralism was coming under scrutiny. German attempts to move forward foreign and security policy integration were not considered to be an open challenge to American involvement in Europe as a 'common defence was considered a very long-term process'.[9] The only circumstances in which a common European defence could be envisaged would be if the United States ever questioned its commitment to European security, something that seems unimaginable in the foreseeable future.

The inclusion of the Petersberg Tasks agreed by the WEU in June 1992 into the Treaty of Amsterdam marked an important step forward in

European security policy. The inclusion of Article J.7(2) to include 'humanitarian and rescue tasks, peacekeeping tasks and tasks of combat forces in crisis management, including peacemaking' was a bold step which clarified to some extent the relationship between the WEU and the EU, without suggesting a fusion. However, this has also placed much greater demands and expectations on CFSP. With the coming into force of Article J.7(2) through the ratification of the Amsterdam Treaty in May 1999, the 'capabilities–expectations' gap[10] could no longer be fudged. Hence the Bremen Declaration of the WEU Council of Ministers that took place on 10 and 11 May 1999 expressed the 'willingness of the European nations to strengthen European operational capabilities for Petersberg Tasks based on appropriate decision-making bodies and effective military means, within NATO or national and multinational means outside the NATO framework'.[11]

The inclusion of the Petersberg Tasks into the CFSP presents Germany, France and the UK with major commitments spanning a wide range of military operations. The decisions made at the Cologne Summit in June 1999 and at Helsinki in December 1999 represent positive strides to meet these commitments. For Germany in particular, the inclusion of the Petersberg Tasks demands a more interventionist German style within the CFSP and means that Germany is no longer able to shirk responsibility in military operations.

Germany has aimed for Qualified Majority Voting (QMV) to be partially extended to questions concerning the CFSP. Opportunities for the use of QMV procedures were agreed at in the Treaty of Amsterdam in an attempt to facilitate CFSP decisions and to create the option of 'coalitions of the willing' conducting missions under EU auspices[12] and leaving room for 'constructive abstention'. Despite this, Germany's stance on QMV exhibits ambivalence, as between federalist and intergovernmentalist conceptions of security integration. Germany also pressed for the appointment of a High Representative for CFSP at Amsterdam to give the EU a more visible face and point of contact in world affairs, a post which has now been filled by former NATO Secretary-General Javier Solana Madariaga. Significantly, the final decision to appoint Solana was taken at the Cologne European Council meeting on 3 and 4 June 1999.

According to Sjursen, 'the internalisation of a European dimension of foreign policy is most advanced and explicit in Germany, where it forms part of the overall strategy of reflexive multilateralism'.[13] This highlights the distinctive German approach to European integration in which policy-makers span the divide between European and domestic level forums and there is a cross-fertilisation of norms and policies in a two-way process. Although the same processes can be recognised in France and the UK, albeit in a much more restricted sense, Germany's main partners are characterised by what has been described as 'nationalistic internationalism', in which policy-makers seek to 'exploit' multilateral institutions for their own national interest.[14] This would equate with the neo-liberal institutionalist paradigm. In Germany, the European project has blurred the divide between what is domestic and what is foreign policy, highlighting the success of Germany's integration. Hill and Wallace have noted the 'transformationalist effects' that the interaction between policy-makers has had on traditional foreign policy-making practices.[15]

Germany has been profoundly affected by involvement in multilateral institutions. Its commitment to institutions has been described as 'exaggerated multilateralism'.[16] Garton-Ash states that 'the Federal Republic was particularly interested in, and became increasingly adept at, not clearly articulating distinctive national positions, but rather feedings its own special German concerns and priorities into a common approach'.[17]

Germany's embeddedness within the EU has reinforced a Europeanist outlook among Germany's foreign policy elites. Central to Germany's overall multilateralist strategy has been the maintenance of close bilateral relations. Significant injections of dynamism into the integration process have resulted primarily from bilateral endeavours between the Federal Republic and its major European partners, most significantly with France. These bilateral relationships will now be examined.

SECURITY RELATIONS WITH FRANCE, THE UK AND THE USA

Franco-German Security Relations

The end of World War Two represented a watershed in relations between France and Germany. It was clear that co-operation between the two Western European powers was crucial for the future peace and prosperity of the continent. The development of Adenauer's *Westbindung* was therefore reliant on close Franco-German relations. The Elysée Treaty of 22 January 1963 was a culmination of efforts since 1945 to construct close Franco-German ties.[18] It committed both parties to strengthen bilateral ties through co-operation on defence issues and also co-operation within the fledgling European Community structures. The Franco-German Treaty of 1988 further elaborated on the Elysée Treaty by establishing the Franco-German Defence and Security Council.[19] Franco-German security consultation takes an institutionalised form based on two underlying aims: first, to prevent the return of military aggression between the two states and, second, to establish a dominant partnership as the 'engine' of

European integration, based on the desire to control Germany within the EC with France providing the policy leads, while Germany provided the economic might.

In the day-to-day business of EU politics, the Franco-German 'co-ordination reflex' results in the tightly knit working relationship which exists at all levels between the two countries. Bulmer *et al.* posit that 'the relationship with France established a settled German preference for strategic partnerships based on a long-term commitment to a strategic project rather than growing out of agreement on a range of technical interests'.[20] The highly institutionalised bilateral relationship between France and Germany has been described by Thomas Pederson as one of 'co-operative hegemony' in which they have been able to secure policy preferences in tandem through a process of close co-operation and through the use of 'side payments' to other member states.[21] Pederson's argument is generally highly persuasive, but it does not provide an adequate explanation of CFSP, where the Franco-German relationship does not dominate to the same extent as in other policy fields. The major difference which exists between the two states in European security policy concerns France's aim of creating *L'Europe puissance*, a powerful Europe more autonomous of the US than at present. However, despite sporadic differences within the Franco-German relationship, the two sides have remained broadly united on the strategic goals of European security policy, largely due to the interwovenness of defence consultations between the two states.

British–German Security Relations

The UK's ability to impact on the EU has been highly circumscribed by the Franco-German 'hard core', despite the recent attempt to shift the balance with the Blair–Schröder Paper.[22] However, in security relations the British–German relationship has been positive due to their close functional interdependence within NATO. The UK has been able to exert considerable influence and prise open the almost exclusive Franco-German 'hard core' in the area of CFSP. The UK's experience and practical expertise in military intervention is likely to ensure it a central role in any future EU military forces. The introduction of EMU and the resulting marginalisation of Britain in the EU's major policy area has made the UK's high-profile stance in the development of ESDP all the more significant.

The UK has adopted a generally guarded stance towards the Franco-German-led Eurocorps.[23] However, at the Anglo-French Summit before the Helsinki European Council meeting, the UK showed signs of adopting a more positive attitude toward the Eurocorps.[24] British participation in the

Eurocorps also represents an area where the UK can play a major role without, in its terms, 'sacrificing' further sovereignty, as co-operation in the Eurocorps resembles that which exists within the (intergovernmental) NATO. Britain's more interventionist attitude towards military engagement was reflected in the UK's 1998 Strategic Defence Review, the aim of which was to outline the future scope of structure of the armed forces according to strategic imperatives rather than financial constraints.[25]

German and British policy-makers have been united in the understanding that the EU must develop a more coherent foreign policy, but the idea of progressing from this to a common defence has often met with British intransigence. The acceptance of the need for an independent crisis reaction capability by British elites has developed in the wake of the ethnic conflict in Kosovo and because of America's reluctance to continue to carry the buck in matters of European regional security. Thränert also posits that renewed British interest in CESDP is the result of wanting to bolster Britain's European standing to strengthen its hand with the USA, to increase Europe's international status, and to prevent any attempt by France to weaken the transatlantic link.[26]

Franco-British Security Co-operation

The primacy of Franco-British security relations within the EU is grounded in intergovernmental approaches to European security co-operation and is cemented by their status as permanent representatives on the United Nations Security Council (UNSC). Furthermore, the extensive post-colonial ties which France and the UK maintain in Africa and other parts of the world give their diplomacy a 'world reach' that Germany has lacked. The Franco-British security partnership has been vital for the renaissance of CFSP since 1998. The Letter of Intent (LOI) on defence co-operation and the declaration on European security signed at Saint Malo in December 1998 by Defence Ministers Robertson and Richard injected a vital dynamism into CFSP. As well as committing both governments to improve the quality of defence co-operation and troop deployment, the LOI strengthens co-operation in the fields of operations, logistics, intelligence, civil/military affairs, media handling, personnel and liaison.[27] The positive impact of bilateral relationships involving France, Germany and the UK in European security results from the lack of exclusivity in these relations. While one eye is always cast on strengthening bilateral co-operation and transparency, the other is continually focused on the impact of such co-operation on other EU member states. The Franco-British tandem in military security affairs is critical due to the military expertise which both states possess and demonstrate in international operations.

The USA's Commitment to Atlanticism and the emergence of the European Security and Defence Identity.

America continues to regard Europe as its most important ally. Geipel posits four key ingredients of the American commitment to Europe: hard economic interests, moral purpose, cultural affinity, and, decisively, the sheer political will of American elites, although since the fall of the Berlin Wall cultural affinity and moral purpose have declined as major factors in the relationship.[28] Central to US–German relations is the high volume of German and American exports and the concern, despite sporadic EU–USA trade quarrels, that these should be allowed to flourish in an open but fair market. While globalisation has placed new and increased demands on national diplomacy, the wide range of common interests which exist between the EU and the USA have necessitated close ties which are in turn reflected in the maintenance of security co-operation. 'Guarded engagement' rather than isolationism will be the hallmark of US foreign policy in the future.[29]

The development of the European Security and Defence Identity (ESDI) within the Atlantic Alliance has been central to the incremental recasting of the transatlantic relationship during the 1990s. The declaration of the North Atlantic Council in Brussels on 10–11 January 1994 stated that the emergence of the ESDI was an 'expression of a mature Europe'[30] and supported the creation of 'separable but not separate capabilities which could respond to European requirements and contribute to alliance security'. [31] Most significantly in this declaration, NATO assets were to be made available for WEU operations through the Common Joint Task Force (CJTF) concept. Ginsberg suggests that the efforts of the EU in the field of CFSP alleviated considerable tensions between the EU and the USA.[32] In addition, the range of options open to both the WEU and NATO were enhanced. The North Atlantic Council summits at Madrid in 1997 and Washington in 1999 elaborated the principles of ESDI. While ESDI has been central to raising the profile of Western Europe within NATO, the United States has been very sure to maintain it position as *primus inter pares* at the head of the Alliance. The military capabilities gap between the United States and European NATO members means that the final decision on future NATO military operations will remain with America.

CURRENT ISSUES FACING GERMAN POLICY-MAKERS IN CFSP

The Kosovo conflict in 1999 provided an important impetus for greater European co-operation in the field of foreign and defence policy. This commitment to the European integration process was emphasised by Chancellor Schröder during the conflict in order to secure public support for German involvement in the bombing of Serbia: 'The integration of Germany into the Western community of states is part of the German *Staatsräson*. We do not want a German *Sonderweg*.'[33] However, the new German government's stance has changed subtly. According to Schröder, 'the new German foreign policy won't be unhistorical. But I believe we have shown in the past 50 years that there is no reason to tie down the Germans, out of fear of the *furum teutonicus* … My generation and those following are Europeans because we want to be, not because we must be. That makes us freer in dealing with others'.[34]

This view is mirrored in the opinion of one of the Chancellor's advisers who stated that he wanted a Europe which is 'worthwhile for Germans'.[35] In the words of Hellmann, 'in Germany's policy towards European integration (as in no other area) Germany's domestic discourse about "national" interests has markedly shifted during the past decade … from a position of supranationalism and "inhibitedness" … based on both Germany's post-war enthusiasm for European integration and its pre-World War II legacy of "Machtpolitik" to a more self-centred, assertive and more "national" position'.[36]

This new Euro-pragmatism has not manifested itself in the area of CFSP as it has in other areas of European integration.[37] The fierce debate over the introduction of EMU (Economic and Monetary Union) is the clearest case study of the waning of the previously unquestioned public consensus on the merits of European integration. Nonetheless there remains broad public support for an enhanced European Union security presence and Germany's responsibility within such a project. Debates on European security in Germany centre on what kind of role Germany should have in any future autonomous European security capability. In many ways, the German public is still wedded to the concept of the Bundeswehr as a purely defensive force. However, Germany must now be *bündnisfähig* (capable of fulfilling the obligations of military alliance membership) and shoulder considerably more responsibility in military operations, as in the bombing of Serbia. The ratification of the Amsterdam Treaty improves the operability of the CFSP by improving decision-making processes, especially by removing the need for unanimous voting in some areas. These developments aimed at increasing solidarity within CFSP by allowing 'coalitions of the willing' to carry out common missions without the need for involvement of all member states. It is this area where Germany's new stance towards Europe is arguably most evident. According to Duke, the provisions contained within the Amsterdam Treaty 'might even encourage national-interest-driven foreign and security policy as opposed to the "mutual solidarity" sought by the treaty'.[38] This is a scenario which Germany will guard against.

The development of the CESDP since the Cologne European Council Summit in June 1999 presents German policy-makers with two important choices. The first relates to the direction in which Germany wants the EU's foreign policy to develop and the extent of the constraints on this policy. Second, Germany must decide what the EU's future role should be. Germany has been described as a *Zivilmacht* (civilian power), relying on military means only as a last resort, but this categorisation is open to question in the light of recent developments in Kosovo.[39] However, Germany appears reluctant to commit to further military involvement in multilateral task forces, while at the same time remaining very aware of its responsibilities as a NATO and EU member. The uneasiness that remains within Germany concerning the deployment of the Bundeswehr for anything other than peacekeeping operations may result in behind-the-scenes efforts to convince its main EU partners of the merits of a minimalist foreign and security policy in terms of the use of military force. Foreign Minister Fischer has been vocal in expressing his continuing view of the EU as a *Zivilmacht*.[40] For Fischer the development of a European security and defence capability is 'not about a militarisation of the EU', rather the EU must be made 'an effective and decisive peaceful power which is able, as was the case in Kosovo, to bolster the rule of law and renounce violence and thereby to consign war as a political tool in Europe to the past'.[41] This view is backed by Angelika Beer, defence spokesperson for Alliance '90/Greens, who maintains that 'the civilian power character of the European Union should not be lost'.[42] While Germany is committed to the development of the CESDP and to react to American calls to take more responsibility in its 'own backyard', the transatlantic link will continue to exert an important gravitational pull. However, a reluctance to develop the CESDP further may lead to frustrations on the part of France and the UK, which feel more comfortable in resorting to armed force. In the changing post-Cold War environment, the CESDP can provide Germany with a multilateral solution for its evolving security needs.

If the CFSP should be truly communitarised (brought into the main treaty structure and put under greater supranational control) and the EU is enlarged to perhaps 28 countries, this would certainly further enhance the EU's role as the most dynamic force on the continent of Europe. Communitarisation of the CFSP implies a common defence budget, greater involvement in CFSP affairs by the European Parliament, the subjection of CFSP to the scrutiny of the European Court of Justice, and, in the last resort, perhaps even supranational control of troops in the European Rapid Reaction Force (ERRF).[43] Extensive enlargement will inevitably signal a dramatic evolution of the EU's geopolitical role in the international system.[44] With this would come added responsibility. The EU might want or have to go it alone without American involvement – a scenario which would pose Germany with tough choices. Ultimately, the EU's enormous economic strength and military potential may lead the EU down the path towards becoming a global power to match the United States and the emerging China.

There has been a notable growth in tension between the United States and the EU in recent times, primarily in economic affairs, but security-related tensions have also been in evidence.[45] The latter have sprung not only from US exasperation at the lack of a European capability in security matters, but also from hints from some European quarters at the development of autonomous European security structures.[46] On a similar line, the EU has also been more concerned about the destabilising impact of Russia on the continent as a whole and has made efforts to bolster co-operation and transparent relations with Russia.[47] In addition, Europeans have been very critical of plans for a US missile shield. This issue is particularly relevant for Germany and its security needs because of the non-nuclear character of German defence. Germany's reliance on the United States for a nuclear shield, according to Fischer, 'was always based on our trust that the United States would protect out interests, that the United States, as the leading nuclear power, would guarantee some sort of order'.[48] Clinton's postponement of a decision on the National Missile Defence (NMD) system has been welcomed by Fischer,[49] but Republicans seem determined to implement the programme, even to the extent of expanding its scope to cover Western Europe.

The main problem with NMD is that it is a fundamentally flawed project with many question marks hanging over it despite assurances from the United States to the contrary. There has been little serious dialogue between both sides of the transatlantic alliance over reaching a compromise concerning the American proposals. NMD is an elite-driven programme which has not been sufficiently 'sold' to either the US public or America's European allies.[50] Despite the ultimate aim of extending the NMD to cover Western Europe, the row over NMD is significant in that it shows up a lack of communication within NATO over the future security provision for the West. This issue is all the more unwelcome because it has emerged at a time when the security architecture is being reorganised to cope with the new demands facing Europe. Transparency and co-ordination within the EU and NATO over future burden-sharing is a prerequisite for the success of any military intervention under ESDP. There must be a two-way process of mutual reassurance in which Europe will be confident of the continued American commitment to European security. In addition, the United States will have to learn to overcome what Lord Robertson has called 'a sort of schizophrenia' over ESDP, in which it seems to welcome moves for a more balanced division of labour in defence matters, while at the same time remaining anxious that a more autonomous European capability could lead to the weakening of transatlantic ties.[51]

What causes most friction between the US and its European Allies is America's continued unipolar vision of the world and its own leadership role in it. Lindley-French identifies the root cause of this as being that 'America is incapable of true partnership because Americans, regardless of political persuasion, feel obliged to lead'.[52] This propensity will inevitably cause major difficulties within transatlantic security relations as the EU's presence in the international community grows and it begins to act more assertively in security affairs. The EU may increase its influence within the Atlantic Alliance, but, while this will give it a greater say in policy matters, the USA remains so far ahead in terms of military capabilities and in the technological Revolution in Military Affairs (RMA) that America will remain the dominant partner for the foreseeable future.[53] Concerns have been voiced within Germany that the future European capability 'might be a shield for Europe, but not America's sword'.[54] The development of a potentially semi-autonomous crisis reaction force, as outlined in the Helsinki Council Declaration in December 1999, has been one of the major issues within the Atlantic Alliance and the EU during the 1990s. Javier Solana has stated that 'putting practical military strength at the top of our agenda should reassure our North American Allies. We are doing what they have urged us to do for decades'.[55]

Calls have been coming from the USA, particularly from the Republican camp, for a clear division of labour between America and Europe, with the US focusing on fighting or preventing wars in the Persian Gulf and Asia, leaving the European states to concentrate on peacekeeping missions. Generally, the Europeans are more willing to commit ground troops in peacekeeping situations than the American. Bearing the legacy of Vietnam, the US prefers to focus on issues which impinge on America's geopolitical role rather than on regional disputes of the kind witnessed in the Balkans. However, such a division of labour and burden-sharing may not be in the best interests of alliance cohesion.

A key indicator of Germany's determination to help concretely in the development of the CESDP will be the fate of efforts to reform the Bundeswehr. Schake *et al.* note the need for Germany to modernise and professionalise its army and, in particular, its crisis reaction troops in order to make a satisfactory contribution.[56] This is a very sensitive issue. Hoffmann and Longhurst argue that:

Essentially, the idea of an All Volunteer Force (AVF) does not 'fit in' with what the Germans see as being the role and purpose of their armed forces. The practice of conscription in Germany has profound meaning, stretching beyond military necessity, party politics and an attachment to economic benefits delivered by Zivildienst ... Conscription is clearly viewed by the mainstream parties as a mechanism to resist fundamental change in Germany's security policies by maintaining a healthy equilibrium and broad interface in civil-military relations.[57]

This evolution in defence and security policy within Germany, while not representing a complete divorce from past German preferences and reluctance to engage in military operations, has impacted on the wider political environment. What would have been politically impossible in the immediate wake of unification can now be justified by German elites in terms of multilateral commitments and the maintenance of international human rights norms. German *strategic culture* defines the realms of the possible and thereby the constraints under which German policy-makers must operate. Longhurst has described the make-up of strategic culture as 'a range of discernible norms, beliefs and ideas which act as a perceptual lens through which objective reality is processed and translated into understandable "facts"'.[58] Strategic culture is, however, an evolving concept, which can be seen in the development of a consensus over the need for a greater European voice in foreign and security policy. This is a case of what Aggestam identifies as 'Complex Learning' – actors going through a process of social learning in which their values and beliefs are altered through continuous interaction.[59]

CHALLENGES FACING GERMAN FOREIGN POLICY ELITES – EUROPE AS A 'FREE RIDER' ON AMERICAN MILITARY STRENGTH?[60]

An analysis of the Balkan Stability Pact is a key indicator of how Germany would like to develop the CFSP. Joschka Fischer invested significant political capital in pressing for EU action in this area. The significance of the Stability Pact for the future of Europe for German policy-makers is very evident in Fischer's remarks that 'with the Stability Pact we must prove that we mean business with our commitment. This is also a question of the political reliability of Germany and Europe's foreign policy'.[61]

Germany also framed the initial efforts to develop a Stability Pact as being in the national interest. 'Due to Germany's pronounced interest in stability in the region, Germany along with its EU partners should undertake the initiative to provide a middle to long-term strategy for the stabilisation of South-east Europe.'[62] The desire evident here to communitarise a German initiative is typical of German European policy-making.

It is noteworthy that major advances towards CESDP were made at the Cologne Council summit. The fleshing out of Fischer's proposals for the Stability Pact for the south-east Balkans marked a clear determination to achieve a better co-ordination of the European's non-military crisis reaction capabilities.[63] Germany's ability to conduct a successful European Council Presidency in CFSP matters was further bolstered by the entry into force of the Amsterdam Treaty on 1 May 1999. The adoption of Fischer's proposals to bring stability to the south-east Balkans was greatly facilitated by the new institutional possibilities created by the new treaty. Clearly, Germany's diplomacy was successful because it acted in accordance with its stated aim to utilise CFSP structures to the full.

Germany would nonetheless prefer the CESDP not to become an institution which demands too much from Berlin. Although Germany has progressed politically along the path towards assuming greater responsibilities in military operations, this movement has not been backed by a complementary reform of the armed forces.[64] Germany has evidently undergone a process of 'foreign policy learning' during the 1990s, but there may be limits to this process.[65] Hence, Germany has sought to influence EU security policy in the direction of non-military endeavours in which political co-operation is more important than military intervention. Germany saw the Stability Pact as a necessary balance to the bombing of Kosovo, as compensation for the destruction which the bombing caused in the region. The Stability Pact may also be viewed as an attempt to gain diplomatic prestige and present a positive image of their European Council Presidency in the first half of 1999. In addition, the appointment of Bodo Hombach as head of the Stability Pact was also a politically expedient move by Schröder to remove a controversial politician from the German domestic stage.

A second major issue which German policy-makers must address is whether Germany should support the communitarisaton of the CFSP, so that EU would replace national control of what is traditionally one of the most jealously guarded areas of national sovereignty. Germany is considered in some quarters a post-national state that is comfortable with the ceding of sovereignty to supranational institutions.[66] But the machinery of decision-making in this area may not be easily transferable to the EU, not even for the Federal Republic. Joschka Fischer clearly sees the ceding of national sovereignty in this area to the EU as a vital part of the integration project.

Thus, in a recent speech to the German Bundestag, he stated: 'The completion of this Europe of integration means … the transfer of the substantial sovereign rights of nation states to the political scope of the European Union … If you want that, then the military level will not remain with the nation-state … Without this development we cannot complete the political goal of a European Union.'[67]

German policy-makers stand out among those of the 'big three' member states in pushing for political union with the inclusion of CESDP structures within the main EU body. France, while being a vocal supporter of deeper integration, will continue to insist on an intergovernmental approach to EU security affairs, albeit not in the strictest sense of the word. The UK, due to the politically extremely contested character of European integration in Britain, would find it very difficult to go down the road of greater supranational control of CESDP. In terms of Putnam's two-level game metaphor, British policy elites are constrained at the international level by ratification difficulties on the domestic level which restrict the scope of policy choices which are acceptable to it at the EU negotiating table.[68]

Fischer's federalist vision of the future of the EU will inevitably clash with intergovernmentalist conceptions in the UK. One may also ask what impact a communitarised ESDP would have on bilateral relations between Germany and the United States. As defence is perhaps the most difficult policy area to communitarise, the CESDP would almost certainly be the final piece in the jigsaw of political union. A more cohesive and powerful EU could put pressure on EU–US relations. Even if this were the case, however, the transatlantic strategic partnership is not a zero-sum game; so the development of a more cohesive and effective CESDP should not dramatically affect security relations.

For Defence Minister Rudolf Scharping, the aim of a common security policy must be that 'Europe speaks with one voice in international affairs and is in the position to decide upon and represent its interests'.[69] Moreover, 'Europe must be politically and militarily authorised to act and take responsibility for European security itself'.[70] Scharping has stressed particularly the need for coordination to avoid costly duplications of resources and proposed the establishment of a Joint Air Transport Command, an area where Europe is especially weak. Scharping in fact proposed the creation of a European Defence Ministers' Council, which had its first informal session in Sintra, Portugal in February 2000, discussing future EU decision-making structures and the strengthening of military capabilities. This informal meeting of defence ministers will be backed up by interim military committees as well as by a delegation of national military experts in the EU Council secretariat. These measures were agreed by EU foreign ministers in February 2000. Moves have also been made by

Britain, France, Germany, Italy, Spain and Sweden to streamline European defence industries. These countries signed a 'framework agreement' for the Organisation for Joint Armament Co-operation (OCCAR), a step which the US sees as unwelcome.[71]

Scharping has also been trying to streamline existing institutions and to improve overall co-ordination in the field of foreign and security policy. The latter concern accounts for his initiative to stage regular, if informal, meetings of member states' defence ministers, building on the 1998 Pörtschach summit. Scharping also supported the establishment of a Political Security Committee (PSC) in the same building as the EU Council of Ministers. Scharping has, however, been hampered in pursuing his policies by substantial cuts in the defence budget, cuts which will hinder his attempts to modernise the Bundeswehr. The reform of the Bundeswehr[72] has provoked intense inter-party debate within Germany, with the CDU/CSU favouring an increase in the defence budget in order to meet the new security demands. The Bavarian CSU has stated that 'the austerity plans of the Red/Green coalition for the German Federal Armed Forces put Germany and its defence capabilities into last place behind its European partners' and that the budget should be raised to DM 50 billion.[73] The opposition parties argue that Bundeswehr numbers should not fall below 300,000.[74] Government and opposition accept the need for the Bundeswehr to remain *bündnisfähig,* but a debate is raging in Germany about how this should be achieved.[75] By reducing still further the ability of the Bundeswehr to conduct unilateral operations, the Red/Green government hopes to increase the dependency of the German military on multilateralism. However, there is uneasiness in both the US and the UK that Germany is really only adapting to current perceived security threats and is not investing in its armed forces as it should to meet the challenges of the future.

What is clear in any case is that the major military member states – France, the UK and Germany – are taking the lead in the preparation of the CESDP. This has led to tension within the EU, especially with the smaller states, which are not always consulted on such matters.[76] The use of *directoires* may become a more frequent occurrence within the CESDP as the necessity for swift and decisive action grows. Germany feels slightly uncomfortable about its position in the *directoire,* as this conflicts with its role as a *Musterknabe* ('model pupil') supporting deeper European integration. It will not therefore want to draw attention to its growing responsibilities within CESDP.

German policy towards the CESDP is affected by competion and conflict between different ministries with their different agendas. Bulmer *et al.* point to the clash between the foreign and finance ministries, the former with its 'positive sum conceptions' of integration and the latter with its 'cost-cutting' ethos.[77] These antagonistic priorities have provoked clashes within the government over CESDP and notably huge row over the Bundeswehr budget, in which cuts were imposed by Finance Minister Eichel. This inter-ministerial wrangling over the future financing of the Bundeswehr was seen outside Germany as a blow to the prospect of developing a viable and powerful European defence force. NATO Secretary-General Lord Robertson, while still UK Defence Secretary, was especially critical of the budget cuts, stating that 'The days of cutting defence budgets are over ... There can be no peace dividend without peace. That is going to dawn on some countries'.[78] This view was echoed by the US Defence Secretary, William Cohen, who asserted that 'now more than ever the alliance looks to German leadership to contribute to the capabilities necessary if we are to continue shaping peace and security into the next century'.[79] However, any suggestion of a German leadership role is viewed with concern by German policy-makers: 'We do not want to dance alone, but rather be the driver of further integration.'[80] At the 73rd Franco-German summit in Toulouse, Schröder and Chirac stressed their 'determination to contribute all their weight so that the EU equips itself with the necessary autonomous means to decide and deal with crises'.[81] The momentum behind Germany's decision to play a larger role in crisis management seems now to be firmly grounded.

The Foreign Ministry under Joschka Fischer actively supports the CESDP, emphasising, for example, as in the Stability Pact, the need for the extension of human rights and democracy to Southern Europe. Despite his unorthodox political background in the Green movement, the pressures of high office have forced Fischer to make concessions and prevented any significant 'greening' of German security policy. Although Fischer has supported the commitment to form a 50–60,000-strong ERRF by 2003, his main emphasis, under pressure from the 'fundamentalist' element of the Alliance '90/Greens, has been on promoting non-military aspects of security. In contrast, Scharping's ministry is ingrained with a pro-NATO stance stemming from the long years of the Bundeswehr's integration into NATO forces and is therefore more likely to emphasis 'hard security' measures.

How much room for manoeuvre does Germany have in the pursuit of new security policies? The upgrading of the European voice and capabilities in regional security issues presents Germany with a new set of priorities and policy choices. The decisions taken by the EU to develop a crisis reaction force were strongly backed by Germany, even though this will result in the increasing use of the Bundeswehr in military operations. There remains distinct unease among the German public concerning the use of the

Bundeswehr, despite the relative 'success' of German involvement in Kosovo. Scharping's commitment at the informal defence ministers' meeting at Ecouen in October 2000 to provide approximately 18,000 troops for the ERRF, almost a third of the total force numbers, signals a great commitment by Germany. The real test, however, will come when the fledgling force takes part in its first military operations. Will the German public continue to support this project if the Bundeswehr suffers losses on the front line?

CONCLUSION

Some initial conclusions can be drawn concerning Germany's evolving CESDP stance. First, Joschka Fischer advocates the development of a CESDP founded on the ideals of *Zivilmacht*, stressing non-military aspects of security in Europe. The Stability Pact is an example of Fischer's emphasis on democracy-building, economic development and respect for humanity as a means of securing stability. This is a clear example of Germany placing its imprint on the CESDP process. Second, this emphasis on non-military security and preventative security measures has affected the German government's decision to cut the defence budget. In defence matters, there appears to be an attempt in some quarters to cling to fundamental principles of the German strategic culture to brake attempts to improve the deployment capabilities of the Bundeswehr. This sends mixed signals to Germany's partners and will continue to result in frustration and tensions unless this issue is resolved. Finally, the broad political consensus favouring an enhanced European capability in foreign and security policy will almost certainly be put under pressure if Germany does develop a stronger military capability and the preference that existed hitherto in favour of non-military crisis prevention is thereby undermined.

Notwithstanding the recent growth of tensions in the Atlantic Alliance, German policy-makers still look to the US to provide Germany's nuclear shield. Germany will therefore continue to pursue a 'British-style' approach to European security aiming at enhancing the European voice *within* NATO rather than at trying to build up a rival venture. The principal CESDP dilemma for Germany is whether it wants to create new machinery for CESDP without first having a clear vision as to how it is going to be used. If Germany cannot affect the process as much as it would like, then it will be forced to make difficult decisions concerning military operations. Performing the Petersberg Tasks, which have been incorporated into the CESDP, will not be easy for the EU, but will rather require a substantial commitment by the member states, including Germany.

The EU's Nice Summit in December 2000 advanced the CESDP further by forging agreement over the broad aims of EU security policy.[82] Despite accounts of a dispute between France and the United Kingdom over the relationship between the CESDP and NATO, a 60-page report outlining the plans for the ERRF was unanimously agreed after only eight minutes of discussions.[83] However, the UK's success in not having defence issues under 'enhanced co-operation' may brake future development of the CESDP. While the relationship between the EU and NATO remains slightly hazy, there has been enough convergence of views on the subject to allow progress on CESDP to be made. The evolving compromise between 'pro-Atlanticists' and 'pro-Europeanists' has been the key to the development of the CFSP during the 1990s.

Germany remains preoccupied by the task of balancing its relations with its European partners against its relations with the United States. American pragmatism and the US's strategic interests will keep the US involved in European security affairs. Germany will continue to push to have its voice heard in security policy negotiations with its major partners to ensure that German interests are considered and that Germany can play an active part in CESDP. For Germany to keep pace with the inevitable consequences of the recasting of the transatlantic security bargains which is under way, German elites must continue to secure domestic approval for a more active role in military operations. To succeed in this, policy-making elites must try to explain, justify and legitimise the role of CESDP in Europe and Germany's security policy. In any case, the current discussions over the future shape of European security institutions cannot be considered as a zero-sum game in which the development of CESDP automatically affects and reduces the quality of transatlantic relations between the USA, Germany, France and the UK. The transatlantic strategic partnership will continue to exist, but in a revised form in which Europe will carry more of the burden in crisis management. Thus, the recasting of security bargains post-Kosovo does not really pose a threat to existing security relations. Rather, this process reflects new geopolitical realities and the new quality of defence co-operation within the EU.

NOTES

The author would like to thank Professor William E. Paterson, Lord Roper and Dr Kerry Longhurst for their helpful comments on earlier drafts of this article.

1. T. Risse-Kappen, *Co-operation among Democracies* (Princeton, NJ: Princeton University Press, 1995).
2. A. Hoffmann, 'Germany in the Age of Crisis Management' (unpublished Ph.D. thesis, Institute for German Studies, University of Birmingham, 1999), p.293.

3. For example, the Federal Republic's refusal to have diplomatic relations with the DDR, embodied in the Hallstein Doctrine, left the Federal Republic open to blackmail.

4. P. Neville-Jones, 'The Genscher-Colombo Proposals on European Union', *Common Market Law Review*, 20/4 (1983), p.658.

5. Ibid.

6. W. Wallace, 'Introduction: Co-operation and Convergence in European Policy', in C. Hill (ed.), *National Foreign Policies and European Political Co-operation* (London: Allen & Unwin, for the Royal Institute of International Affairs, 1983), p.10.

7. R.C. Eichenberg, 'Dual Track and Double Trouble. The Two-level Politics of INF', in P.B. Evans, H.K. Jacobson and R.D. Putnam, *Double-Edged Diplomacy: International Bargaining and Domestic Politics* (London: University of California Press, 1993).

8. M. Jopp, 'The Strategic Implications of European Integration', *Adelphi Paper*, No.290 (London: Brassey's, 1994), p.9.

9. Ibid.

10. C. Hill, 'The Capabilities-Expectations Gap or Conceptualising Europe's International Role', *Journal of Common Market Studies*, 31/3. See also C. Hill, 'Closing the Capabilities-Expectation Gap?', in J. Peterson and H. Sjursen (eds.), *A Common Foreign Policy for Europe? Competing Visions of the CFSP* (London: Routledge, 1998).

11. Declaration of the WEU Council of Ministers, Bremen, 10–11 May 1999, para. 4.

12. E. Regelsberger and M. Jopp, 'Und sie bewegt sich doch! Die Gemeinsame Außen- und Sicherheitspolitik nach den Bestimmungen des Amsterdames Vertrages', *Integration*, 20/4 (1997), pp.255–63.

13. H. Sjursen, 'CFSP and EU Enlargement', in B. Tonra and T. Christiansen (eds.), *CFSP and Beyond: Theorising European Foreign Policy* (Proceedings of the Conference Held at the Centre for European Studies at Aberystwyth in May 1998), p.17.

14. Ibid.

15. C. Hill and W. Wallace, 'Introduction', in C. Hill (ed.), *The Actors in Europe's Foreign Policy* (London: Routledge, 1996), p.6.

16. J. Anderson, 'Hard Interests, Soft Power, and Germany's Changing Role in Europe', in P.J. Katzenstein (ed.), *Tamed Power: Germany in Europe* (Ithaca, NY: Cornell University Press, 1997).

17. T. Garton-Ash, *In Europe's Name* (London: Vintage, 1993), p.262.

18. Treaty between the French Republic and the Federal Republic of Germany Concerning Franco-German Co-operation (The Elysée Treaty), Paris, 22 Jan. 1963.

19. Protocol to the Treaty of 22 January 1963 between the Federal Republic of Germany and the French Republic on Franco-German Co-operation, Article III.

20. S. Bulmer, C. Jeffery and W.E. Paterson, *Germany's European Diplomacy: Shaping the Regional Milieu* (Manchester: Manchester University Press, 2000), p.53.

21. T. Pederson, *Germany, France and the Integration of Europe: A Realist Interpretation* (London: Pinter, 1998).

22. The Third Way/Die Neue Mitte, Tony Blair and Gerhard Schröder, http://www.labour. org.uk/lp/new/labour/docs/PMSPEECHES/THIRDWAYPURPLEBOX.HTM.

23. M. Clarke, 'British Security Policy', in K.A. Eliassen (ed.), *Foreign and Security Policy in the European Union* (London: Sage, 1998), p.135.

24. Joint Declaration by the British and French Governments on European Defence at the Anglo-French Summit on 25 November 1999 in London, http://www.dgap.org/english/tip/tip2/gbfr251199_p.html.

25. T. Dodd and M. Oakes, 'The Strategic Defence Review White Paper', *House of Commons Research Paper*, 98/91, p.10.

26. O. Thränert, 'Wie die Europäer sicherheitspolitisch erwachsen werden wollen. Über die Perspektiven der Beziehungen zwischen EU und NATO und eine neue Rollenverteilung', *Frankfurter Rundschau Online*, 24.07.2000 http://www.f-r.de/fr/spezial/qveuropa/t2015007.htm.

27. M. Oakes, 'European Defence: From Pörtschach to Helsinki', *House of Commons Research Paper*, 00/20, Appendix I.
28. G. Geipel, 'The Future of Atlanticism', in C.C. Hodge (ed.), *Redefining European Security* (New York and London: Garland Publishing Inc., 1999).
29. J.E. Rielly (ed.), *American Public Opinion and U.S. Foreign Policy Report 1999* (Chicago: The Chicago Council on Foreign Relations, 1999).
30. The Declaration of the Heads of State and Government Participating in the Meeting of the North Atlantic Council in Brussels on 10–11 Jan. 1994, para. 1.
31. Ibid., para. 6.
32. R. Ginsberg, 'Transatlantic Dimensions of CFSP: The Culture of Foreign Policy Co-operation', in E. Regelsberger, P. de Schoutheete de Tevarent and W. Wessels (eds.), *Foreign Policy of the European Union: From EPC to CFSP and Beyond* (London: Lynne Rienner Publishers, 1997), p.314.
33. Regierungserklärung von Bundeskanzler Gerhard Schröder im Deutschen Bundestag zur Aktuellen Lage im Kosovo am Donnerstag, 15 April 1999, in Bonn.
34. 'Comment and Analysis: Germany's Moderniser', *Financial Times* interview with Gerhard Schröder, 10 May 1998.
35. 'Survey-Germany: Horsetrading on EU Finance', *Financial Times*, 1 June 1999.
36. G. Hellmann, 'Beyond Weltpolitik, Self-containment and Civilian Power: United Germany's Normalising Ambitions', *Institute for German Studies Discussion Paper 99/10* (University of Birmingham, 1999), p.53.
37. M. Knodt and N. Staeck, 'Shifting Paradigms: Reflecting Germany's European Policy', *European Integration Online Papers* (EIoP) 3/3 (1999), http://eiop.or.at/eiop/texte/1999-003a.htm.
38. S. Duke, 'From Amsterdam to Kosovo: Lessons for the Future of CFSP', *Eipascope*, 2 (1999), p.7.
39. However, Hanns Maull continues to apply the term *Zivilmacht* to Germany despite Berlin's involvement in Kosovo. See H.W. Maull, 'Germany and the Use of Force: Still a Civilian Power?', *Trierer Arbeitspapiere zur Internationale Politik*, 2 (Nov. 1999).
40. Rede zum Ende der deutschen Presidentschaft in der Europäischen Union: Rede des Bundesministers des Auswaertigen Joschka Fischer vor dem Europäischen Parlament am 21 Juli 1999 in Straßburg, http://www.auswaertiges-amt.de/6_archiv/2/r/r990721a.htm.
41. Ibid.
42. 'Die EU muß Zivilmacht bleiben: Gastkommentar Angelika Beer', *Die Welt*, 27 July 1999, http://www/welt.de/daten/1999/07/27/0727fo122982.htx.
43. For a British view on the possible state of European defence in the year 2010, see C. Grant, 'European Defence from 2010 – A British View', *Challenge Europe On-Line Journal*, The European Policy Centre, 21 Oct. 2000, http://www.theepc.be/Challenge_Europe/text/memo.asp?ID=178.
44. C. Hill, 'The Geopolitical Implications of Enlargement', *EUI Working Papers Series*, Robert Schuman Centre for Advanced Studies, RSC No.2000/30.
45. The current EU–USA dispute over US tax breaks for exporting firms is bringing EU Trade Commissioner Pascal Lamy into intense confrontation with the US Treasury, which if allowed to develop may escalate into a full-blown trade war. S. Taylor, 'Walking the Tightrope in US Tax Dispute', *European Voice*, 21–27 Sept. 2000.
46. F. Bonnart, 'U.S. Starts to Fret Over EU Military Independence', *International Herald Tribune*, 24 May 2000.
47. See Common Strategy on Russia of 4 June 1999, Annex II, Presidency Conclusions, Cologne European Council Presidency, 3 and 4 June 1999; Common Strategy on Ukraine 1999, Annex V, Presidency Conclusions Helsinki European Council Presidency 10 and 11 December 1999.
48. Ibid.
49. J. Fischer, 'Towards a New Transatlantic Partnership: The United States, Germany and

Europe in an Era of Global Challenges', Herbert Quandt Lecture by Joschka Fischer, Federal Minister for Foreign Affairs, 15 Sept. 2000 at Georgetown University, Washington DC, http://www.auswaertiges-amt.de/2_aktuel/index.htm.

50. J. Hoagland, 'So Here Comes Missile Defence Without a Cork', *International Herald Tribune*, 28 Feb. 2000.

51. 'The Ageing Alliance', *The Economist*, 23 Oct. 1999, www.economist.com/.

52. J. Lindley-French, 'Leading Alone or Acting Together: The Transatlantic Security Agenda for the Next US Presidency', *Occasional Papers*, 20, The Institute for Security Studies, Western European Union (Sept. 2000), p.6.

53. For an analysis of the Revolution in Military Affairs, see R.P. Grant, 'The RMA – Can Europe keep in Step?', *Occasional Papers*, 15, The Institute for Security Studies, Western European Union (Sept. 2000).

54. R. Heine, 'Bahr plädiert für europäische Sicherheitsunion', *Berliner Zeitung*, 23 June 2000, http://www.BerlinOnline.de/aktuelles/berliner_zeitung/politik/.html/23artik24.html.

55. D. Buchan and Q. Peel, 'Defence: US warns EU over Proposal', *Financial Times*, 7 Feb. 2000, http://www.ft.com/hippocampus/q340e46.htm.

56. Kori Schake, Amaya Bloch-Lainé and Charles Grant, 'Building a European Defence Capability', *Survival*, 41/1 (Spring 1999), p.26.

57. A. Hoffmann and K. Longhurst, 'German Strategic Culture and the Changing Role of the Bundeswehr', *Welt Trends*, 22 (Spring 1999), p.162.

58. K. Longhurst; 'German Strategic Culture: A Key to Understanding the Maintenance of Conscription in Germany? *Institute for German Studies Discussion Paper* 98/6 (University of Birmingham, 1998).

59. L. Aggestam, 'Role Conceptions and the Politics of Identity in Foreign Policy', *Arena Working Papers* WP99/8, http://www.sv.uio.no/arena/publications/wp99_8.htm.

60. H-D. Genscher, 'Europa als Kostengänger amerikanischer Stärke?', speech before the WEU Assembly in Paris, 20 June 1984, *Bulletin*, No.75, 27 June 1984, pp.662–5.

61. Regierungserklärung zum Stabilitätspakt für Südosteuropa abgegeben durch den Bundesminister des Auswärtigen Joschka Fischer am 27. Januar 2000 in Berlin, http://www.auswaertiges-amt.de/6%5Farchiv/2/r/r000127a.htm.

62. Zum Stabilitätspakt für Südosteuropa, http://www.auswaertiges-amt.de/6%Farchiv/inf%2Dkos/hintergr/stabdt.htm.

63. Conclusions of the European Council Meeting in Cologne, 3–4 June 1999, para. 56.

64. P.H. Gordon, 'Franco-German Security Co-operation in a Changing Context', *Franco-German Relations and European Integration: A Transatlantic Dialogue – Challenges for German and American Foreign Policy* Conference Report, 16 Sept. 1999 (Washington: American Institute for Contemporary German Studies), p.78.

65. H.W. Maull, 'Germany and the Use of Force: Still a Civilian Power?', *Trierer Arbeitspapiere zur Internationale Politik*, 2 (Nov. 1999), p.2.

66. E. Pond, 'Germany in the New Europe', *Foreign Affairs*, 71/2 (Spring 1992), p.115.

67. Bundesminister Joschka Fischer am 3 December 1999 vor dem Deutschen Bundestag (excerpts), http://www.auswaertiges-amt.de/6_archiv/2/r991203a.htm.

68. R. Putnam, 'Diplomacy and Domestic Politics: The logic of Two-Level Games', *International Organization*, 42/3 (1988).

69. R. Scharping, 'Europas Stimme in der Allianz', *Die Zeit* No.8, 18 Feb. 1999, http://www.zeit.de/zeit/tag/aktuell/199908.identitaet_.htm.

70. Ibid.

71. A. Nicoll, 'Moves Towards a Security Pact', *Financial Times*, 23 July 2000.

72. See *Gemeinsame Sicherheit und Zukunft der Bundeswehr: Bericht der Kommission an der Bundesregierung, 23.Mai, 2000*. Vorsitzender: Richard von Weizsäcker.

73. 'Stoiber sieht keine Anlass für Reduzierung der Streitkräfte', *Handelsblatt*, 19 May 2000, http://www.handelsblatt.de.

74. 'CSU sieht wenig Spielraum für kleinere Armee. Weniger als 300,000 Mann "politisch

unbegründbar"', *Berliner Zeitung*, 20 May 2000, http://www.BerlinOnline.de/wissen/berliner_zeitung/archiv/2000/0520/politik/.

75. See 'Mehr Kräfte für Auslandseinsätze nötig', *Kölner Stadt-Anzeiger*, 9 March 2000, http://www.ksta.de/politik/205125.html; P. Breuer, 'Rot-Grün zu realer Sicherheitspolitik nicht fähig', http://www.cducsu.bundestag.de/texte/breue95i.htm.
76. 'Große Mitglieder übernehmen Planung für Europa-Korps', *Die Presse Onlineausgabe*, 2 Dec. 1999, http://www.diepresse.at/.
77. Bulmer *et al.*, *Germany's European Diplomacy: Shaping the Regional Milieu*, p.6.
78. 'Europe Seizes Military Role', *The Guardian*, 12 May 1999.
79. 'US Assails German Plans to Cut Defense', *Boston Globe Online*, 2 Dec. 1999, http://www.boston.com/globe/.
80. J. Fischer, 'Wir wollen kein Soli tanzen', *Der Spiegel* No. 48, 23 Nov. 1998.
81. R. Graham, 'Europe: Defence – Pledge on European Capability', *Financial Times*, 31 May 1999, http://www.ft.com/hippocampus/qe3e96.htm.
82. See Presidency Conclusions – Nice European Council Summit Meeting 7, 8 and 9 Dec. 2000, http://www.presidence-europe.fr/pfue/static/acces3.htm.
83. B. Groom, 'Leaders in Agreement Over Plans for Defence', *Financial Times*, 8 Dec. 2000, www.ft.com/.

Germany in Europe: Return of the Nightmare or Towards an Engaged Germany in a New Europe?

WOLFGANG WESSELS

THE FUNDAMENTAL PATTERN: A PARADOXICAL COMBINATION

The European Debate between a Nightmare and a Leadership Scenario

Both in ancient[1] history and in contemporary discourse,[2] the character and role of the 'teutonic' Germans have attracted considerable attention. *L'incertitude allemande* may even be one of the most recurrent and controversial issues in the historical and political analysis of the European construction.

Given a high and permanent interest of its neighbours, the public discourse within Germany quite often does not match the scope and intensity of that in European arenas. The intra-German debate on its foreign and European policy is quite often confronted with a paradoxical situation: the search of the German soul is more intensively pursued by its neighbours than in an open discourse within Germany.

With a certain bewilderment most Germans witness two major schools of thought which offer controversial and opposing lines of argument. On the one hand, there is a perception influenced by the long shadow of history. In this view, Germany's economic weight, its geo-political position and some internal developments raise fears that Germany will try to re-establish a central hegemonic position using the EU only as an alibi: the same old wine disguised in a more prettily decorated bottle so to speak. Whatever Germans do – whether obstructive or supportive – it is interpreted in view of an imperial strategy to dominate its region.[3] Taken to the extreme, such an orthodox-realist view of the balance of power on the European continent would expect that traditional geopolitical power structures will revive traditional conflict behaviour. The nightmare is described as Germanisation via unionisation.

On the other hand, the perceived strength of the Federal Republic of Germany, and especially its pro-European declarations, leads to hopes and

Wolfgang Wessels, University of Cologne

even demands for a German leadership[4] within and for a wider and deeper European Union. In this view European neighbours ask for a strong German engagement for the sake of a common European good. The self-described low-key profile of Germany in terms of what some call a 'civilian power'[5] or a 'trading power'[6] is then not believed – or, from the other perspective – not hoped for.

The Internal Debate: A Low Profile, a Permissive Pro-European Consensus and a Post-Nationalist Attitude

Confronted and compared with intense debates on German European and Foreign policy, the intra-German discussions over the second half of the twentieth century were and are rather low key: no projection of military power was thought of, the pro-Western and pro-European attitudes were seldom really disputed. Though certain key projects like NATO membership in the 1950s, *Ostpolitik* in the 1970s and the creation of the EMU in the 1990s were topics of controversy, an overall pro-European consensus was and is dominating, enabling the political leadership to act without major constraints inside the West German political system.

Given the post-war German performance as *Musterschüler* (the best pupil in class) and the high budgetary investment as *Zahlmeister* (paymaster), the nightmare view of some neighbours was perceived as an unfair continuation of outdated experiences turned into prejudices; the demands for military out-of-(NATO)-area engagements were declined as improper and leadership projects in the EC and the EU were launched always as a French–German proposal (watch the order). A shift from *Machtbesessenheit* (power addiction) to *Machtvergessenheit* (power negligence)[7] described a fundamental mental disposition; some even characterised this role perception – somewhat unfairly – as a 'Swiss attitude' writ large: Germany was and is seen as being highly interested in world and European affairs – presenting optimal and 'just' solutions – but keeping its engagement restricted to economic means of considerable size. The German view of the world and its role were described as 'post-modern' or 'post-nationalist'.[8]

Core Functions of European Integration: (Re)turn to Western Europe, External Influence and Effective Problem-Solving

West European integration was always more than an issue of limited economic goals and regulations: for the early Federal Republic it was an instrument and a framework for the (re)turn to the group of Western democracies and for stabilising its own parliamentary system. This process helped Germany to regain voice and influence in Europe and beyond; it also backed up the NATO shield with indirect, soft security measures. Of course, it was also perceived as another means of keeping the 'German question' open and defending the difficult position of (West) Berlin.

Besides these basic foreign and German policy interests, the evolving functions of what is now known as the EU served Germany as a means to tackle problems for which Germany – like other EU members – was and is too small. For a broadening range of crucial topics of everyday politics – be they trade, positions in international fora, environmental protection or the fight against international crime – the EU was perceived as what could be described as an 'optimal problem solving area'[9] – though by many not as an optimal single currency area[10] – or at least a better one than just the national arena.

Many of these motives resembled the basic interests of other members and applicants of the 1990s. By the regular enlargement of the scope of issues allocated to the European level the fundamental interests in the common system have been deepened and extended up to the beginning of this century.

AFTER 1989: RENAISSANCE OF HISTORICAL PATTERNS OR A NEW VISION AND MISSION?

Reunification as the Return of History: Germanisation via Unionisation

The end of the bipolar system and the creation of an again larger Germany resuscitated hidden or dormant suspicions *vis-à-vis* Germany. The nightmare scenario was invoked by many and in many European countries. Given the long shadows of history these instinctive reactions were perhaps less of a surprise but certainly a great disappointment to many German politicians who could point to their established democratic records in the post-war period. In this perspective – which was put forward especially by American and British voices[11] – the end of the East–West confrontation on German soil meant a final post-war emancipation of Germany from its strings which would allow Germans to pursue their bad 'old' policies. In this school of thought the European Monetary Union with the 'German' model for the European central bank was understood as the continuation of German dominance by other means, to paraphrase the German military strategist Clausewitz. The strong declaratory pressure for EU enlargement towards 'its' Eastern neighbours was and is also interpreted by some as another sign of the attempts to run Europe from Berlin. Thus both deepening and widening were interpreted as reinforced strategies to pursue Germanisation via Unionisation.

Unionisation as the Straightjacket to Bind the German 'Gulliver'[12]

From another perspective, careful and thoughtful politicians relaunched Monnet's post-war strategy of domesticating the 'German beast' by integrating it into a strong 'supra'-national European framework. In this perspective the Maastricht Treaty and especially Monetary Union were perceived as the proper means to communitise the German Mark as the most important power assets of Germany for building a hegemonic position. Some even referred to this the Maastricht Treaty as a new 'Treaty of Versailles'. Enlargement is then also considered to reduce the German freedom of manoeuvre and to help some of its deeply concerned Eastern neighbours to get an additional protection via the strong EU institutions and its binding rules.

Unification as a Step towards Living in a Peaceful Europe

Strangely enough, these worries, perceptions and strategies did not find a dominant place in German thinking. For the public, the major orientation was not to think in terms of a new power exercising a strong influence in Europe or even the world. German citizens are more interested in personal welfare and luxury; the search for a *Platz an der Sonne* (a place in the sun) as a catch-word for colonial expansion during the times of imperialism seems outdated as popular beaches can be reached in a two-hour flight 15 times a day from Düsseldorf airport alone. The economic and social problems, not least in the new Länder, have reduced even more the perhaps high-flying ambitions of the early days immediately after the fall of the wall. Indeed, opinion polls even indicate a withdrawal of attention from the national policy arena to local issues, with Europe increasingly becoming an important political space to watch.[13]

Living in peace with all of one's neighbours is viewed as an asset that is increasingly taken for granted. Moral issues of European and international relevance remain high on the list of public attention. Opinion polls on national pride indicate a trend towards post-national orientations.[14]

The political elites also do not show many signs of a new assertive spirit: some Western observers were even troubled about Germany's cautious inward-looking attitudes and behaviour.[15] The latest change in government, with a new 'post-war' generation, did not lead to an overall reappraisal and realignment of Germany's positions. After initial declarations that he would pursue a more interest-oriented foreign policy – including in relation to EU budgetary claims – Chancellor Schröder has rapidly learned to continue pursuing long-standing German strategies. Sending a contingent of German soldiers 'out of area' to Bosnia and Kosovo was perceived by many in Europe as a small step towards normalcy. However, for the German understanding of its post-war role it was a great leap, involving intense debates within both coalition parties, especially the Greens, who as long-standing pacifists had to come to grips with a military intervention for humanitarian reasons.

Except for going ahead with the diplomatic recognition of Croatia, the foreign policy of Germany did not show major signs of breaking out of the Western and European group. Even the claim for a permanent seat in the UN Security Council is publicly not perceived as an important symbol of regaining world status.

Indeed, quite often in the immediate post-unification period the 'shock' of again being important in a new Europe led to an even closer adherence to the Western and European groupings that had proved to be supportive of Germany: both NATO and the EU remain central problem-solving arenas, following the idea that the more we are living in a different, changing and complex world, the more we need to strengthen the known and existing frameworks. The larger room of manoeuvre is viewed only to a limited extent as an opportunity for an *Alleingang* (going it alone). Rather, it is seen as a source of greater uncertainty in which the familiar Union is needed to deal with the new challenges. Thus, in general, Germany's perceptions and strategies in the 1990s hardly differ from those of post-war years. What is considered as a unique success generates its own positive reputation and strength.

AND THE FUTURE ...

The '1905' and the '1945' Nightmares turned into a New Vision and Mission

Germany's rather cautious reaction and its reflex of sticking to successful organisations cannot, however, be interpreted as a short-term transitional period of keeping post-war attitudes while adapting to a new power status. It is a basic and partially instinctive reaction to what could be called the '1905' trauma of being encircled by a hostile coalition of neighbouring countries, and to the '1945' nightmare of being a front-line state in the core of a disastrous conflict. To prevent any repetition of these constellations vital national interests urge in a realist view that the positive post-Second World War experiences should also be applied to the East as they were developed in the West. That means in concrete terms that Eastern enlargement of both NATO and the EU, as well as other initiatives such as the 'Weimar triangle' (trilateral consultations between Germany, France and Poland) are envisaged to serve the fundamental interests of not being a front-line state anymore as was the case in the Cold War period, and of not being isolated again as during the first half of the century.

To achieve this kind of peaceful order, some elites in the Federal Republic understand it to be of overriding national interest to build the bridge towards Central and Eastern Europe. The vision to create a larger democratic and prosperous Europe is thus declared a specific mission of German policies, albeit there is no master plan yet to prevent the potential social and economic strain of integrating the applicant countries.

Beyond and Below the Visions: In Search of Effective Policy Frameworks

Perhaps most important for explaining the high degree of institutional continuity is the awareness that the integration construction was and is not only an issue of high national politics, but of jointly dealing with similar or identical problems in a more efficient and effective way than the traditional nation state, even one the size and weight of a unified Federal Republic, could possibly do. The dramatic reforms towards a communitisation of the asylum and immigration policy and the more effective co-operation in police and judiciary matters as put in the Amsterdam Treaty[16] at the end of the last century are a telling example of the rational analysis of member governments that they cannot solve problems of a global and especially European nature on their own. Transnational networks reduce the influence of state intervention, governments find themselves sharing their influence with social and economic actors. As the legitimacy of the member states depends on the satisfactory performance of solving urgent problems of their societies,[17] unionisation is often a natural exit from national shortcomings.

A New Generation of the Berlin Republic: Towards a More British or Gaullist Strategy?

But is such a set of expectations not itself a time-bound analysis, turning into an illusion as the new visions based on the nightmare interpretation of German history in the twentieth century might wane with a new generation that has no personal experience of the Second World War and that looks at the world from the more grandiose architecture of the 'Berlin republic'? Politicians and administrations might turn to defend narrow budgetary and other short-term interests. Faced with concrete costs, the vision for an enlarged Europe would then turn into declaratory policy. The German government might become more British in the defence of its own narrow interests and more Gaullist regarding how the European Union should be institutionally structured and behave in the international system. Xenophobia and Fascist tendencies, especially in the eastern Länder, might add to the impression that some old patterns and habits are returning. The decline in pro-European attitudes and the majority that opposes the euro could be interpreted as a rapid decrease in the diffuse permissive consensus concerning European integration.[18]

These worries need to be discussed seriously, but this reading is less pessimistic than these considerations. The fundamental pro-Western attitudes and considerations are taken for granted by at least the coming generation of political elites; even if they are more relaxed and less geared to draw explicit lessons from the past. The shadow of history will remain in the sunken memory of this group too, however. Some have common experiences with their fellow generations in other EU countries. The existing institutional structures and manifold networks increasingly lead to a founding 'community'[19] by which Europeans learn to live and work together in common frameworks.

The Berlin panorama might change foreign policy outlooks but the functional necessities and offers will remain. Moving the capital to Berlin has not changed the map of interests. Also the claim that after unification Germans could finally be more oriented to pursuing 'their' own interests does not look convincing. In the last 50 years German positions always promoted what was then considered to be of major national interest – sometimes more and sometimes less openly, but in most cases with considerable success. Unlike its self-chosen modest role in foreign and security policy, German leadership in European integration affairs is a long-standing trend. Even if the German government did not always have its way in the intergovernmental conferences leading to the Maastricht and Amsterdam treaties on the European Union, the crucial decisions (for example, in economic and monetary matters) have a clear German imprint. Future and long-term trends will, of course, also depend on the success or failure of the EU itself in dealing with future problems, worries and interests. If other member states or institutions block major policies, disappointment might increasingly change interest definitions to other fora and strategies. According to a spill-over logic, German attitudes will thus also be deeply affected by the investments and the engagement of other EU members.

CONCLUSIONS: A 'NORMAL BUT ENGAGED' MEMBER STATE

European Normalcy

Apart from overly pessimistic and overly enthusiastic evaluations of Germany's European policy, we could also interpret the German role after unification as that of a normal European state, one, however, with special engagements. Continuity is higher than expected, not only because of deeply rooted attitudes, but also because of a rational analysis of the opportunities, constraints and risks that has partially increased after unification. The debate about the reform of the Bundeswehr is an adaptation to new European defence concepts as outlined by NATO and EU bodies.

This normalcy also includes continuing inconsistencies, such as between the more persistent defence of short-term interests on the one hand (for example, German agriculture), and longer term visions of an enlarged and deepened EU on the other hand.

Widening and Deepening: Dealing with Dilemmas

Whatever the day-to-day mood of the public or the elites might be, the overall foreign policy relevance and the crucial role of the EU for problem-solving will lead to further investments in the EU. German concepts and interest will continue to flow into the shaping of a more effective and efficient set-up. However, these goals call for decisions of considerable importance balancing especially demands to enlarge towards a union of 27 members with a high degree of diversity and the pursuit of sound policies via good governance. How to deal with this unique experiment will be a major issue for and within the Germany and EU overall. Beyond some general declarations that both widening and deepening are important, there are no simple answers for German decision-makers. The range of options, each of which looks reasonable, is broad. Quasi-constitutional steps are taken with increasing speed, although incrementally and inconsistently, especially by the European Council. The risks of irreversible decisions being taken are considerable.

Towards a Core Europe

Major disappointment about an inefficient, overstretched and blocked EU of 21 or even 28 member states is bound to give rise to repeated projects of a 'core Europe',[20] or even a *directoire.*[21] As the provisions for 'enhanced co-operation', as formulated in the Amsterdam treaty, will only constitute an 'inflexible flexibility', concepts for projects among the able and willing members will need to be discussed as potential fall-back positions. As illustrated by speeches of the Foreign Minister Joschka Fischer and President Jacques Chirac, both countries want to keep their freedom to move ahead without being blocked by hesitant partners. But forms of differentiation and flexibility are no easy solutions and might even offer temporary seductions by which the necessary investments in a larger union are postponed.

The road map for the future of the EU is not clear, as the German strategy for the union needs further debate. The responsibility of German leaders will remain large.

NOTES

1. Tacitus, *Germania. De origine et situ Germanorum Liber* (Stuttgart: Reclam, 1977).
2. See among others Paul B. Stares, *The New Germany and the New Europe* (Washington: Brookings, 1992); Karl Kaiser and Hanns W. Maull (eds.), *Deutschlands neue Außenpolitik, Bd. 1, Grundlagen* (Munich: Oldenbourg, 1994); Karl Kaiser and Hanns W. Maull (eds.), *Deutschlands neue Außenpolitik, Bd. 2, Herausforderungen* (Munich: Oldenbourg, 1995); Karl Kaiser and Joachim Krause (eds.), *Deutschlands neue Außenpolitik, Bd. 3, Interessen und Strategien* (Munich: Oldenbourg, 1996); Alan W. Cafruny and Glenda G. Rosenthal, 'The State of the European Community. Theory and Research in the Post-Maastricht Era', in Alan W. Cafruny and Glenda G. Rosenthal (eds.), *The State of the European Community: The Maastricht Debates and Beyond* (Boulder, 1993), pp.1–16; Hans-Peter Schwarz, *Die Zentralmacht Europas. Deutschlands Rückkehr auf die Weltbühne* (Berlin: Siedler, 1994); Christian Hacke, *Weltmacht wider Willen. Die Außenpolitik der Bundesrepublik Deutschland* (Stuttgart: Ullstein, 1988); Michael Staack, 'Großmacht oder Handelsstaat? Deutschlands außenpolitische Grundorientierungen in einem neuen internationalen System', *Aus Politik und Zeitgeschichte*, B12 (1998), pp.14–24; Gregor Schöllgen, 'Geschichte als Argument. Was kann und was muß die deutsche Großmacht auf dem Weg ins 21. Jahrhundert tun?', *Internationale Politik*, 52/2 (1997), pp.1–7; Paul Michael Lützeler, '"Großmacht" Deutschland? Essay über die Perspektive von außen', *Internationale Politik*, 52/2 (1997), pp.8–14; Robert Picht, 'Deutsch-französische Beziehungen nach dem Fall der Mauer: Angst vor "Großdeutschland"', in Rudolf Hrbek, Mathias Jopp and Barbara Lippert (eds.), *Die Europäische Union als Prozeß: Verfassungs-entwicklungen im Spiegel von 20 Jahren der Zeitschrift integration* (Bonn: Europa Union Verlag, 1998), pp.325–38; Simon Bulmer and William Paterson, 'Germany in the European Union: Gentle Giant or Emergent Leader?', *International Affairs*, 72/1 (1996), pp.9–32; Helga Haftendorn, 'Gulliver in der Mitte Europas. Internationale Verflechtung und nationale Handlungsmöglichkeiten', in Kaiser and Maull (eds.), *Deutschlands neue Außenpolitik*, Bd.1, pp.129–52; Michael W. Richter, 'Deutschlands europäische Rolle nach dem Ost-West-Konflikt: Konziliator im übernationalen Interesse?', in Gottfried Niedhart, Detlef Junker and Michael E. Richter (eds.), *Deutschland in Europa. Nationale Interessen und internationale Ordnung im 20. Jahrhundert* (Mannheim: Palatium, 1997), pp.48–74.
3. These views are reported in Bulmer and Paterson, 'Germany in the European Union'.
4. See William Wallace, 'Deutschlands zentrale Rolle: Ein Versuch die europäische Frage neu zu definieren', in Hrbek *et al.* (eds.), *Die Europäische Union als Prozeß*, pp.316–24.
5. See François Duchêne, 'Die Rolle Europas im Weltsystem: Von der regionalen zur planetarischen Interdependenz', in Max Kohnstamm and Wolfgang Hager (eds.), *Zivilmacht Europa – Supermacht oder Partner? Die Rolle Europas im Weltsystem* (Frankfurt: Suhrkamp, 1973), pp.19–26; Hanns W. Maull, 'Zivilmacht Bundesrepublik Deutschland. Vierzehn Thesen für eine neue deutsche Außenpolitik', *Europa-Archiv*, 10 (1992), pp.269–78; Knut Kirst and Hanns W. Maull, 'Zivilmacht und Rollentheorie', *Zeitschrift für Internationale Beziehungen*, 2 (1995), pp.283–312.
6. See Staack, 'Großmacht oder Handelsstaat?'.
7. Hans Peter Schwarz, *Die gezähmten Deutschen. Von der Machtbesessenheit zur Machtvergessenheit* (Stuttgart: Deutsche Verlags-Anstalt, 1985); and Schwarz, *Die Zentralmacht Europas*.
8. Hans Peter Schwarz, 'Das deutsche Dilemma', in Kaiser and Maull (eds.), *Deutschlands neue Außenpolitik, Bd. 1, Grundlagen*, pp.81–97.
9. Rudolf Hrbek and Wolfgang Wessels, *EG-Mitgliedschaft: ein vitales Interesse der Bundesrepublik Deutschland?* (Bonn: Europa Union Verlag, 1984); and Josef Janning, 'Bundesrepublik Deutschland', in Werner Weidenfeld and Wolfgang Wessels (eds.), *Jahrbuch der Europäischen Integration 1998/1999* (Bonn: Europa Union Verlag, 1999), pp.325–32.
10. Rolf Caesar and Hans-Eckart Scharrer, *Die Europäische Wirtschafts- und Währungsunion. Regionale und globale Herausforderungen* (Bonn: Europa Union Verlag, 1998).
11. John J. Mearsheimer, 'Back to the Future. Instability in Europe after the Cold War',

International Security, 15/1 (1990), pp.5–56.

12. Haftendorn, 'Gulliver in der Mitte Europas. Internationale Verflechtungen und nationale Handlungsmöglichkeiten', pp.129–52.

13. Elisabeth Noelle-Naumann, 'Die öffentliche Meinung', in Weidenfeld and Wessels (eds), *Jahrbuch der Europäischen Integration 1998/1999*, pp.311–16.

14. Noelle-Naumann, 'Die öffentliche Meinung'; Europäische Kommission, *Eurobarometer. Die Öffentliche Meinung in der Europäischen Union*, 51 (July 1999).

15. Wolfgang Wessels, 'Zentralmacht, Zivilmacht oder Ohnmacht? Zur deutschen Außen- und Europapolitik nach 1989', in Peter R. Weilemann, Hans Jürgen Küsters and Günter Buchstab (eds.), *Macht und Zeitkritik* (Paderborn: Ferdinand Schöningh, 1999), pp.389–406.

16. See Peter Christian Müller-Graff, 'Justiz und Inneres nach Amsterdam – Die Neuerungen in erster und dritter Säule', *Integration* 4 (1997), pp.271–84; Jörg Monar, 'Legitimacy of EU Action in Justice and Home Affairs: An Assessment in the Light of the Reforms of the Treaty of Amsterdam', in M. den Boer, A. Guggenbuhl and S. Vanhoonacker (eds.), *Managing the New Treaty on the European Union* (Maastricht: European Institute of Public Administration, 1998), pp.205–28; Jörg Monar, 'Justice and Home Affairs in the Treaty of Amsterdam: Reform at the Price of Fragmentation', *European Law Review*, 23/4 (1998), pp.320–35.

17. See Fritz W. Scharpf, *Governing in Europe. Effective and Democratic?* (Oxford: Oxford University Press, 1999).

18. Noelle-Neumann, 'Die öffentliche Meinung'.

19. See, for example, the work by Karl W. Deutsch, especially Karl W. Deutsch *et al.*, *France, Germany and the Western Alliance: Study of Elite Attitudes on European Integration and World Politics* (New York: Scribner, 1967).

20. Christian Deubner, *Deutsche Europapolitik: Von Maastricht nach Kerneuropa?* (Baden-Baden: Nomos, 1995); Karl Lamers, 'Kerneuropa – flexible Methode der europäischen Integration?' *Wirtschaftsdienst*, 10 (1994), p.495.

21. Joseph Janning 'Dynamik in der Zwangsjacke – Flexibilität in der Europäischen Union nach Amsterdam', *Integration*, 4 (1997), p.290.

Germany's Power and the Weakening of States in a Globalised World: Deconstructing a Paradox

ANNE-MARIE LE GLOANNEC

It is somewhat ironical to ponder Germany's power at a time when radical changes due to globalisation vastly limit the efficiency of state actions world-wide. Certainly, it was legitimate for politicians and analysts as well as for the broader public, both inside and outside the country, to examine the broad implications of Germany's reunification[1] for Europe and the world. Reunification actually did trigger thoughts, mingled sometimes with satisfaction, sometimes with concern, about the nature of Germany's power. The transfer of the capital to Berlin in 1999 and the coming of political age of a new generation rekindled all these thoughts and concerns. In any case, one wondered whether changes were to be expected and, if so, what kind. Generally it was assumed that, as a result of reunification, Germany would increase its power, becoming 'a' power, a political power, whereas formerly it had been primarily a centre of economic power. From the early 1990s, Germany's power became the focus of numerous articles and books – though the term was always more or less qualified, as one spoke of Germany as a *Zentralmacht* ('central power'), as a *Weltmacht wider Willen* ('world power against its will') or as a *Zivilmacht* ('civilian power').[2] Chancellor Gerhard Schröder himself did not shy away from referring to Germany as an important power, a *grosse Macht* ('big power'). But he avoided the word *Grossmacht* ('Great Power'), a word laden with past history and certainly closer than *grosse Macht* to the concept of a superpower which was later coined: a *Grossmacht* it was not, rather a *grosse Macht* it was supposed to be.[3] The statement nonetheless went further than any to date from a German politician. Prior to Gerhard Schröder's election, Peter Katzenstein had written: 'The Germans have eliminated the concept of "power" from their political vocabulary.'[4] The statement has since then lost its validity.

It was generally recognised that an increase in territory and population alone would not arithmetically strengthen Germany's clout, that the country

Anne-Marie le Gloannec, Centre Marc Bloch, Berlin and CERI, Paris would have to bear the costs of reunification and would therefore run into temporary difficulties, and that an increase in GNP was not to be expected immediately. Nonetheless, most analysts, in Germany and abroad, considered that the transformation of Germany's status in Europe would bring about changes. Reunification – which entailed the removal of those constraints which had weighed on the country – had a 'liberating effect on the *potential* for German diplomacy', as two well-known observers of Germany put it.[5] Reunited and sovereign, Germany was returning to the centre of Europe as its 'Zentralmacht', a 'Gulliver' (to borrow Helga Haftendorn's slogan), 'in theory ... free', as Hanns Maull wrote, 'to return to the role of one of Europe's Great Powers'.[6] Some indeed lamented Germany's reticence to exercise power, as two famous book titles exemplified, or – and it may be somewhat different – its reluctance to take over responsibilities. Others, in particular some politicians and public opinion in countries surrounding Germany, feared its renewed clout. But, in any case, most analysts thought that Germany's power had increased, not weakened.[7] Behind analyses of the more immediate impact of reunification lurked the issue of the longer term changes it would bring about – in Germany's internal fabric as well as its power. Yet another way to analyse changes in the light of reunification was to wonder whether the reunified Germany was going to alter its commitments.

Certainly a reunited Germany did not put into question its membership in NATO, let alone in the European Community or in any other organisation. A number of those who wrote in the following decade stressed that Germany remained embedded in the international system, all the more so as globalisation was advancing swiftly. In this respect, multilateralism as well as the integration of Europe remained – more than ever – the name of the game which the federal government was ready to play. Nonetheless, within this framework, the question remained open as to whether it would entirely stick to former priorities or subtly reformulate some of its interests and whether it would change its style or modify some of the substance of its foreign policy. As Karl Kaiser and Hanns Maull put it: 'Doesn't it mean a new foreign policy which can say "no"?'[8] The very notion of interests was eventually reformulated, as the expression 'national interest' – qualified and singular – became somewhat popular in political discourse. The same Karl Kaiser, a long-time analyst of Germany's foreign policy and an advocate of multilateralism, contended in 1994 that Germany's foreign policy had now to face 'the challenge of defending, more than formerly, its own viewpoint which will stand for the interests of the country in multilateral frameworks'.[9]

The issue was therefore how change and continuity were going to combine with one another, how much change and how much continuity were to be expected? Another way of putting the question was to ponder Germany's 'normalisation'. As Germany was liberating itself from previous constraints, it was becoming a more 'normal' country, a country like any other country in Western Europe at least.[10] Did this mean that it was to liberate itself from its previous commitments, at least from what has been called 'excessive' or 'reflexive multilateralism', which led it to favour integration over sovereignty, a sovereignty that it did not have until 1990?[11] And did 'normalisation' mean not only the recovery of sovereignty, but also its assertion?

To answer these questions, analysts attempted to examine German power through the prism of its resources, somewhat like Hans Morgenthau, one of the founding fathers of the study of international relations. From this perspective, one of the main sources of Germany's power was economic. Yet deducing power from resources – economic or not – may be somewhat venturesome. While most analysts underline the difficulties encountered by Germany in the wake of reunification, difficulties deemed temporary, though severely affecting the economy and finances of the country, the main problem of converting economic power into political clout was sometimes, but not always, acknowledged. As William Paterson has stressed, it does not suffice to enumerate the possible sources of power and to extrapolate from economic to political power because 'the political impact of economic standing is notoriously difficult to measure *inter alia* because economic power, unlike military power, is often in private hands'.[12] It is true that certain economic resources, such as the budgetary ones, may be directly transferable into political power, enabling governments, for example, to provide side-payments to others. But power also accrues from other, non-economic resources, such as the internal make-up of countries, their political and administrative organisation and personnel, the support of public opinion, and, last but not least, the credit that foreign governments and public opinions are ready to give a particular government or state. Most importantly, power results from the will of political leaders to use these resources.[13] Does this type of analysis, however, suffice to account for Germany's or for any other country's power?

As a vast body of literature on the topic shows, the particular configuration of this globalised world, the dynamics of a globalised economy in particular, the spread and interconnections of flows of all sorts and the development of a multi-tiered governance limit the power of states and the efficiency of their actions. Is it possible in this context to speak, if at all, of great powers? Germany certainly does not belong to the category of 'middle powers', as Gunther Hellmann aptly points out, but rather to that of states 'which one would hardly call today Great Powers (*Grossmächte*) though they behave as big powers (*grosse Mächte*), in other words those states which declare themselves fit for the "G8" or for the "Contact Group" and which practise an ad-hoc diplomacy in exclusive circuits, beyond official international organisations, such as the UN or the OSCE, or again the EU or NATO'.[14] Yet we may still wonder what big powers are, if we look at the role and action of the Contact Group to which Germany belonged, but in which a single state – the United States, by far the most powerful state in the world – was able to impose its policies on all others.

As most authors writing on Germany's role in the post-Cold War era have argued, the lesson appears to be that, save for the United States or some so-called rogue states, German governments, like most others, can only act within multilateral frameworks.[15] The country is embedded in a network of organisations and institutions, intergovernmental or supranational, from which it derives resources and power and which help to shape its identity, as the constructivist approach stresses. It would suffer vastly from severing its roots in those organisations, were it ever to do so. In other words, unless one considers suicide as a choice, leaving NATO never was a choice for a reunified Germany, and very few raised this demand. A *Sonderweg*, a unilateral policy, would have weakened, not strengthened it, by depriving it of means of action and influence.[16] One could even argue that a long-time membership and practice of international organisations has turned to the country's advantage. As Gregor Schöllgen and Chancellor Schröder after him have contended, Germany's long practice in international organisations, the knowledge and flair that its diplomats have acquired over the years in tackling the many constraints that limited its margin of manoeuvre during the Cold War –have endowed it with a kind of comparative advantage, a know-how about dealing with limitations in multilateral frameworks.[17]

In other words, an enumeration of the – possible – sources of German power may provide us with little understanding of the nature of German power, of its structures and hence of the capacity for Germany to shape its environment, embedded as it is in the system, European and international, from which it derives its strength. Quite mechanical in itself, a mere enumeration of resources does not render a full picture. Rather it is necessary to turn to an analysis of the European structure to capture the nature of Germany's power. In this context, an analysis of Germany's power in the pre-1989 – so-called Cold War – era might be fruitful. As a divided state borrowing its security from outside sources, Germany was an exceptional, semi-sovereign, state. Yet it did gain in power and exercised a considerable influence both on its partners and on the European system for nearly three decades. In 1990, it turned out to be an exception again, but in the reverse sense: not only did it regain its formal sovereignty, but it was also the single state on the European continent that increased its territory and population while elsewhere federations broke up, violently or otherwise. Nowadays it is just a state like any other, semi-sovereign 'in the same way that all states except, arguably, the United States are'.[18] Is it indeed more powerful than it used to be? Is Germany a Gulliver or just a little 'more equal' than others? And what is Germany's power in a system, the structure of which has been dramatically modified not only by reunification, but also by the introduction of an economic and monetary union? What is the nature of this power in a globalised world and in an integrated Europe? The argument here is that the changes which the European system has undergone in the past decade are more far-reaching than Germany's reunification, so that the structure of German power has changed and this power has become more diffused and arguably diluted. While the country could earlier on exercise a semi-hegemony over Western Europe in the monetary area, the further integration of the EC has altered the European structure and deprived Germany of a major power source. Certainly, other kinds of changes have taken place, changes which can be called circumstantial – a term which implies that they will not necessarily last – like the current German government's attempt to exercise its clout in Europe. The combination of both circumstantial and structural changes – called henceforth systemic so as to apply the adjective structural only to 'structural power' (as defined below) – may be awkward and somewhat paradoxical. We may be led to believe that the country definitely has more power than formerly, yet this impression may actually be misleading.

SEMI-HEGEMONY AND THE DIFFUSION OF POWER

It has often been said that integration served Germany well, whether in multinational fora, such as NATO, or in the supranational venture that is the European Community/Union. After the war, the leaders of Germany, a country diminished both politically and economically, had few other choices than to pursue a policy aimed first and foremost at restoring the credit and sovereignty of their country – albeit the course which the Social Democratic Party under Kurt Schumacher's leadership sought to steer. Actually Germany succeeded in obtaining both, or rather it gradually gathered respectability and increased its margin of manoeuvre, short of the ultimate sovereignty which came with reunification. In so doing, it also assured its security, both political and economic, by gaining access to American protection and to European markets. It also shaped its new identity based on co-operation, interaction and integration within intergovernmental and supranational organisations, as the constructivist approach has shown. The Atlanticist identity of the German military is evidence for this if any is needed.

Within these frameworks, Germany increased its power, not through the sheer fact of being a member of NATO and the European Community/Union, but rather because it set up the biggest and most efficient army on the European continent while becoming its most important economy and a major economic power world-wide. Yet it became a major military and economic contributor *because* it was integrated, *because* it fitted the European and world economy. It also became the United States' major ally on the continent *because* it was indispensable to the defence of the Western part of the continent. For this reason, too, it may be said that integration served the country well. And, in turn, Germany's major military and economic role was accepted by its neighbours and partners *because* it was embedded within multinational or supranational settings. In the military area, the Bundeswehr was an integral part of NATO – to an extent unmatched by any other army – and in the economic area the German economy was enmeshed with the other economies of the European Community.

In this latter dimension, the socio-economic system of the Federal Republic was very well adapted to the world market both in producing goods that were bought world-wide and having an institutional framework that facilitated and benefited from a strongly export-oriented policy, a formula which came to be known as 'the virtuous circle'.[19] Germany specialised in the production of high-quality equipment and chemical products that remained in almost limitless international demand, regardless of price. Far from hindering exports, the strong currency and higher prices led to increased growth, higher wages and, ultimately, internal stability. External growth and internal stability thus complemented each other. But while the Bundeswehr was closely integrated within NATO, indeed it is the most closely integrated of all NATO armies, Germany's increasing economic might raised problems.[20] Put simply, its wealth brought some disadvantages to its partners. In trade, in particular, German surpluses meant deficits for others. In the 1970s and 1980s, these imbalances threatened to undermine the cohesion of the European Community: for the system to last, 'the weak ha[d] to be either bribed or forced to continue playing a game they los[t]'.[21] At the same time, especially from the 1970s on, the Federal Republic constrained the fiscal policies of its partners, through the increasingly close intra-Community trade relations – and Germany's partners' deficits – and through stricter monetary rules, such as the 'Snake' and later the European Monetary System (EMS). A system of fixed parities compelled the other parties to these arrangements to pursue tight monetary policies in spite of their growing trade deficits with the Federal Republic and in spite of their own different preferences. In other words, Germany's partners had to adopt Germany's deflationary policy.

Though the gains and losses that accrued from Community arrrangements cannot be measured simply in terms of trade surpluses and budget contributions and therefore do not lend themselves to a cost–benefit analysis, it can be said that Germany thus came to dominate the European economies by the mere virtue of its 'structural', 'non-intentional power', as well as by the fact that it shaped major decisions in the Community through its 'constitutive power'. This is to take up the distinctions established by Simon Bulmer who, following Stefano Guzzini, establishes four categories of power. Two of these – 'deliberate power' and 'institutional' or 'constitutive power', which refers to efforts to shape the constitutive rules of the European Union – are intentional, involving the deliberate projection of national interests. The other two categories are not intentional. The first category is called (too vaguely, in my view) 'unintentional', which may be equated with 'structural power', while the second is called 'empowerment', referring to the fact that 'the EU facilitates the disposition of a German agent power', notably through the similarities in their respective political systems.[22] These categories will be useful here. It may be necessary, however, to introduce another category of power, that of semi-hegemony, which combines 'economic dominance', that is, structural power, with an ideological dimension of power. The latter dimension is absent from most works on Germany, though it is undergoing a kind of comeback. Andrei Markovits and Simon Reich have applied to the exercise of German power in Europe a well-known political science notion, that of hegemony, that is, legitimate leadership. The notion of *semi*-hegemony is used here to characterise the exercise of German power in one area, that of economic and monetary affairs.[23]

The notion of semi-hegemony allows us to answer the following question. If the relationship between Germany and its partners was asymmetrical, if the latter suffered from trade deficit and from a deflationary policy they did not want at first, how did the system function? Certainly, as the hub of all kinds of commercial and financial networks and the anchor of monetary stability, Germany retained a kind of veto power over all EC enterprises. This structural power was accepted by Germany's partners, and was thus *legitimised*. Several facts favoured this acceptance of Germany's structural power. First, as often emphasised in the literature on German power, Germany made side-payments, whether under the guise of financial contributions to the EC budget, including the creation of a new regional fund in exchange for subscribing to the Single European Act, or through direct loans, such as one to Italy in the 1970s. Germany thus helped countries with balance-of-trade deficits to go on abiding by the rules of the game or bribed them into accepting further constraints. Put differently, the role of politicians was to allay the effects of the structural power that the country exercised. There were two actors: the Bundesbank, the role of which was to take decisions according to national parameters – decisions which affected other countries and which they perceived negatively – and the government, which had to take decisions fitting broader interests and soothe these countries. Contrary to much of the literature on Germany's power in Europe, this policy was not necessarily 'selfless' or meant to satisfy other countries' expectations, though the latter is less misconceived. Germany's political authorities did so in order to keep the system functioning, a system which benefited Germany. Their objective was to sustain a system in which Germany's economic dominance threatened the overall balance – commercial, financial and political.[24]

The second fact that contributed to the legitimisation of German power is that Germany increasingly became a model, at least in some areas. Certainly in the 1970s many believed that this model could not be successfully imitated by others. One reason for this scepticism was the belief that if other countries successfully copied the German model, the formula could no longer be applied to the Federal Republic. Germany would thus lose its position as a major exporter. Moreover, the model's success appeared to rest, at least in part, on German social and cultural traits, something which made its adoption by other countries questionable. By the 1980s, however, the original scepticism about the applicability of the German model had dissipated and other countries had come to consider some of its characteristics worth adopting. First and foremost, deflationary politics became increasingly widely accepted. France was the first country, among the inflationary ones, to follow Germany's lead, after the disastrous two-year attempt to establish 'socialism in one country' between 1981 and 1983. Other characteristics of the German socio-economic system were praised as well and adapted if not adopted. Hence, for example, closer co-operation between banks and industry, the German system of vocational training, and the practice of conflict-resolution by gathering employers and trade unions around the same table were advocated by successive French governments – until these practices were themselves transformed in the wake of reunification and globalisation! In short, many actors abroad began to realise that Germany's success rested on a combination of macroeconomic and microeconomic traits, all worth imitating.

This amounted to a clear reversal of the previous widespread rejection, on the French Left, for example, of the German model which Chancellor Schmidt had advocated in the 1970s. This increasing acceptance of the German model certainly eased the problems associated with German dominance within the Community. Those countries – France, first and foremost – that accepted Germany as a model more easily accepted the country's position. There was very little talk of France leaving the EMS, while Great Britain, for example, hardly accepted either the German model or the European Community. Certainly there was some criticism, even in France, but it became more muted – although it rebounded in more recent years, in the form of the criticism directed against *la pensée unique*, that is, against deflationary policies and the necessity to take heed of economic constraints and international markets. In any case, the adoption of Germany's economic model was due to a combination of factors – in particular, to the idea that there was literally no choice but to abide by EC rules to tie in German power (that is, to accept Germany's dominance and influence as a way to reduce it), as well as to the influence of some agents, in particular that of the business elite on the *classe politique* in France, a detailed study of which still remains to be done.

Germany's economic dominance, however, did not translate into political leadership within the European Community. Domestic and international factors account for this lack of German leadership. First of all (this has been well documented by Simon Bulmer and William Paterson, among others), a number of peculiarities of the German system, sectorisation, for example, undermined the overall coherence of German policy. Also, while West Germany did not even seek political power because it was expected not to do so, the European Community prevented West Germany or, theoretically, any other country, from bidding for hegemony by pooling resources and decision-making. To that extent, the European Community functioned – and still functions – as a mechanism for the *diffusion of power*, to coin an expression akin to that of the *balance of power* which formerly dominated the continent. At best, Germany shared initiatives with other governments, mainly the French, to devise monetary arrangements or launch intergovernmental conferences.

In any case, Germany did not exert and could not exert a political hegemony over Europe, not only because it did not have the resources to do so, for instance the credit, which its neighbours denied it, but also because the mechanism of diffusion of power prevented it from doing so. It exercised a limited kind of hegemony in the monetary area, the reason why it is preferable to call it a semi-hegemony.[25] This was made possible not only because the country had the resources – a strong currency backed by a strong economy and a tight monetary and fiscal policy – for so doing, but also because the European system allowed it. The monetary arrangement, which had been devised outside the European Community framework, did not amount to a monetary union. Power was not shared or pooled in a supranational institution as would later be the case. Various currencies were merely pegged to the Deutsche Mark – though the margins of exchange-rate fluctuation were defined by common agreement. The burden of adjusting economic and budgetary policies to maintain the parity of these currencies with the DM was borne by the other states, not by Germany. The monetary system allowed for a semi-hegemony, instead of diffusing power as the European Community did.

THE DIFFUSION OF POWER AND THE DEFINITION OF SHORT-TERM INTERESTS

The institution of an economic and monetary union (EMU) was precisely intended to reverse this unilateral system. EMU has indeed dramatically changed the system of power in Europe, diffusing German power in the monetary and economic dimension as well. Yet just as the weaker members of the monetary arrangements had to be bribed to stay in the old system, the Federal Republic of Germany had to expect advantages from the future EMU to accept it, that is, to agree to give up its monetary independence and the Deutsche Mark. Besides gaining acceptance from its partners, which worried about reunification, and thereby consolidating political stability in Europe, Germany could expect through EMU and the accompanying creation of supranational frameworks to secure increased monetary and economic stability, although not automatically. Stability would ensue from the institutionalisation of the German economic and monetary model, which had already been adopted in a number of countries in the 1980s. However, this institutionalisation meant going a step further in establishing the German economic and monetary system as the prevailing model in Europe, because it anchored this model *de jure* in Europe, it enshrined it in a constitution. Actually, several devices were designed to establish EMU following the German model. Since Germany was the essential pivot of the mechanism, the German government retained a veto power over the whole venture and could thus impose its blueprint on its partners. The criteria for entry and, even more so, the so-called Stability Pact and the independence of the European Central Bank all bear the mark of German decision-makers. To these points one could also add the nomination, for better or for worse, of Wim Duisenberg as head of the ECB. Germany played a crucial role in shaping the rules of EMU. It exerted a constitutive power, backed by its structural power, and the necessity to have Europe's main currency and main economy inside the new European arrangements and not outside them. As a result, the German government created an environment which was as congenial as possible for the German economy, ensuring as best as it could that German preferences for low inflation and a stable currency would subsequently be respected.

The functioning of EMU, which does not need further explanation here, has so far not matched these expectations. One should, however, underline that with a new coalition in power in Berlin political preferences have changed somewhat. Hence, Chancellor Schröder let it be known that a weak Euro might be in Germany's interest. Simon Bulmer argues that the adoption of German rules and norms empowers the country by facilitating the articulation of German interests.[26] But what is one to make of this argument if and when these interests, subjectively defined, change abruptly? In any case, the fate of the European currency since its inception shows that the mechanisms which Germany devised are not necessarily conducive to the transposition of German policies to the European level. As the dominant economy in Europe, the country plays an important role and is a major parameter in the European decision-making process. However, German decision-makers, central bankers or politicians cannot shape policy outcomes as they formerly did within the EMS since, in the EMU, these outcomes are basically the product of a number of inputs, economic and political, German and non-German. In other words, Germany's power has changed. Its structural power has certainly become more diffuse, more diluted, more tolerable to its partners, which sometimes criticised Germany's monetary semi-hegemony over Europe. At the same time, it has become a less useful tool in the hands of German decision-makers. Germany exercised strong constitutive power in the foundation process of EMU. However, once the rules of EMU had been devised, the process has largely escaped German will, showing the limits of empowerment. In this sense, Germany's power in Europe has changed. Whereas formerly it occupied a semi-hegemonic role in one limited, but nonetheless very important, area, the situation is now one in which it has a more diffuse power in all areas.

Moreover, the creation of EMU may prove to be the last major case of the exercise of constitutive power by a German government – at least in these European frameworks. For the foreseeable future, the Federal Republic does not have the capacity to shape any other constitutive rule in the same way it did the EMU rules, where the issue is that of the revamping of European institutions, EU enlargement, or the constitution of a European defence. As far as European defence is concerned, the major breakthrough, both in terms of institutions and in terms of means, occurred because both British and French governments agreed on the primary question of creating a defence dimension within the European framework. Germany joined the initiative only later. Despite the creation of a German rapid reaction force (*Krisenreaktionskräfte* – KKK), which will comprise up to 150,000 men, its military capabilities are also more limited and less suitable for projection than the British or the French ones. The drastic cuts in the German defence budget will not allow for major changes in this situation, at least not under the present coalition. As for enlargement and closer integration, Germany certainly has some weight. In particular, it retains a power of veto, as shown, for instance, by the limitations it placed on the transfer of provisions pertaining to security and home affairs from the third to the first 'Community' pillar in the Amsterdam Treaty. But here the mechanism of power diffusion operates fully, depriving any federal government of the capacity to shape rules decisively or single-handedly and enabling other states, big or small, also to exercise influence. Certainly, a parallel may be drawn between the two cases of devising the EMU rules and the use of a veto power during the Amsterdam negotiations, since in both cases, German federal authorities, non-governmental or non-federal agents exerted a decisive influence on EU affairs, the Länder in the latter case and the Bundesbank in the former.[27] Yet preventing the introduction of qualified majority voting in provisions pertaining to security and home affairs is, by scope, intent and nature, very different from devising EMU rules. The latter is an overwhelming case of Germany shaping EU rules, the former is only one of many instances of member states, Germany or others, using their veto power.

In other words, as a consequence of the diffusion of power within the EU, Germany's exercise of decisive influence over the terms of EMU may have been exceptional and its constitutive, or institutional, power may turn out to be much more limited than this case would suggest. Yet power is not absent from Germany's tool box. First, its structural power still exists. This structural power, as we have seen, provides the country with means of influence. Though structural power by itself is not sufficient to allow the exercise of intentional power, it is necessary to provide the means for it, giving an actor a key role without which German authorities, for example, could not have blackmailed their partners into accepting their own version of EMU. And, regardless of the strains placed on German finances by the burden of reunification, the country remains the main economy on the continent, in terms of GDP, of financial resources, or of the multiplicity and presence of social actors abroad. Moreover, these actors – economic, social, political, whether they are lobbies, enterprises, party-political foundations, the Federal Constitutional Court or the Länder – develop and maintain channels of communication, build up and extend connections and contacts, and propagate norms, standards, guidelines and even models. In short, they reproduce to some extent the German institutional fabric, which Simon Bulmer considers as being at the root of empowerment. Yet the question of how connections and contacts, the propagation of norms and rules, and institutional transfer and adaptation translate into political power – if they do – still begs explanation.[28] One hypothesis is that political connections and political credit may accrue from these various channels. If so, this would mean that in an age of global networks Germany derives comparative advantages from its specific, dispersed institutional make-up. But, again, who would derive benefits from these comparative advantages – non-governmental institutions or the government? And, in the former case, would the government be able to draw on this? Is it also not possible that institutional dispersion means incoherence, the inability of the government to arbitrate between various requirements and interests? (If this were the case, Germany would be one of the first post-modern states.) In other words, how do resources (structural power) and agents (state and non-state) combine? Can governments in fact still devise a clear policy line and exercise deliberate power in the EC/EU? Is the veto-power of the Länder, which are able to prevent the further transfer of sovereignty to the EU in certain areas, a source of strength, as sometimes argued, or a source of weakness? In other words, does the diffusion of power – inside the country, through the multiplicity of non-state actors, and outside the country, through the particular mechanism of the EU – allow for German leadership in Europe?

If it does, as volatile coalitions may become the rule in a wider Europe of almost 30 members, Germany will have to rely more than ever on coalition-building, on its capacity to arbitrate between various agents taking part in the decision-making process. Credit and capabilities are essential for this task. Credit may derive from Germany's specific location and make-up. Even if it turns out that the multiplicity and actions of agents of all sorts outside the country do not produce many advantages to Germany, at least credit may be one of them, credit based on an appreciation of Germany's capabilities and expectation of positive results. Whether Germany's credit has increased since reunification is difficult to measure, though the number and importance of state visits to Bonn and nowadays Berlin may provide some indication.[29] But credit alone is not enough – the willingness and capacity to strike coalitions and to mediate or arbitrate between actors is also required. The previous German government was good at building coalitions in Europe, against the French if necessary, as the example of Wim Duisenberg's nomination as head of the ECB underlined. The current government demonstrated its ability at diplomatic intermediation in 1999 when, using its connections and credit, it brought Russia back in the Balkan game, negotiated, with Russia, Serbia and the Finnish EU presidency, the end of the NATO strikes against Serbia and launched a Stability Pact for the Balkans, taking in a sense a revenge for being shunned by its French and British partners during the Rambouillet negotiations on Kosovo.

However, arbitration may prove to be difficult and the difficulty of the enterprise may in turn deter the government, in particular where other resources, such as financial or public support, are required. At a time of limited financial resources and dwindling public enthusiasm for European integration, the current coalition as well as the previous one have sometimes preferred to adopt a give-and-take approach to the EU[30] rather than 'footing the bill', as Chancellor Schröder more or less put it, regardless of how crucial it was to help the broader EU system function in the interest of Germany itself. Certainly, former Chancellor Kohl had been the first one to complain about the size of Germany's contribution to the EU budget. Yet Chancellor Schröder was somewhat cruder in expressing this sentiment, complaining as he did about German money being 'wasted' (*verbraten*)[31] and declaring the reduction of the German budgetary contribution to be a major policy goal ahead of the 1999 EU Berlin Summit, at which, however, he eventually limited his demand, preferring the summit to succeed under the German presidency.

In other words, since reunification German governments have sometimes preferred to define Germany's interests in terms of short-term possession goals rather than in terms of long-term milieu goals – to combine the categories provided by Martin Wight and the dichotomy introduced by Arnold Wolfers. One might add that never has a government so clearly spoken of national interests as though national interests had not led previous governments in the 50 years of partition. As we all know, the defence of national interests – especially those which are conceived of as short-term returns on investment – should not be misconstrued as hegemony or leadership. On the contrary, such behaviour may indicate weakness, an inability to lead, that is, to arbitrate between sectoral interests. It remains to be seen whether short-termism is a temporary approach, linked to a conjunction of limited public support and financial resources and whether other developments, be it the consolidation of public finances, the resurgence of public support for European integration and enlargement, or the willingness of a German government to demonstrate leadership, may alter the definition of German interests, this time in favour of broader, European, parameters. Another conceivable, 'hybrid' outcome is that in spite of consolidated finances and renewed public support for the EU, future German governments lose the taste or the willingness to take broader, European parameters into consideration. If so, we would have a combination of structural power, however diffused it might be, and of a give-and-take European policy which might deprive Germany of the necessary backing of its partners.

Short-termism may not just correspond to the personal preferences of today's political leaders, such as Chancellor Schröder. It may also very well be the future, more fluid, game in the EU. In a wider and more diverse Europe, as mentioned earlier, it will be easier to strike coalitions than it will be to maintain a Franco-German axis which meets the resolute opposition of smaller countries. Short-termism also stems from the technicalities of current and future negotiations. Simon Bulmer, Charlie Jeffery and William

Paterson have stressed this evolution.[32] If short-term attitudes become more characteristic of EU politics in the future, it is likely that the federal government will go on stressing its thirst for a 'return on investments'. At the same time, the use of deliberate power by the German government may turn out to be much more difficult than expected. This is explained not only by dwindling resources, such as financial resources, which, for instance, limit Germany's military clout, but also by the very nature of the European system which ensures an extreme diffusion of power and in which governments must form coalitions with others in order to achieve their policy objectives. In this scenario, the federal government might be better advised to eschew the deployment of deliberate in favour of other types of power.

NOTES

1. The word 'reunification' is used here as it is more common, in English and French, than 'unification', which is used in German to stress the absence of similarity between the first unification, in 1871, and the process which took place in 1990.

2. See Hans-Peter Schwarz, *Die Zentralmacht Europas. Deutschlands Rückkehr auf die Weltbühne* (Berlin: Siedler, 1994); Christian Hacke, *Die Außenpolitik der Bundesrepublik Deutschland. Weltmacht wider Willen?* 'Frankfurt am Main/Berlin: Ullstein, 1997); Hanns W. Maull, 'Zivilmacht Bundesrepublik Deutschland. Vierzehn Thesen für eine neue deutsche Aussenpolitik', *Europapolitik*, 10 (1992), pp.269–78.

3. 'Germany is well advised to see itself as a big power (*grosse Macht*) in Europe, as our neighbours have already long done'. Gerhard Schröder, 'Eine Außenpolitik des "Dritten Weges"'?' quoted in 'Forum: Auf dritten Wegen ins dritte Jahrtausend?' *Gewerkschaftliche Monatshefte*, 50/7–8 (1999), pp.392–6. Gregor Schöllgen, however, refers to Germany as a *Grossmacht*: 'Zehn Jahre als europäische Grossmacht. Eine Bilanz deutscher Außenpolitik seit der Vereinigung', *Aus Politik und Zeitgeschichte*, B 24, 9 June 2000. Gunther Hellmann also uses this word in his latest article: 'Rekonstruktion der "Hegemonie des Machtstaates Deutschland" unter modernen Bedingungen? Zwischenbilanzen nach zehn Jahren neuer deutscher Außenpolitik', paper presented at the 21st Congress of the Deutsche Vereinigung für Politische Wissenschaft, Halle/Saale, 1–5 Oct. 2000, ahttp://www.rz.uni-frankfurt.de/fb03/prof/hellmann.html. For an alternative viewpoint, one may look at Hartmut Elsenhans: 'Reif für die Weltpolitik? Gedanken zur außenpolitischen Elite Deutschlands', *Welt Trends*, 25 (Winter 1999/2000), as well as the replies to Elsenhans in *Welt Trends*, 28 (Fall 2000).

4. Peter J. Katzenstein (ed.), *Tamed Power. Germany in Europe* (Ithaca/London: Cornell University Press, 1997), p.2.

5. Simon Bulmer and William E. Paterson, 'Germany in the European Union: Gentle Giant or Emergent Leader?' *International Affairs*, 72/1 (1996), p.30. See also Helga Haftendorn's apt remark that 'There can be no doubt that the disappearance of the structures of post-war Europe will fundamentally change the conditions of German foreign policy'. Helga Haftendorn, 'Gulliver in der Mitte Europas. Internationale Verflechtungen und nationale Handlungsmöglichkeiten', in Karl Kaiser and Hanns W. Maull (eds), *Deutschlands neue Außenpolitik, Bd. 1: Grundlagen* (Munich: Oldenbourg Verlag/Forschungsinstitut der Deutschen Gesellschaft für Auswärtige Politik, 1994), p.129.

6. See Schwarz, *Die Zentralmacht Europas*; Haftendorn, 'Gulliver in der Mitte Europas'. Bulmer and Paterson also referred to Gulliver, 'Germany in the European Union'. The last

quotation is from Hanns W. Maull, 'Germany and the Use of Force: Still a "Civilian Power"?', *Survival*, 42/2 (Summer 2000), p.69.

7. Schöllgen, *Angst vor der Macht*. *Die Deutschen und ihre Außenpolitik*; Hacke, *Die Außenpolitik der Bundesrepublik Deutschland*. Among others, Arnulf Baring and Hans-Peter Schwarz have called for a stronger role for Germany. See Arnulf Baring, *Deutschland, was nun?* (Munich: Goldmann Verlag, 1992), and Schwarz, *Die Zentralmacht Europas*, as well as, outside Germany, Andrei S. Markovits and Simon Reich, *The German Predicament: Memory and Power in the New Europe* (Ithaca/London: Cornell University Press, 1997).

8. Karl Kaiser and Hanns W. Maull, 'Einleitung: Die Suche nach Kontinuität in einer Welt des Wandels', in Kaiser and Maull (eds.), *Deutschlands neue Außenpolitik, Bd. 1*, p.xxiv.

9. Kaiser, 'Das vereinigte Deutschland in der internationalen Politik', in Kaiser and Maull, *Deutschlands neue Außenpolitik, Bd. 1*, pp.8 and 9.

10. See i.e. Philip H. Gordon, 'The Normalization of German Foreign Policy', *Orbis*, 38 (Spring 1994), pp.225–43; Gunther Hellmann, 'Nationale Normalität als Zukunft? Zur Außenpolitik der Berliner Republik', *Blätter für deutsche und internationale Politik*, 44/7 (July 1999), pp.837–47. Philip Gordon has provided a definition of normalisation, meaning the attenuation of the constraints which have weighed on Germany since World War II and the development of an international behaviour more like that of other large Western states. I will refrain from using this notion, as it may be implicitly, willingly or not, normative and as it is, moreover, used in the internal debate, referring to Germany's past.

11. Cf. Jeffrey J. Anderson and John B. Goodman, 'Mars or Minerva? A United Germany in a Post-Cold War Europe', in Robert O. Keohane, Joseph S. Nye and Stanley Hoffmann (eds.), *After the Cold War: International Institutions and State Strategies in Europe, 1989–1991* (Cambridge: Harvard University Press, 1993), pp.23–4; Jeffrey J. Anderson, 'Hard Interests, Soft Power, and Germany's Changing Role in Europe', in Katzenstein (ed.), *Tamed Power*, pp.80–107; and idem, *German Unification and the Union of Europe. The Domestic Politics of Integration Policy* (Cambridge: Cambridge University Press, 1999), p.227.

12. William E. Paterson, 'Beyond Semi-Sovereignty: The New Germany in the New Europe', *German Politics*, 5/2 (Aug. 1996), p.173.

13. See, in particular, Paterson, 'Beyond Semi-Sovereignty'.

14. Gunther Hellmann, 'Nationale Normalität als Zukunft?', p.341.

15. See, for example, the four volumes edited by the Deutsche Gesellschaft für Auswärtige Politik, *Deutschlands neue Aussenpolitik*; vol. 1 *Grundlagen* (edited by Kaiser and Maull); vol. 2 *Herausforderungen* (edited by Kaiser and Maull); vol. 3 *Interessen und Strategien* (edited by Kaiser and Joachim Krause); and vol. 4 *Institutionen und Resourcen* (edited by Kaiser and Wolf-Dieter Eberwein) (Munich: Oldenbourg, 1994, 1995, 1996 and 1998).

16. In this respect, I disagree entirely with Hanns Maull, who writes in an otherwise very thoughtful article: 'In theory, Germany was (after unification) free to return to the role of one of Europe's Great Powers': Maull, 'Germany and the Use of Force', p.69. As to the construction of identities through international interaction, see – as most exemplary on this topic – Katzenstein (ed.), *Tamed Power*.

17. Gregor Schöllgen, 'Die Berliner Republik als internationaler Akteur. Gibt es noch eine deutsche Interessenpolitik?', *Außenpolitik*, 2 (1998), pp.27–37; Schröder, 'Eine Außenpolitik des "Dritten Weges"?'.

18. Paterson, 'Beyond Semi-Sovereignty', referring to Katzenstein's famous book.

19. Bernard Keizer, 'La République fédérale d'Allemagne: puissance extérieure', in *Statistiques et Etudes financières*, hors série (Paris: Ministère de l'Economie, Direction de la prévision, 1980), p.35.

20. I have already developed this analysis in 'The Implications of German Unification', in Paul B. Stares (ed.), *The New Germany and the New Europe* (Washington, DC: The Brookings Institution, 1992), pp.251–78, from which this is taken, as well as in 'Les fortunes d'un modèle', in A.-M. Le Gloannec (ed.), *L'Allemagne après la guerre froide. Le vainqueur entravé* (Brussels: Editions Complexe, 1993), pp.17–70, and 'The Purpose

of German Power', in Zaki Laïdi (ed.), *Power and Purpose after the Cold War* (Oxford/Providence: Berg, 1994), pp.35–53.

21. Wolfgang Hager, 'Germany as an Extraordinary Trader', in Wilfrid L. Kohl and Giorgio Basevi (eds.), *West Germany: A European and Global Power* (Lexington: Lexington Books, 1980), pp.5 and 15–16.

22. See, expanding on Stefano Guzzini's 'Structural Power: The Limits of Neo-Realist Analysis', *International Organization*, 47 (Summer 1993), pp.443–78, Bulmer, 'Shaping the Rules? The Constitutive Politics of the European Union and German Power', in Katzenstein, *Tamed Power*, p.76; Bulmer and Paterson, 'Gentle Giant or Emerging Leader?'; and Paterson, 'Beyond Semi-Sovereignty: The New Germany in the New Europe'. The notion of 'economic dominance' was coined by François Perroux, *L'économie du XXème siècle* (Paris: PUF, 3ème édition 1969). Michael Kreile elaborates on this concept in: 'Will Germany Assume a Leadership Role in the European Union?', in Heurlin (ed.), *Germany in Europe in the Nineties*. The concept of structural power is used by Susan Strange among others.

23. The concept has not been applied often to the Federal Republic. As Arnulf Baring notes in 'Germany, What Now?', in Baring (ed.), *Germany's New Position in Europe. Problems and Perspectives* (Oxford/Providence: Berg, 1994), p.17 (n.5): 'Germany's precarious situation as a "demi-hegemon" in Europe was first described by Ludwig Dehio' in 1961 while Jochen Thies and Hans-Peter Schwarz had applied it 'to the external situation of the reunited Germany'. Others have spoken of a hegemon. See in particular Andrei S. Markovits and Simon Reich, 'Should Europe Fear the Germans?', *German Politics and Society*, 23 (1991), and idem, *The German Predicament*; as well as Reinhard Rode, 'Deutschland: Weltwirtschaftsmacht oder überforderter Euro-Hegemon', *Leviathan*, 19 (June 1991), pp.229–46; William Wallace, 'Germany as a "Natural Hegemon"', in *The World Today* (1995); and Hellmann, 'Rekonstruktion der "Hegemonie des Machtstaates Deutschland" unter modernen Bedingungen?'. Hellmann, however, does not offer a definition or a discussion of the concept. For reasons made explicit in this article, I prefer to use the term semi-hegemon (or demi-hegemon, although semi-hegemon may also refer to the semi-sovereign or the semi-Gulliver idea that other authors have described). See my 'Les fortunes d'un modèle'. In the other two articles cited in note 20, I describe the mechanisms of German structural power and ideological domination without, however, using the concept of hegemony or semi-hegemony, introduced in *L'Allemagne après la guerre froide*. Charlie Jeffery and William Paterson resort to Markovits' and Reich's approach to develop their own concept of empowerment in 'Germany's Power in Europe' (Birmingham: University of Birmingham, Jean Monnet European Centre of Excellence and School of Social Sciences, The Birmingham Discussion Papers, n° ESRC-IGS2000/10), 64 pp.

24. Jeffery and Paterson use the word 'selfless' in their otherwise extremely nuanced and stimulating analysis ('Germany's Power in Europe', p.33). Anderson speaks of a way of meeting other countries' expectations, see 'Hard Interests, Soft Power, and Germany's Changing Role in Europe', in Katzenstein (ed.), *Tamed Power*, p.85.

25. Markovits and Reich exaggerate the resources of Germany and underestimate the role of the European Community/Union in their otherwise stimulating interpretation.

26. Bulmer, 'Shaping the Rules?', p.50.

27. As Jeffery and Paterson underline in 'Germany's Power in Europe', p.15.

28. Two research programmes should be mentioned here – 'One or Several Europes', conducted by the Institute of German Studies of the University of Birmingham, and 'The Role of Non-State Actors in Transnational Relations: The Case of Germany', which is being carried out at the Centre Marc Bloch, Berlin. The conclusion that Simon Bulmer draws from the existence of a 'nice fit' between German and EC/EU institutions may be hasty: see, e.g. Eiko R. Thielemann, 'Institutional limits of a "Europe of the Regions": EC State-Aid Control Meets German Federalism', *Journal of European Public Policy*, 6/3 (Sept. 1999), pp.399–418. In a forthcoming book, Green Cowles, Caporaso and Risse also show the absence of such a nice fit: see Maria Green Cowles, James Caporaso and Thomas Risse (eds.), *Transforming Europe. Europeanization and Domestic Change* (Ithaca, NY:

Cornell University Press, 2001).

29. See e.g. Pond and Schoenbaum, *The German Question and Other German Questions*, p.210.
30. See the very informative book by Anderson: *German Unification and the Union of Europe*.
32. Simon Bulmer, Charlie Jeffery and William Paterson, *Germany's European Diplomacy. Shaping the Regional Milieu* (Manchester/New York: Manchester University Press, 2000), pp.8 and 53.
31. Rede des Bundeskanzlers auf der Bundesdelegiertenkonferenz der SPD zur Europawahl 1999 am 8. Dezember 1998 in Saarbrücken, quoted by Hellmann, 'Rekonstruktion der "Hegemonie des Machtsstaates Deutschland"', p.63.

Germany, *Quo Vadis*? A View from the Diplomatic World

PHILIPPE DE SCHOUTHEETE

Seen from the viewpoint of the daily activities of the Council and COREPER (Committee of Permanent Representatives), reunification has had little or no perceptible impact on the European policy of Germany. The latter seems to constitute a case of *'plus ça change, plus c'est la même chose'*.

This is, in fact, not very surprising if one takes into account the lack of change in the foreign policy establishment of the country. It has remained largely unaffected by reunification:

- no members of the diplomatic service of the GDR were introduced in the German foreign service;
- the foreign policy advisers of the Chancellor are largely the same as they were a decade ago;
- the upper reaches of the Ministry of Finance have not changed meaningfully in the last few years.

Combined with political stability at the highest level, these facts imply that the basic triangle (head of government, foreign affairs and the Finance Ministry) which, in Germany, as in most other European countries, largely determines European policy, has gone through the reunification process without experimenting any substantial change. Political stability is underpinned by technocratic stability. The main advisers of the government are drawn from a bureaucracy whose members have spent their whole administrative career, in some cases with great enthusiasm, in a culture of European integration.

Needless to say, this stability has been very reassuring for Germany's partners in the European Union, especially for those, like Belgium, who share the basic orientations of Germany's European policy. What are those orientations? They can be summarised in six points:

Philippe de Schoutheete, Belgium

1. Fundamental support for *European integration* as a basic policy objective. This support is channelled through the Community system and therefore implies support for the European institutions in general, with a particular accent on the European Parliament. The specific case of the Amsterdam negotiation is dealt with separately (see below), but, in general, over the years, the attitude described above has been maintained.

2. Support for *economic and monetary union*, as a major policy objective, with a strong Euro as a prerequisite. This point needs no further comment: EMU would not have appeared in the Maastricht Treaty if Germany had not wanted it to be there and Chancellor Kohl clearly staked his political career on its success.

3. *Free trade:* Germany has been traditionally on the liberal side of the permanent internal Community debate on foreign trade issues. This remains true after reunification, for instance in the end-game of the Uruguay Round in the autumn of 1993. Every now and then there is a specific case where the basic rule is forgotten, generally in agriculture (for example, potatoes or sour cherries), but these are marginal deviations on issues which are politically sensitive but economically negligible.

4. Firm accent on the *Franco-German relationship* without alienating smaller countries. As a former representative of a small country in the European negotiating process for a number of years, I can say without hesitation that, of all Belgium's big neighbours, Germany has been the most sensitive to the preoccupations, sometimes the complexes, of smaller member states, and especially its neighbours. Recent examples of this could easily be found in the Amsterdam negotiations, where there was some tension between big and small countries. Now some will say that there are good historical reasons for this attitude but, whatever the reasons, the fact is important, and it goes a long way towards explaining why, in Belgium at least, Franco-German leadership is not a problem. There is no feeling of outside imposition.

5. Conciliatory attitudes in cases of tension or conflicting views with the *United States*. This policy, which has deep and obvious roots in the Cold War period, seems to have been constantly maintained, even after the implosion of the Soviet Union and the disappearance of the Berlin Wall. It is an integral part of German European policy.

6. Openness towards *Central and Eastern Europe*. Germany played an important role in the decision taken by successive European Councils,

starting in Copenhagen in 1993, to open negotiations with a dozen Eastern and Central European countries. The significance of this decision and the difficulties which are likely to arise from it are largely underestimated by public opinion, in Germany also. But the basic objective – that the eastern borders of Germany should no longer be the European Union's borders – remains nonetheless. To quote a high-ranking German diplomat: 'Germany wants Western countries on its Eastern border.'

For the sake of completeness, two more points must be mentioned. They may not be fundamental to the European policy of Germany, but they are nonetheless significant, and concern policy issues where German attitudes have clearly undergone a change in the last few years (though not necessarily as a consequence of the reunification process). They concern the budget contribution and the free circulation of persons.

7. *The budgetary problem* is not new in the internal debate in Germany. Already in the middle of the 1970s, one could read articles in the German press about Germany being Europe's 'milking cow' (*Milchkuh Europas*). But the demand for a reduction in Germany's EU budgetary contribution has recently become more insistent, more general and it has meanwhile been taken up by prominent political figures. It is likely to play a significant (and probably negative) role in the discussions on Agenda 2000.

8. *The free circulation of persons*, including political asylum and immigration, has become a major issue as a result of a massive influx of refugees, including several hundred thousand from former Yugoslavia, combined with a high level of unemployment. In these circumstances such a backlash was inevitable. It does not imply a major policy change, but it is a matter of concern.

In both these cases the major new influence has been not so much German reunification as the increase in the power of the Länder in European policy. This phenomenon requires an assessment of the general political climate *vis-à-vis* European affairs in Germany.

Although German policy decisions on European affairs today are not significantly different from what they were ten years ago, the political climate in which the debate is conducted has clearly changed in the course of the decade. In the Maastricht negotiations, at the beginning of the 1990s, Germany was pressing strongly for further integration and calling for political union. In the Amsterdam negotiations, six years later, Germany was more reluctant. Indeed, it opposed some institutional modifications, including the increased use of qualified majority voting in some sectors. It is significant that Germany deliberately declined to associate itself with the declaration on institutional reform which Belgium, France and Italy made in the margin of the Amsterdam Treaty. In former years Germany would undoubtedly have subscribed to such a declaration.

Various causes are commonly mentioned for this change in political climate: the passing of the generation which has some personal memories of the war, a downturn in the economic cycle in recent years, the increased power of the Länder, and the effects of reunification. All these factors, and probably some others, have had some impact and assessments of their relative weight could differ. Poor performance in the economic field is probably the main factor. It is a fact, well substantiated by research, that the development of European integration – not only in Germany but all over Europe – is linked to the economic cycle. It progresses when the economy is booming and comes to a standstill during economic recessions. In the present case this well-known cyclic phenomenon is compounded by a structural element, namely a loss of confidence in the economic and social system as a whole. The virtues of the *soziale Marktwirtschaft* are put in doubt in the face of mounting unemployment. Given that, at the same time, the loss of that symbol of German stability and success – the Deutsche Mark – is approaching, it is no wonder that hesitation and *Angst* abound!

In the measure in which it is cyclical, this analysis is reassuring. It is in the nature of the economic cycle to go up after having come down. The implication of this is that with an upturn in the economic cycle there should be renewed dynamism in Germany's European policy. This will probably prove to be true, but only up to a point. One should not underestimate the weight of other factors, which are not of a cyclical nature and of which two in particular deserve to be highlighted.

In the first place, reunification has incorporated the new eastern Länder into the German political landscape. The public in former East Germany was not involved in the European unification process in the 40 years between 1950 and 1990. Knowledge and understanding of what the Community is, how it works, what it can and cannot do, how and why it came into being is disquietingly limited even in the western part of the continent. But it is practically non-existent in that other part of Europe to which the GDR once belonged. Frustration and irritation about 'Brussels' is not unknown even among the founding members. However, in the eastern Länder, this sentiment can easily be grafted on to the more general frustration *vis-à-vis* the *Wessies*. The communication problem on European affairs is general, but in some places it is worse than in others.

Second, the Länder have acquired a greater weight in European affairs as a result of constitutional changes agreed during the Maastricht Treaty ratification process in Germany. Experience so far shows that their attitude on European issues is frequently defensive. Their ministers and officials (unlike federal politicians and civil servants) are not directly exposed to the socialisation effect of repetitive contacts, ministerial meetings and European Councils. On the contrary, they fear the consequences of these meetings for their own powers of decision. All over Europe (not least in Belgium) an enhanced attachment to the region or regional identity (in French we speak of a *réflexe identitaire*) is perceptible. It can easily lead or be linked to a form of Euro-scepticism.

What conclusion should one then draw from these diverse insights? In the aftermath of the next elections and in the context of a more rapidly growing economy, German policy on Europe will demonstrate renewed dynamism. Basically, however, German policy on Europe is not worse, but also not better, than the European policies of other member states. There is an inherent weakness in all European policies, which is also the weakness of German policy. There is no overriding project, no long-term view of what the European Union should be and should do in the new century, and no presentation that is convincing enough to brush aside and overcome parochial interests and incipient Euro-scepticism. 'Building a united Europe implies historical analysis and a long-term view', writes Jacques Delors.[1] Isn't that precisely what is missing?

Donate Kluxen-Pyta makes the point repeatedly in a recent essay. She writes: 'A prospective view of a united Europe in a concrete political form is totally absent from the political debate in Germany'; 'Europe is a subject which provokes a limited interest'; 'There is vagueness about Europe and its political future'; 'Monetary union is the only point of reference of the Community, in face of disappearing ambitions'; and, finally, 'What is missing most of all is a common political public opinion'.[2] This last point is one which Dominique Wolton[3] has been making in France and which this author underlines in *Une Europe pour Tous*: 'Without a public space, without the Greek agora or the Roman forum, there is no debate, therefore no true democracy.'[4]

Although these comments may seem depressing, they are not, in fact, aimed at German policy in particular. They concern European policy in all member states. All the member states have very serious problems, notably in the field of communication with public opinion. 'Today, while Europe has a very heavy agenda to face, doubts about its future are creeping in', as Delors has noted.[5] Nonetheless, so far as German European policy is concerned, as the former Belgian Prime Minister and Foreign Minister, Pierre Harmel, argued in a recent book, 'Germany, like every other European power, knows very well that the political stage has become global. She knows also that she cannot, alone, manage a world policy ... If

Germany is today reunified, as we have always wished, it is because she has been, in every instance, faithful to her European and Atlantic commitments'.[6]

This assessment of German European policy is widely shared. The diplomatic community, both inside and outside the European Union, is, of course, professionally interested in the outcome of the 1998 German elections. It tries to weigh the impact of the introduction of the Euro and to judge the consequences of an economic upturn. It accepts that the timetable of important policy discussions, for instance over Agenda 2000, may be delayed so they do not get mixed up in pre-electoral domestic political confrontation. But basically the assumption holds that for any German government, just as for governments of other member states of the Union, there is no credible alternative to European integration. No significant voice, either within or outside Germany, puts this principle into doubt. This is despite the fact that various commentators have alluded to a so-called *Britishisation* of German European policy, implying that in future this policy will be less committed to integration, more sceptical towards new integration proposals, more doubtful about common policies and less supportive of common institutions, that is to say, closer to the views formulated in London up to 1997. I have serious doubts about the validity of this analysis. Foreign policy is about the maximisation of a country's influence in external affairs, in economic, political, military, moral or cultural terms. That, after all, is what diplomats, in general, are paid for. Now the European policy of the previous British government (I leave 'New Labour' in peace) arguably brought that country's influence on the affairs of the continent to its lowest level since the Napoleonic Wars. I would be very surprised if any other European country, let alone a major regional power like Germany, would want to imitate a foreign policy which has had such obviously disastrous consequences for the external position of the country which has practised it.

NOTES

This text was completed in April 1998.

1.   Jacques Delors, foreword in Philippe de Schoutheete, *Une Europe pour Tous* (Paris: Odile Jacob, 1997), p.v.
2.   Donate Kluxen-Pyta, 'La Nation et l'Europe: le Débat Allemand', in *France Allemagne: Le Bond en Avant* (Paris: Odile Jacob pour Notre Europe, 1998), pp.65–112.
3.   Dominique Wolton, *La Dernière Utopie* (Paris: Flammarion, 1993), chapter 9.
4.   De Schoutheete, *Une Europe pour Tous*, p.94.
5.   Delors, 'Et Maintenant?' in *France Allemagne: Le Bond en Avant*, p.199.
6.   Pierre Harmel, *Temps Forts* (Brussels: Editions Racine, 1993), p.143.

Germany, *Quo Vadis*? A View from Poland

JERZY KRANZ

Any Polish analysis of current German foreign policy must depart from a few basic facts about Polish foreign policy and Polish–German relations. In 1989, Poland did not change its borders or its geography. But its geopolitical location did change. The idea of Poland's 'return' to Europe is wrong in an historical and cultural sense, but it is true in terms of geopolitical categories. It is striking that nobody speaks of the former German Democratic Republic (GDR) 'returning' to Europe, in spite of the fact that a half a century of Communist dictatorship in eastern Germany proved to have more important psychological consequences than in the case of Poland. Poland did not 'return' to Europe after 1989. Rather Europe has assumed a new political structure.

The anti-Communist opposition in Poland spoke out strongly in support of German unification in 1989 on the understanding that this would be a station on the way to European unity and that Germany would not be the only country that would benefit from the historical opportunity that had emerged at the end of the Cold War. After having denounced the division of Europe and Germany for a period of 50 years, it would have been inconceivable for it if this process had stopped at the stage of German unification.[1] At the same time, Poland rejected the idea of either Germany or the Central European region becoming neutral. In other words, Poland did not want the withdrawal of Soviet troops to be limited just to the GDR. It was also opposed to the Warsaw Pact or the COMECON being transformed into instruments of Soviet domination in another form.[2]

Traditional Great Power politics – in particular Russian and German policy – threatened the very existence of the Polish state and Poland's national identity from the end of the eighteenth century onwards. This historical experience leads us today to want to see our neighbours' policies embedded within a strong European framework. Poland therefore strives to avoid any marginalisation of Central Europe that could otherwise turn the region into a 'play ground' on which various big powers contend for influence. Only the Eastern enlargement of the EU and the NATO will definitively put an end to this chapter of history in general and the post-Second World War Yalta era in particular.

Jerzy Kranz, Polish Ambassador to Germany

Poland's over-riding goal consists in trying to make the political changes that took place in Europe in 1989 irreversible. Corresponding to this goal, it wants to ensure that Poland is integrated into the – political, economic and military – structures of European and transatlantic co-operation from which it had been cut off as a result of the agreements struck immediately after the Second World War. Although the possibility of a revival of Russian power must not be under-estimated, at least over the time span of the next decade, it is not fear of the Russians that is pushing Poland towards European structures. The main concern and goal of Polish policy is rather internal, regional and hence at the same time European stability.

Poland's current foreign policy is neither pro- (nor anti-) Russian nor pro- (nor anti-) German; it is pro-European. Poland has chosen the European option because of long-term political calculations. Its aim goes a bit further than assuring the Poles' security and well-being – it is to ensure that the new Europe has a peaceful future. In other terms, there are no longer any specifically Polish arguments in favour of the strengthening and Eastern expansion of European structures. Instead there are problems and challenges that confront Europe as a whole.

Poland appreciates the current situation in Europe in which it is not obliged to choose between an alliance with the Russians against the Germans and the reverse. The Poles have no reason to play upon any rivalries between Germany and Russia. Similarly, Poland knows how to appreciate a situation such as the present in which the Germans, anchored in European structures, are not tempted to go their own way and search for a German–Russian entente. After a long period of conflict, Poland and Germany are linked today by a community of interests founded on common values and goals. The transformation of Polish–German relations since 1989 constitutes a kind of political success story.

THE CONTEXT OF POLISH–GERMAN RELATIONS

Polish perceptions of German foreign policy are grounded in particular in the analysis of Germany's attitudes towards Central and Eastern Europe, the transatlantic alliance (NATO) and the EU.

Germany's involvement in Central Europe is primarily motivated by its own interests. For the Germans, this region is a sphere of political and economic influence, but also a potential source of instability. It would, however, be wrong to think that the region could become a political client of Germany or serve as a buffer zone against the Russians.

The fundamental question is whether German policy towards this region is subordinated to its policy towards Russia. For a long time in history,

Germany was very attached to the notion of having only one partner to its east, namely Russia.[3] This tradition is old and creates a kind of psycho-political difficulty even if the political constellation in Europe has changed diametrically since 1989. The upshot of this is that a more intensive German–Polish dialogue concerning Germany's policy towards Eastern Europe constitutes an important pre-condition of co-operation between Berlin and Warsaw.

Does Germany need an *Ostpolitik* in the sense that this was known in the post-Second World War period? The Polish answer is negative, for this *Ostpolitik* treated the countries subjugated by the Soviet Union as a bloc. In other words, important issues concerning the region were resolved in Moscow and the Western powers knocked first of all, if not only, on the doors of the Kremlin.

The Polish goal is not at all to marginalise Russia. It would nonetheless be an historical paradox, with serious consequences, if issues relating to Central Europe were still to be resolved, as they were in the past, by the West in collaboration with Moscow. The last few years show that this tendency, motivated by consideration of Moscow's allegedly legitimate interests, dies somewhat hard.

For its part, the Russian leadership does everything it can to discuss the problems of Central Europe over the heads of the countries concerned, hoping to encounter an understanding attitude in Germany.[4] To impose its political preferences, Moscow has pursued a shrewd policy of alternating threats emphasising its power with threats stressing its weakness and the dangers that could ensue from this.

Some hesitations in German foreign policy result especially from the fact that the Western countries do not have a coherent long-term conception of the system of security in Europe and Russia's place in this system. This dilemma, which is rooted in a lack of clarity as to Moscow's interests and prospective long-term foreign policy, is of fundamental importance for European stability and for Polish–German relations.

The well-known slogan of German policy towards Central and Eastern Europe – not to create new divisions or cleavages – quite simply glosses over and ignores the fact that the Cold War division of the continent must not be equated with the lines that divide it today. These divisions exist and will always do so, but they are of a completely different kind to the barbed-wire fences of the past.[5] This German argument echoes the Russian one, according to which NATO in its old form was not an element of division, but a NATO enlarged to include Poland would be.[6] In the same vein, the arguments made in some circles in Germany concerning the dangers of a disequilibrium in Europe or of Russia being isolated are aimed in the wrong direction.[7] In fact, nobody wants an equilibrium ('cemetery peace') which would be based on an imperialistic Russia dominating, in a different form than in the past, either Central Europe or some countries that were formerly part of the Soviet Union.

Poland's goal is not to find itself in a gray zone where the big powers compete with one another for influence. With the changes of 1989, which is genuinely an historical turning point, the tendency for Central Europe to be dominated by Russia or Germany has disappeared. The partnership between Poland and Germany implies support for Polish aspirations to become a member of NATO and the EU, but this objective can not be reduced to an anti-Russian alliance. Poland does not envisage confronting Germany with the choice: us or Russia. Moreover, it is not in the interests of Poland when Moscow tries to frighten the Poles by wheeling out the argument of German expansionism or when stereotyped arguments are made in Germany to the effect that Poland is dangerous for Europe because of Poles' alleged Russophobia.[8] Actual developments in the last few years disprove this kind of reasoning.

A non-enlarged NATO would be condemned to failure, for it would not be capable of mastering the new problems that have arisen with the removal of the iron curtain. The existence of Communist regimes in Europe surprised nobody in the last few decades, but their fall has provoked general consternation and revealed the absence of any pan-European political conceptions. It is striking how much time has been taken in the last few years to conceive a scheme for European security that has still not been completely realised today.[9]

Not to enlarge NATO is in the interests of Moscow, which will doubtless pursue a policy of trying to divide the NATO allies and reduce the American presence in Europe. If, in the past, the Soviet menace enhanced cohesion in Western Europe, the reduction of the Russian menace could lead to a weakening of the cohesion of both NATO and the EU. Paradoxically, the disappearance of the blocs could, in unfavourable circumstances, lead to a weakening of European security.

Potential conflicts in Europe can arise today as a result of political or economic instability in certain parts of the continent, but also as a result of certain big powers seduced by the prospect of having a zone of influence in this region pursuing a policy of coercion (*Machtpolitik*). The Eastern enlargement of NATO and the EU must put an end to this temptation – this is an objective shared by Poland and Germany.

The anchoring of Poland in European structures enhances stability in Europe and boosts Polish–German co-operation. This perspective assuages Polish fears in respect of German–Russian dialogue, for Warsaw and Berlin are going to co-operate within the framework of the same organisations. It also enhances the prospects of Polish–Russian co-operation, which was marking time, owing to Moscow's hostility to Poland's accession to NATO. Since 1989, Germany has seen its interests as being in stability and in developing good relations with the countries of Central Europe as well as in maintaining close relations with Moscow. The Germans seem to have understood that instability in Central Europe or a German–Russian alliance at the cost of this region have too often menaced peace in Europe. It remains nonetheless true that Germany's policy towards Poland or other countries in the region is more rational than its policy towards Russia, which seems sometimes to be made on the basis of 'gut feelings'.[10]

GERMANY AND EUROPEAN SECURITY

Devising a new structure for European security is a challenge for everybody. NATO and the EU already exist and have done a remarkable job. Their future, however, depends on Europe adapting itself to new, long-term demands, foremost among them their enlargement and the evolution of their functions. The coming years will be decisive for the new political shape of the European continent. The fundamental goal of German foreign policy in this respect is to create a system that will guarantee the participation, in different forms, of the United States and Russia.

Apart from the maintenance of the American presence in Europe, which Germany supports very strongly, one of the main problems of European security consists in defining the role and place of Russia in the system, in particular if one considers Russia's uncertain political and economic development. It is too early to bury the hope for democracy and a positive economic evolution in Russia, but, for the moment, it is proving difficult to rely upon such a scenario.

German policy in the domain of European security is very active and takes account of the interests of Washington and Moscow (without forgetting Germany's other partners). Chancellor Kohl often lets the different actors in Germany play their own roles, while, however, reserving the right of final decision to himself.[11] His foreign ministers, Messrs Genscher and Kinkel, have occasionally displayed a tendency to let themselves be carried away too much by the interests, pledges and menaces of the Kremlin.[12] In this context, the attitude of the Defence Minister, Volker Rühe, has been notable for its clarity and decisive support for NATO's Eastern enlargement.

While Germany has based its security policy on the transatlantic partnership and a strong and effective NATO, Bonn is still exposed to diverse pressures coming in particular from Washington, Paris and Moscow. Consequently, Germany will pursue a differentiated policy, trying to balance between various European capitals, without, however, modifying its top priority, which is to strengthen the role of NATO. The structures and functioning of NATO and the EU must in any case be strong and effective enough to retain Germany's interest.

Pursuing this policy will encounter occasional problems, as witnessed by certain Franco-German difficulties in relation to the EU's evolution and the reform of NATO. As for NATO enlargement, the Germans referred at the beginning to American reticence. Then, once Washington's decision had been taken (in 1994), they put the emphasis on negotiating the reform of the alliance and on not provoking or humiliating the Russians.[13]

It is noteworthy that, while the policy regarding European (military and economic) integration conducted by Austria, Finland and Sweden is considered in Germany as something natural, Polish policy in this domain is perceived above all in the context of Russian interests.[14]

During the presidential election campaign in Russia in 1996, German politicians were to the fore in warning against any decision relating to NATO enlargement before the results of the election. President Clinton did not share this view and did not hesitate to speak out openly in favour of the enlargement. This example demonstrates that American policy, even if it occasionally hesitates, constitutes a decisive element for the development of the situation on the European continent (Bosnia constitutes a further example.)

It goes without saying that consulting or searching for a compromise with the Russians is, as such, nothing out of the ordinary. German initiatives in this area have become more pronounced since unification, a fact which testifies to the more important margin for political manoeuvre Germany has possessed since 1989. In German conceptions, the dominant concern consists in stabilising Russia, but Germany's support for Russia is focused above all on political issues, its economic engagement remaining very limited (hence, the volume of Polish–German trade is presently larger than than between Germany and Russia).

On the one hand, it can be observed that German support for the enlargement of NATO (and the EU) is a kind of function of a compromise with Russia.[15] Without contesting this approach, the essential question for Poland remains knowing the limits of this compromise, knowing to what extent Germany is prepared to accept Russian interests without undermining the stability and confidence of Central Europe. This question cannot be answered in the abstract, but it is a potential field of divergences between Bonn and certain Central European capitals.

On the other hand, it is true that, since the agreement between NATO and Russia in 1997 and the invitation to the three countries (Poland, Hungary and the Czech Republic) to join NATO, the problem of Russian objections to enlargement has been relegated to secondary importance. If some issues relating to security (for example, disarmament and the role of the OSCE) continue to concern European security policy-makers, they will be debated in a modified political configuration and are probably going to occupy a diminished role in relations between Poland, Germany and Russia. At the same time, another topic is going to play an increasingly important role – that of the reform and enlargement of the EU.

GERMANY AND THE EASTERN ENLARGEMENT OF THE EU

The strengthening and Eastern enlargement of the EU constitutes a further common objective for Poland and Germany. The danger for the Germans and the Poles is that the Oder–Neisse border becomes a line that separates different parts of Europe in terms of political stability and economic prosperity. Former Foreign Minister Genscher has rightly judged that prosperity cannot be achieved in the West so long as it is faced with instability in the East. This political dimension of the EU's Eastern enlargement is well anchored in the minds of the German leaders, to a lesser extent in those of some southern countries which see European integration as a primarily economic process.

Since they do not want to be the eastern bastion of the EU, the Germans support Poland's aspirations to become a member. These aspirations require the support not only of the government, but also of the German population.[16] However, the strengthening of European integration is proving to be increasingly difficult, in the light of the level of integration already attained and opposition to integration (sometimes of a populist character) in Western Europe. It is noticeable that the political dimension of integration has become less evident for the citizens of the EU member states. This trend may be dangerous for Europe. In this regard, the Franco-German tandem has a big role to play as a guarantor of integration. The co-operation between Paris and Bonn has thereby become more complex since German unification (partly because of the strengthening of the international position of Germany and France's desire to maintain a status equal to Germany's). Even if a more open European policy in London could facilitate the evolution of the EU, the Anglo-German alliance will hardly replace the Paris–Bonn tandem.[17]

At the same time, it should be borne in mind that opinions in Germany towards the deepening and enlargement of the EU have become more nuanced in the last few years. In the past, it was rather the advantages of European integration that were stressed in Germany, while today its defects are increasingly emphasised.

Some German politicians (including the leaders of some of the federal states) are inclined to slow down the integration process. It is interesting that this attitude is driven largely by domestic political considerations.[18] The Germans seem increasingly exasperated by their internal difficulties, and also by the debates about reform of the EU and the financing of the EU budget, by finding a European solution to the problem of immigration, or by the uncertainties surrounding the Euro – all these issues have led to a kind of Euro-scepticism.[19] Difficulties in the implementation of the common foreign and security policy or, indeed, of monetary union, and in particular the issue of the co-ordination of economic policies and policies to combat unemployment, could lead to tensions and frustrations that, in the case of Germany, could have important political consequences (Germany's difficulties, after all, are often Europe's). Such an internal climate would put Germany's European policy to a severe test.

If it is true that the Maastricht Treaty constituted a kind of Franco-German *Flucht nach vorn* in the face of German unification, the Treaty of Amsterdam shows that, without jeopardising the *acquis communautaire*, German policy has grown more prudent.[20] German policy is beginning to emphasise the advantages of intergovernmental co-operation in extending the scope of operation for national policies.[21] It will be interesting in this context to follow the German attitude towards the concept of flexibility (reinforced co-operation) enshrined in the Treaty of Amsterdam.[22]

From the Polish viewpoint, Germany's support for the EU's enlargement seems solid. One can nonetheless anticipate that federal government's resolve will be put to the test by the population's growing euro-scepticism, the pressure of some federal states (German federalism does not make the federal government's job any easier nowadays) and differences of interest between Poland and Germany that will emerge when some sectoral issues are negotiated in connection with the enlargement.

GERMANY'S PRIORITIES

Germany's foreign policy priorities include the following:

- The strengthening and continuation of the Atlantic Alliance.[23]
- The deepening of the EU in conjunction with the introduction of the monetary union.
- The maintenance of the Franco-German tandem in the European integration process.
- Bringing Russia into international and especially European co-operation.
- The Eastern enlargement of NATO and the EU with a view to ensuring political and economic stability in Central and Eastern Europe.

- Enhancing the importance given to economic considerations, in particular controlling the globalisation process and expanding in markets beyond Europe (for example, in Asia).

Reconciling these priorities will not be easy. In implementing such a foreign policy, Germany will be confronted by some problems and challenges, in particular:

- Being able to co-operate with Washington, Paris and Moscow on issues where there is a big distance between the three powers (without nonetheless becoming 'everybody's darling', an expression used at the time of unification by Willy Brandt).
- The possibility of things going badly wrong in Moscow.
- Some anxieties relating to the issue of a European defence identity (reconciling the US military presence in Europe with the European identity, including some possible divergences between Bonn and Washington concerning the role of instruments of economic pressure).
- Difficulties in co-ordinating policy between Bonn and Paris, particularly in relation to the military wing of NATO, deepening the EU and the operation of the monetary union.
- The search for a compromise between Germany's policies towards Moscow and towards the countries of Central Europe.
- The fear of being obliged to defend NATO's interests against Russia or to build up Central Europe's security in a period of tension between Moscow and NATO.

CONCLUSION

German unification has led to an enlargement of the action radius of its foreign policy. This results not only from the removal of the 'iron curtain' in Europe, but also from the existence of effectively independent states to the east of the Oder–Neiße (a product of the disappearance of the Soviet *Diktat*), from the modification of the role of NATO and the deepening of the EU.

It does not seem that German foreign policy is suddenly changing its character, neither by becoming isolationist nor by giving absolute priority to the West or the East. Germany's Western integration will not be abandoned, but will rather be complemented by a new policy towards the East (one which will break with the old concept of *Ostpolitik*) and a more pronounced involvement in European affairs. Germany does not hide the fact that the political and economic stabilisation of Eastern Europe constitutes one of its objectives, but it does not want to do this alone and is seeking support in this task from its allies in the EU and NATO. Even if some people criticise this approach, it seems to correspond to the long-term interests of all Europeans. The evolution and effectiveness of German foreign policy depend at the same time on the attitudes taken by its principal partners – by France, by Britain and by the United States (especially concerning the functioning of the EU and NATO).

In the future direction of German foreign policy it is rather continuity that will prevail, with the emphasis being on multilateralism while not excluding a certain amount of freedom in bilateral ties and policy conducted outside of the European and transatlantic structures. The danger currently faced by Germany (and some other EU countries) consists in their focus on domestic social and economic difficulties that can have a harmful influence on foreign policy in general and on the development of a new political architecture for Europe in particular.

It is often argued in Germany that Bonn's foreign policy was above all to multiply the number of options and that the definition of national interests was neglected. This criticism seems to be somewhat ill-founded. This problem is often posed in relation to national identity and to the role – the decline or strengthening – of the nation-state. In fact, this is an artificial dilemma. The facts show that the role of the nation-state acting alone is diminishing, particularly given the globalisation of (not only economic) problems and the insolubility of these issues at the national level. The EU and NATO prove, moreover, that the nation-state can gain some influence in multilateral structures. In this context, Germany realises its national interests, which often converge with those of its partners, in a multilateral framework.[24]

True, the German political class has preferred since 1945 to talk primarily of European interests, but this did not prevent the Germans at all from pursuing their national interests (for example, through the former *Ostpolitik*, which at the outset provoked a certain amount of distrust among the Americans). At the present time, the problem does not come down to the absence of the pursuit of national interests or their inadequate implementation, but to knowing what these interests are, whether they are coterminous with those of Germany's principal partners and in what way they can be promoted. The new constellation in Europe encourages Germany to set new emphases and goals, but the main thing is that German foreign policy continues to be pursued in the framework of multilateral structures, something which is advantageous both for Germany and Europe. Does Germany have another choice than European and transatlantic multilateralism? Theoretically yes, but to force the Germans to choose a single option (the USA, the EU, Russia and/or Central Europe) could prove dangerous for the interests of the Germans themselves and of Europe. It does not look as though the Germans are tempted by this kind of perspective.

Translated from the French original by Douglas Webber

NOTES

(Text written in March 1998)

1. One other difficulty related to the official recognition by the united Germany of Poland's Western border. The Polish Prime Minister Mr Mazowiecki did not want to rely on Chancellor Kohl's word alone, but expected formal undertakings. Mr Kohl still holds this against him today. This chapter was definitively closed by the two agreements concluded between Poland and Germany in 1990 and 1991 respectively.
2. The West had some hesitations about this process. So far as Germany is concerned, the attitude of Foreign Minister Genscher towards Moscow was fairly accommodating, especially *vis-à-vis* the Soviet wish to reduce the impact of German unification on the former Eastern bloc (including concerning the extension of NATO to the territory of the former GDR).
3. It should be remembered that, from the middle of the eighteenth century until 1939, the German political class thought that a Polish state was a nuisance and an obstacle to the pursuit of an imperialistic German policy towards Eastern Europe.
4. There is no lack of examples of this phenomenon in relation to NATO enlargement: Yeltsin's letter to the four Western powers in 1993, the (Franco-German) idea (supported by Moscow) of a five-power summit just before the decisive NATO meeting in 1997, Yeltsin's proposal to give security guarantees to the Baltic states and, earlier, to Poland, and Primakov's letter to the Western powers in 1997 concerning the Baltic states' security. Moscow's goal consists in drawing the Germans into a trap and confronting them with the choice: Russia or Central Europe. France, concerned to compete with the Americans or the Germans, has the illusion of being able to become a soloist in the concert composed and conducted by Moscow.
5. To observe this, it suffices to cross Poland's eastern border by car. Unfortunately, however, politicians, including the German ones, travel only by plane.
6. According to Mr Primakov, Russian Foreign Affairs Minister, relations between Moscow and Budapest would not suffer through Hungary's accession to NATO (*Frankfurter Allgemeine Zeitung*, 20 Feb. 1998, p.1).
7. This remark applies not only to some politicians, but also to some well-known German political scientists. In fact, if the Russians are menaced, it is by themselves, that is to say by their economy, which has fallen behind those of the West by decades, by the problems of Russian democracy and by their historical complex of being a besieged fortress.
8. See on this issue the remarks made by Arnulf Baring in the *Frankfurter Allgemeine Zeitung*, 11 March 1998.
9. It would be an illusion to believe that not enlarging NATO could strengthen or conserve its effectiveness. Of course, new problems will surface with its enlargement, but, all things considered, the overall impact on European security will be positive.
10. 'One is beginning to get the impression that Germany's foreign policy increasingly draws a distinction between two classes of partners: on the one hand, a small circle of big powers, in whose deliberations and decisions Germany participates or strives to participate and, on the other hand, a multiplicity of middle-sized and smaller countries. For East-Central Europe, such a change becomes noticeable in particular when German foreign policy

accedes to Russian pressure for it to be recognised as a great power (a claim which is questionable in the light of objective circumstances) and holds back from criticising obvious negative developments in Russia, while, on the other hand, Bonn behaves harshly towards the smaller Czech Republic or, for example, indicates to the three Baltic states, whose independence was destroyed in 1939–40 by a German–Russian conspiracy, that their accession to NATO is intolerable for Russia' (Ch. Royen, 'Das wiedervereinigte Deutschland und seine ostmitteleuropäischen Nachbarn', unpublished conference paper, Nov. 1996).

11. In a televised interview on 8 December 1994, Kohl stated: 'My conception for preserving peace ... is that we do everything to prevent any new confrontation emerging between the USA and Russia ..., that we do everything to ensure that Europe, in as far as it is represented by the European Union, does not allow any such confrontation to arise.' In his speech to the diplomatic corps in Bonn on 16 December 1994, Kohl emphasised:

> The Atlantic Alliance is the guarantor of security and stability not only for its own members, but also for all of Europe. An important foundation of it remains the close connection with North America and the permanent stationing of American soldiers in Europe ... A gradual enlargement of NATO has to be seen in close relationship with the enlargement of the European Union and the WEU [West European Union] as part of a pan-European security strategy. Such a strategy must be developed in close contact with Russia. Russia rightfully expects a place that corresponds to its status and dignity. The accession of new members to NATO must therefore be complemented by broad cooperation above all with Russia and the Ukraine.

12. In a speech to the Chicago Council on Foreign Relations on 19 April 1995, Klaus Kinkel said: 'We cannot show less understanding and patience towards the democratic forces in Moscow than we showed in former times to the Communist apparatchiks. As long as Russia says "yes" to a partnership with Europe and the USA, we have to say "yes" to a partnership with Russia.' In his speech to the International Bertelsmann Forum at Petersberg on 20 January 1996, Kinkel went further:

> The enlargement of the EU, not to mention that of NATO, cannot be achieved with our backs to Russia! The potential candidates for accession must also know this. Against this background, I have welcomed President Kwasniewski's emphasis on an active Polish *Ostpolitik* ... I say today to Russia: we have faith in the reform forces in Russia and reckon with the reforms' success ... The creation of a community of interest between Russia and the European Union is also the real high road (*Königsweg*) to common security in Europe. I am convinced therefore that, from the perspective of our Polish or Hungarian friends, the priority must be accession to the EU, not that to NATO.

13. The argument concerning the 'humiliation' of Russia constitutes an example of a half-truth, for it is not necessary to take as a humiliation the fact that Russia had to give up its quasi-colonial empire in Central Europe. The Russians even seem sometimes to expect some kind of compensation from the West for this unexpected 'loss'.

14. Chancellor Kohl said in a televised interview on 12 October 1993: 'Russia is our most important and most powerful partner in the East. That is the first fact. And the second reaction to this must be that we develop the most intensive possible relations with Russia. That means that we must now support the group of reformers around Boris Yeltsin ... Anything that comes after Yeltsin will very probably be much more difficult and, what is more, for us much more expensive.'

15. While the Germans have indicated their support for a future accession of the Baltic states to the EU, they do not hide their reticence when it comes to a NATO enlargement in this region. Bonn is evidently satisfied with the charter signed in 1998 by the United States and the three Baltic countries.

16. Note the speech by Klaus Kinkel to the *Liberales Gesprächsforum* in Hamburg on 12 November 1996:

> The enlargement is in our enlightened self-interest, it means peace and stability for the whole of Europe. We will also profit from it economically, for only as a big pan-European community will we have a chance in the global competition of tomorrow ... For German business, Central and Eastern Europe has become one of the most important growth markets worldwide. Roughly a half of the entire EU's trade with the Central and East European reform states is conducted by Germany ... The Central and Eastern European countries' share of our foreign trade now exceeds 9 per cent and has thus overtaken our trade with the USA ... Almost one tenth of German foreign direct investments go today to Central and Eastern Europe. Germany is the biggest foreign investor in the region. The fear that every Deutsche Mark invested in Central and Eastern Europe will ultimately endanger jobs at home is groundless. Our companies' investment activities are motivated by the goal of capturing new and potential markets. German companies identify low labour costs only as the second-most important motive. The transfer of production to surrounding countries is a successful recipe worldwide and unavoidable in the era of globalisation ... The German Institute for Economic Research has proven unequivocally in a study that the opening of Eastern Europe creates more jobs for us too. Certainly, the growing division of labour between Western and Eastern Europe will necessitate further structural change in our country.

17. It should be noted here that the Euro and the Stability Pact have been primarily the fruit of the common purpose of France and Germany, the negotiations between Paris and Bonn having been marked by high drama. One can conclude from these episodes that Germany is ready to strongly support the concept of European integration.

18. The future of Germany and its foreign policy depends to a large extent, it should be noted, on the solution of acute domestic social, economic and political problems (including those linked to the challenges posed by globalisation). It is accepted that the German economy and the level of social protection (which has been growing more or less constantly since the years of the economic miracle) can not grow without limits. In the absence of a decisive reform (postponed partly because of unification), frustration threatens German society, something which can have consequences for German foreign policy.

19. Note the objections raised by the Bavarian Prime Minister, Edmund Stoiber, concerning the EU's third pillar (*Frankfurter Allgemeine Zeitung*, 9 and 11 March 1998) as well as the analysis of the Christian Democrat, Elmar Brok (*Frankfurter Allgemeine Zeitung*, 16 March 1998).

20. It is paradoxical, but attributable to changing circumstances, that, whereas in the past the inconveniences caused by the need for unanimity were criticised, the emphasis today is put rather on the dangers of majority voting. The concept of flexibility, incorporated in the Amsterdam Treaty, may enable certain obstacles created by the need to achieve unanimity among all the member states to be circumvented.

21. According to an account of a seminar in Berlin,

> State Secretary von Ploetz from the Bonn Foreign Office stated openly the view that German European policy had become 'more British': The Germans asked themselves increasingly what benefits forfeiting sovereignty in this or that issue-area would bring and whether it would not be better to stick to loose cooperation ... "I'm no pro-integrationist", added Kohl's European policy adviser [Joachim Bitterlich], thus making clear what Kohl had suggested on earlier occasions: for the federal government, the expansion of EU competences (*Vergemeinschaftung*) is no longer an article of faith and if better (that means, Bonn's desired) results can be achieved by the normal method of loose cooperation outside of the rules of the EU, then there is no reason to go further

along the course of integration ... It is clear therefore that the Germans are asking more than ever about the costs and benefits of European unification

(*Frankfurter Allgemeine Zeitung*, 30 Oct. 1997). See also *Le Monde*, 1 Nov. 1997.

22. The concept of reinforced co-operation, in the guise of a 'hard core', was mentioned already in the Schäuble–Lamers paper on European integration.

23. 'Without Germany's support and cooperation with Germany, the United States would not be able to remain a "European power" after the end of the Cold War. Great Britain, France and Russia, for different reasons, could not be the partner that America wished ... That this insight still applies today is proven by America's strong support for NATO membership for the three countries that are so essential for Germany's "strategy": Poland, Hungary and the Czech Republic' (S.F. Szabo, *Frankfurter Allgemeine Zeitung*, 2 July 1997, p.2).

24. It should be noted, however, that Germany does show some interest in the concept of a more or less formalised European *directoire* (an idea to which Moscow is also favourable). An example of this is the 'contact group' in the Yugoslavian crisis.

German Foreign Policy and Transatlantic Relations since Unification

ANDREW DENISON

Like 1989, 1999 was a watershed year for the Federal Republic of Germany. The September 1998 elections had already set the stage by ending Helmut Kohl's 16-year tenure as Chancellor. Gerhard Schröder's new Red–Green government then entered 1999 facing a war over Kosovo, the move from Bonn to Berlin and the replacement of the Mark with the Euro. The new government also held the EU and G8 presidencies and used them adroitly to facilitate agreement between NATO, Russia and Yugoslavia over terms to end the Kosovo war. Finally, it was in December 1999 that Kohl admitted to having secret party accounts. The ensuing revelations about a deeply corrupt CDU left Kohl's reputation destroyed and Germany's political opposition in a nose-dive.

Changes in views on the use of force have been especially striking. In 1991 German protesters filled the streets against the Gulf War and Bonn stayed out of the fight, writing a $10 billion cheque to the US Treasury instead. In 1999 German pilots were firing HARM missiles into Yugoslav air defence sites, urged on by Foreign Minister Joschka Fischer (leader of the eco-pacifist Green/Alliance 90 Party) and supported by clear majorities in opinion polls and the Bundestag.[1]

Germany has changed, but not into a predatory power from the past – as so many feared at the time of unification. The Federal Republic is also not the 'West Germany' of the Cold War. Germany is a country undergoing metamorphosis as the face of its society changes, as the world of which it is a part changes. This change is not, however, entirely divorced from enduring norms – deeply felt and rooted in the lessons of a dark history – that inform policy-makers' actions and find a strong resonance among Germany's political class. Germany remains a country seeking to work with others to advance ends that go beyond Germany's own immediate self-interest. Co-determination in the stabilisation of its international environment is very much at the top of the German policy agenda. With the Cold War over and Germany no longer the most heavily armed region of the

Andrew Denison, Transatlantic Networks, Königswinter, Germany world, Germans are also increasingly comfortable about no longer being consumers, but producers of stability and security. Germany in this 'producer' role is new, but it fits with Germany's basic beliefs about foreign policy and the rapidly evolving international system.

Aspiration is there. Resources are the problem. Germany has been through ten years of economic stagnation, compounded by daunting unification costs. Whether the issue is funding the Balkan Stability Pact, adhering to the Monetary Union's own Stability Pact, or mustering a 150,000-strong intervention force, Germany is strapped for cash. The country's public sector is almost 49 per cent of GDP, the annual public deficit a bit above two per cent, and public debt at 63 per cent of GDP.[2] Unemployment has remained at a costly ten per cent throughout the decade. 'Die Arbeitslosigkeit macht die Aussenpolitik kaputt' (unemployment is undermining foreign policy). The country is ranked seventeenth in NATO defence spending as a proportion of GDP. Germany's spending (24 billion Euros in the year 2000) is at 1.5 per cent of GDP, while France and Britain spend 2.8 and the US 3.2 per cent. Germans would argue, however, that they spend more on foreign policy and development assistance. The Americans would retort: 'Trade not aid! It's foreign direct investment and market access that make for development.' The economic models compete. The burden-sharing debate continues.

Germany is a country that places much value on 'continuity'; it is a country with deeply held political principles, clearly articulated in its 1949 Basic Law and still held high in political discourse. Germany is a country ever-afraid of its past.[3] It is a country that values the lessons of the Long Peace, the 50 years that made the second half of the twentieth century so much better than the first. Germany is an internationalised country, economically and in terms of its political culture. 'Westbindung als Staatsräson' (Western integration as a basic parameter of government policy) remains a central principle.[4] The country's body politic responds sensitively to words from foreign capitals. A European Germany, an Atlantic Germany: these concepts are very much a part of Germany's self-image of *Eingebundenheit* – of being tied into something larger than itself. The United States of America also continues to loom large in Germany's political world, being a primary frame of reference, politically, economically, culturally and strategically.

Continuity in the face of change? This seems a valid conclusion for Germany a decade into unification. All the same, reconciling basic norms with changing realities is not easy. New conditions, domestic and international, mean old norms clash with one another in new ways. What has this implied for the change that has occurred? How have guiding principles manifested themselves? Has Germany become more assertive, more militaristic, more unilateralist? Finally, what does all this mean for relations with the United States? These are the questions addressed below.

CHANGE AND CONTINUITY

Germany is a country with many faces, some historical, some modern, some not even German. It is the Reichstag remade by a British architect; it is the Potsdamerplatz that has risen from the ashes and is now dominated by the Mount Fuji-like roof of Sony headquarters; it is the million-strong Love Parade under the Brandenburg Gate. Germany is also dressing up for Sunday afternoon walks, or sitting at one's very own *Stammtisch* at the local bar, or attending the wine and beer festivals celebrated in every little town and village from the Rhine to the Oder.

Germany's culture remains rich, but it has become more dynamic, more diverse and more international. Berlin Kreuzberg is said to have the largest Turkish population outside Turkey. Germany will need to add 200,000 foreign workers to its labour force every year for the next 20 years to keep the ratio of tax-paying to pension-collecting individuals the same as today. As Europe has opened, so has Germany, now a main avenue of East–West transit. Germany's uniquely German Autobahn restaurants leave one certain that Europe is not only Mediterranean, but also Slavic, even Central Asian. Germany is becoming more European in the broadest sense of the word.

Germany's transformation naturally raises the question of what has remained the same. In Germany's case, it is apparent that co-existing with the changes of the past decade are very fundamental lines of continuity. There has been no unilateralist backlash. Germany is more tightly tied to the European Union than ever before. Nor does Germany believe it can play a strong role in Europe without a strong transatlantic partnership. Germany may be willing to use military force – even without a mandate from the UN Security Council – but it remains highly unlikely that Germany would ever use force alone.

The Schröder government's mantra as it entered office was 'continuity', continuity even as it led the country into war and the international community towards a Fischer Plan/G8 arrangement for achieving a Serbian withdrawal from Kosovo. Analysts as different as Hanns Maull, purveyor of the view that Germany is a 'civilian power', and Hans-Peter Schwarz, who maintains that Germany is Europe's 'central power' have claimed that continuity characterises German foreign policy.[5]

Germany, like the Federal Republic of old, remains a country with a lofty set of political principles – global solidarity, world peace, Atlantic community, European Union, shared prosperity, social justice, equal living standards between Germany's east and Germany's west. Germany also remains a country with a conservative strategy and pragmatic tactics – predictable, consensual and workable, but often quite slow.

Combining change and continuity is not always easy. The public discourse shows no lack of ideas about how to address shortcomings and bring about change: more flexible labour markets, better small business conditions, less government spending, EU enlargement, modern military forces for humanitarian intervention. Consensus politics and entrenched interests prevent action. The gap between rhetoric and reality generates cynicism. The task of reconciling old norms with new realities progresses slowly. Change is incremental. But change does occur. Moreover, the outside world, long a factor in moving Germans to change, has not declined in importance.

To say the outside world still shapes German behaviour is not to engage in retrograde realism. The state is not a closed box, but an opening one. Globalisation means dissolving borders. Economies, governments and societies have all grown more inter-operable. Germans are among the world's most active tourists. Making up a third of Germany's economy, foreign business transactions play twice the role they do in the US economy. Germany is wired into Europe and the world like never before. International events do affect Germany, in terms of policy, in terms of economics, demographics and culture. Germany's response, however, is based on traditions, habits, outlooks and institutions that remain very 'German'.

GERMANY'S FUTURE: A LOOK BACK

Ten years ago, the question of how German foreign policy would change after unification and the end of the Cold War was hotly debated. Most assessments, especially from the realist perspective, held that the thrust of German foreign policy would necessarily change, because the conditions that had created that foreign policy had changed so dramatically. Most realist observers at the time of unification foresaw a Germany that would be more assertive, more independent, and a potentially dominant power in Europe and the world.

These assessments have predicted the trend, but have been wrong about the pace, degree and nature of change. While noting what is new and different from before, it is important not to exaggerate the degree to which German foreign policy is changing. Germany has become somewhat more assertive of its own national interest, less averse to using military force as a tool of foreign policy, and less passively multilateral than it once was. But these changes have been smaller and have occurred more slowly than many observers initially assumed they would. In the case of Germany, the realist view that the structure of the international system determines foreign policy is thus too limited. The liberal view, in its institutionalist and constructivist guise, with its argument not to forget domestic politics, institutions and political culture, is proving more relevant. Certain bedrock principles remain. They will shape the way Germany asserts its power. Numerous international commitments and institutions reinforce this pattern.

The nature of the international system has certainly changed, more dramatically for Germany than any other European country. The change in German foreign policy, though real, has been much less dramatic. This in itself is an argument that points to other agents of change than Germany's external environment. Germany's relations with the rest of the world have been conditioned by national habits of reticence and restraint, by a strong inclination to multilateralism and by the consensual politics of its own institutions[6] – as well as by a preoccupation with its own debilitating economic problems.

When change has come to Germany's foreign policy, it has not entirely fit the pattern of a rising power, lost and all alone. Instead, Germany has been weaving an ever-denser web of trans-European integration, tying itself down (*Einbettung/Einbindung*) in the process of seeking a Europe of greater co-ordination and co-determination. This Europe is Germany's vocation today as much as it ever was. The official 'tenets' of German foreign policy are still described in very integrationist terms:

- peaceful co-operation with our neighbors in a spirit of partnership;
- continued development of the North Atlantic Alliance (NATO) and transatlantic co-operation where Europe must assume a greater share of the responsibility;
- deepening and broadening the EU which must become a partner fully capable of acting in all areas on the global stage;
- Europe-wide co-operation in the OSCE;
- strengthening the international organisations, first and foremost the UN, and an active role for Germany in these organisations;
- a special responsibility for democracy and stability in Central, Eastern and South-Eastern Europe and the promotion of sustainable development in the countries of the South.[7]

These views reflects a belief that what is good for the community of nations can also be good for oneself.

More novel is a new 'global' perspective that has entered the German discussion of its foreign policy role. In 1995, the then Federal President Roman Herzog called for a 'globalisation of German foreign policy',[8] provoking an on-going discussion of this issue. Germany's foreign policy role has grown larger than Europe. Yet the norms that define Germany's role on this more global stage have changed much less. Talking about the 'globalisation' of Germany foreign policy or Germany as a 'global player' is accepted; describing Germany as a world power (*Weltmacht*) is not, although speaking of Europe as a *Weltmacht* has become acceptable, even in vogue. Meeting new challenges while remaining true to time-tested principles remains the proclaimed objective. The German government still speaks in terms of restraint and responsibility, even as it looks to new horizons:

> At the threshold of the 21st century, the parameters of German foreign policy have fundamentally changed ... The most obvious manifestation of these changes is globalization, transcending national borders through the internationalization of communication and business. Germany is willing to assume greater responsibility in this changing world.[9]

It is thus clear that the rhetoric of the integrationist Germany, the 'civilian power', is still very much alive. But what about the reality? Is there actually a new assertiveness, a new militarism, a new unilateralism to be found in the events of the past decade?

A NEW ASSERTIVENESS?

Germany has often been on centre-stage in Europe over the past decade. The hand of the Kohl and Schröder governments is quite visible when looking across the institutional landscape of today's Europe. Germany has frequently asserted its view of how Europe should be organised, from NATO enlargement to European Monetary Union. Germans themselves speak of being more *selbstbewusst*, a term that is difficult to translate, but implies an assertive self-confidence based on self-awareness. Germans often describe Germany as a 'motor' of European integration. They are more reluctant, however, to see Germany as a 'leader', which, in German, translates, of course, into *Führer*.

George Bush's May 1989 call for a 'partnership in leadership' between Germany and America left Bonn feeling awkward and Bonn's European partners wary. Still, it signalled a pronounced American desire to see Germany assuming a larger role in Europe. The US Deputy Secretary of State, Strobe Talbott, speaking in Bonn shortly before the Kosovo War, echoed this objective, stating: 'We recognize and welcome the role of the Federal Republic at the epicentre of these processes — expansion and integration, broadening and deepening.'[10] Despite American urging, the idea of German leadership, if it comes at all, always comes in a way that makes it sound synonymous with Franco-German or even European leadership. Where German leaders have changed their tone is in regard to 'influence'. It has become entirely legitimate for Germany to seek greater influence in return for greater contributions. In other words, being 'responsible' can also be a source of influence.

Germany's new assertiveness has often been discussed with regard to Germany's early insistence on recognising Croatia and Slovenia in 1991, when most of Europe wanted to wait. Yet the international reaction to this step showed Germany that it was not conducive to good foreign relations to take action before their partners did. Germany would have to seek influence through the institutions by seeking others' approval for specific initiatives. All the same, from EMU to NATO and EU enlargement, from the G8 plan and the Stability Pact(s), German leaders have demonstrated their belief that 'German models and concepts for order can contribute to European solutions'.[11] They have also sought a greater role in other international institutions, whether a seat on the UN Security Council or their man at the head of the International Monetary Fund. They have seen many of their ideas adopted. This has been accompanied by a certain renaissance of strategy. The Germans are thinking harder about ways to shape their environment, to protect the common interest. Thus, 'international civil–military relations' are becoming the key to foreign policy, according to the Bosnian trouble-shooter and former minister in Kohl's government, Christian Schwarz-Schilling.[12] The Bundeswehr is thinking and commissioning studies about what the next two or three decades might bring. There is an urge to operationalise the concepts of conflict prevention and crisis management.

There is a new self-confidence, as Sebastian Harnisch has concluded from a number of studies looking at the degree and nature of any new German assertiveness or 'self confidence'. Harnisch adds, however, that 'this increased self-confidence went into the customary institutional context of Germany foreign policy (the EU, NATO, CSCE/OSCE and the UN), thereby also contributing to the changing structure and mission of these organisations'.[13] Germany has become more assertive, but it has largely done so in the framework of multilateral institutions and with an eye to its most important partners.

Where more '"selfish" assertiveness' has occurred, this has usually been a function either of Germany's pressing need to reduce its public spending or of the growing role of the Länder governments in the area of European politics. It was largely the Länder that stopped Kohl from accepting greater majority voting on Justice and Home Affairs (Pillar III) in the EU's Amsterdam Treaty.[14] One can therefore argue that the 'normative frame of reference for this increased self-confidence remains the tradition of the "Bonn Republic" with its solid anchoring (*Einbindung*) in the Western community of values'.[15]

Germany has shown greater assertiveness, but it has remained multilateralist. Germany, according to Harnisch and other Trier-based research, still fits the 'civilian power' model,[16] but it has grown more assertive in pursuing this role. The country has come to pursue something akin to 'assertive multilateralism'. Underlying this practice is the continued belief, as in industrial relations, that 'co-determination' can facilitate action without backlash.

A NEW MILITARISM?

Proponents of the new militarism argument need only to compare Germany during the Gulf War with Germany today. During Operation Desert Storm, Germany's domestic debate raged even over the minor issue of deploying training aircraft to Turkey. Troop deployment or major involvement in the area was out of the question. Since then Germans have fought in an air war over Yugoslavia, playing a small though important role in the suppression of enemy air defence. They are policing a sector in Kosovo, headquartered in Prisren, said by many observers to be one of the 'better run' towns in Kosovo. In June 2000 they announced plans to triple the size of their crisis reaction forces, from 50,000 to 140,000. Has a new militarism come to Germany?

Whether it has or not, it is clear that German participation in Allied Force, and the widespread public support it found, was the culmination of a decade-long process of re-orientation. Reconciling the Federal Republic's traditional foreign policy values with the exigencies of war in the Balkans has not been easy. A large part of the German political culture, particularly strong in the Social Democratic and Green parties, was strongly opposed to German military intervention anywhere. In a landmark decision, the Federal Constitutional Court ruled in July 1994 that out-of-area combat operations were not a violation of Germany's Basic Law – as long as they were 'approved by parliament' and took place in 'mutual collective security organisations' (including NATO and the WEU). Nevertheless, numerous SPD and Green deputies voted against German participation in Deliberate Force over Bosnia in September 1995. (German aircraft, armed with anti-air defence missiles did fly over Bosnia, though they never fired any weapons.) In 1996, it seems, a significant shift occurred. Some combination of the lessons of Srebrenica, the success of NATO's Implementation Force (IFOR), and continued Allied pressure for Germany to do more moved large majorities in the SPD and the Greens to vote for a 'combat mission' (that is, robust rules of engagement) for 3,000 Bundeswehr soldiers in Bosnia as part of NATO's follow-on Stabilization Force (SFOR). The Bundestag vote on this deployment was 499–93 and was not even widely debated.

The discussion then moved from whether Germany might be involved in the use of military force to whether such force required a UN Security Council mandate. A majority in the SPD and the Greens still insisted that such a mandate was necessary. When the parties took power, their coalition agreement asserted:

> The participation of German armed forces in measures to maintain world peace and international security is tied to the observance of international law and German constitutional law. The new federal

government will actively support maintaining the United Nations' monopoly on the use of force and strengthening the role of the Secretary General.[17]

THE KOSOVO STORY

It was precisely this divisive issue that the newly elected team faced – even before it had been officially inaugurated. Schröder and Fischer, who were in Washington in October 1998 as members of a government-elect while US envoy Richard Holbrooke was negotiating with Slobodan Milosevic in Belgrade, found themselves urged by the White House not to veto any NATO action. Soon, however, it was not enough for Germany simply not to veto any such action. Just back in Bonn, Schröder and Fischer were confronted with a revised White House request: to raise the pressure on Milosevic by having the Germans commit to full Bundeswehr participation in the operation, at least in NATO staffs, on NATO's Airborne Warning and Control Systems (AWACS) and in other 'indirect' forms of combat – and all this without a UN mandate. With the deployment of OSCE observers in Kosovo, the coalition was given a bit of time, but not much. In March 1999, Schröder, Fischer and Defence Minister Rudolf Scharping had to rise to the challenge of keeping the German people behind participation in NATO's air war (and their own governing coalition from collapsing over the means and motives of Allied Force). They succeeded, winning praise both at home and abroad.

Germany resorted to military force in Kosovo because the arguments in favour of 'continuity', 'alliance solidarity' and 'human rights' outweighed the arguments against a 'militarisation of foreign policy' and a 'violation of international law' (or at least of the government's coalition agreement). Those who see post-unification German policy as characterised by continuity see Kosovo as a supporting case. Hanns Maull, for example, makes the following argument:

> As a result of those challenges, and in response to new demands on German security policy both from within and without, Germany has shifted to a security posture which in principle accepts the need for German participation in military intervention outside the traditional NATO context of collective defense. While clearly representing an important evolution, this new security posture does not constitute a fundamental departure from Germany's post-war foreign policy identity as a civilian power.[18]

Germany's contribution to Allied Force also gave it a real voice in the diplomatic efforts to achieve a Serbian withdrawal, to keep Moscow 'on board' and to gain some sort of *post facto* UN legitimisation of the military intervention. This, at any rate, was the standard text used (particularly as a defence against budget cuts) by Scharping in the months following the war. Germany is still more reluctant to enter into military operations than other countries may be in the same situation, but the distance it has travelled since 1991 is remarkable. Germany will use force again in the future and a UN mandate will not be the most important criterion shaping such decisions. Yet this 'normalisation' stops when it comes to using force alone. It will be a long time before the German public will accept Bundeswehr actions without some sort of international legitimacy – and political risk-sharing. The 1994 constitutional ruling stating that the constitutionality of military action is dependent on it taking place in mutual collective security organisations would also be a big hurdle to take.

BUNDESWEHR REFORM

The importance of international expectations is also seen in the issue of Bundeswehr reform. Germany's new military role needs to be triangulated within the context of NATO, the EU and its most important partners. NATO's Defence Capabilities Initiative and the EU's Headline Goal are important frames of reference. Germans did not consider it unusual when Defence Minister Scharping invited the US Secretary of Defence, William Cohen, to speak to a Bundeswehr audience in Hamburg on the need for German military modernisation.[19] Yet even with international legitimacy and a clear plan, reform is still very much dependent on funding. The high priority given to reducing public spending in Germany likely means little funding will be forthcoming for such a project. Scharping has secured the Schröder government's tentative approval for embarking on such a reform, winning initial support from the Federal Cabinet for his 'Cornerstones of Fundamental Renewal' on 14 June 2000. But he has not yet acquired the necessary funds.

Largely backed by the findings of an independent commission on 'Common Security and the Future of the Bundeswehr' and a series of Bundeswehr–business agreements, the Ministry of Defence proposes big changes in Germany's armed forces: to cut total Bundeswehr strength by a third to 255,000; to increase rapid reaction forces by two-thirds to 150,000; to make serving as a 'citizen in uniform' a profession fit for a high-tech economy, with commensurate compensation and training; to open 'all careers' to women; to streamline procurement and services by adopting modern business practices and by drawing industry into a 'strategic partnership' with the Bundeswehr; and, above all, to give Germany the military capabilities it needs to promote 'inclusive security' for itself, for its allies and for regions more distant.

The objectives of Bundeswehr reform are thus clear. The open question is that of money. Without Germany, the EU's largest and richest country, Europe's new headline-grabbing goals will amount to little. Germany's alleged 'new militarism' is not the problem. The problem is rather the huge gap between aspiration and reality, both in Germany and in Europe. This, in turn, is the real threat to transatlantic relations. For the EU to proclaim 'autonomy', but not to be able to sustain it militarily, could quickly lead to resentment and recrimination across the Atlantic and within Europe.[20]

A NEW UNILATERALISM?

Is Germany shunning its European and Atlantic links, seeking instead the 'greater' manoeuvring room of a unilateralist foreign policy? Germany's integrationist impulse has certainly run up against domestic and foreign obstacles. International institutions, from the EU to the UN, seemed especially inept during the first half of the 1990s, as when Germany's 1993 UN peace-keeping deployment in Somalia went down with the US Blackhawks over Mogadishu. The burning Balkans left many disillusioned with internationalist rhetoric and conference diplomacy. Germany has also had difficulty towing the integrationist line in the face of allies – France, Britain and the US – very much more inclined to independent actions.

All the same, the lessons of 50 years of peace run deep. Multilateralism is still a core interest. Germans still hold that Europe is necessary to accommodate German power and that Germany can guarantee good relations with its many neighbours only if balance-of-power politics is replaced by concert and co-operation. Integration and sovereignty are not mutually exclusive, but can be mutually reinforcing; a stronger European Union can also mean a stronger Atlantic partnership; and a widening European Union can also be a deepening European Union.

For Germany, the challenge of multilateralism has been very much caught up in the twin challenge of deepening and widening, both of NATO and, to an even greater degree, the EU. Deepening and widening, particularly in the case of the EU, are each difficult to achieve in their own right. These tasks are made to seem all the more confounding by the widespread perception that they are mutually exclusive. Reconciling the desire for deepening and widening has thus been one of Germany's main foreign policy challenges since the fall of the Wall. Consternation has often been the result.

Enthusiasm for the European project, particularly for Economic and Monetary Union (EMU) has certainly wavered over the years. The notion of a United States of Europe has largely faded from the country's political vocabulary. Europe's costs are a cause of grumbling; some politicians are tempted to seek political gain from an anti-European stance (though they rarely succeed). Schröder himself made some noise during the 1998 election campaign about paying too much into EU coffers, but once he was in power the issue fell by the wayside. As one says in Brussels, campaigning against Europe is one thing, governing against Europe is another. When it came to pushing through Agenda 2000 at the March 1999 Berlin EU Council summit or gaining more votes in the EU Council than the less populous France or Britain at the treaty revision negotiations at Nice in December 2000, the German government was much more deferential than election campaign rhetoric might have led one to believe. Where the Schröder government has pushed is on enlargement, particularly enlarging the accession group. Fischer played an important role in getting the 1999 Helsinki Summit's approval for adding Turkey to the membership negotiations.

Widening, many Germans maintain, is best reconciled with deepening through 'flexible' or 'differentiated' integration. This 'different strokes for different folks' approach to doubling the membership of the EU has drawn criticism from some quarters because it allegedly implies a new unilateralism. From the 1994 Schäuble–Lammers proposal for a 'hard core' to the Amsterdam Treaty's 'constructive abstention' and 'reinforced co-operation' Germans have favoured an EU that can be both large and capable of moving faster than the slowest member(s), who would nevertheless still enjoy the 'stabilising influence' of the Union. This 'leaving-some-behind' approach is a modification of the integrationist impulse, but by no means its end. Indeed, it is more likely that European integration would come to a halt in the absence of such modification. Hence 'flexibility' is Germany's own way of reconciling the fundamental paradox of multilateralism: individual initiative – leadership – is sometimes the best catalyst for co-operation.

In step with this notion of core and periphery, in a May 2000 speech at Berlin's Humboldt University Foreign Minister Fischer has also weighed in with his 'personal' view of European finality. Fischer laid out a vision of a Europe with a federation of nation states at its core and with parliamentary accountability assured through a bicameral legislature of national and local representatives.[21] In a significant gesture to the French, Fischer thus explicitly brought the nation state back in. And true to the German bicycle theory of integration, he insisted the process must move forward, because the choice is 'integration or erosion'. Closer union is seen as the only way to accommodate greater diversity.

Beyond Europe, Germany has not so much abandoned international institutions as sought a greater voice in them. German models to the front, a German place on the UN Security Council, a German banker at the IMF – some might see a certain German pushiness in its behaviour on these issues. Still, it is less unilateralism than assertive multilateralism. German chancellors are not yet flying solo when it comes to showing up in some world hot-spot to save the day.

If German unilateralism is hard to see in today's Europe, what are the prospects for tomorrow? The new Europe is one of striking (and enduring economic) diversity – particularly between East and West. Bringing the highly heterogeneous group of 13 EU Associates into the Union will force a fundamental reorientation of the EU's role – flexible integration may be the goal, but institutional gridlock and a backlash against Europe remain clear dangers. Should the European project not be up to this transformative task, the bicycle of European integration might indeed crash, leaving Germany much more alone. Yet even then it is highly unlikely that such a 'disembedded' Germany would be anything like the Germany of days gone by – at least as long as there was a clear Atlantic link.

The much more likely outcome is that Germany will be part of a unifying Europe, a Europe encompassing more states, and, if perhaps fitfully, a Europe seeking to be a unitary actor on the world stage. How America deals with this Europe then becomes Germany's most important transatlantic issue.

GERMANY'S 'NEW ATLANTICISM'

That transatlantic relations would change in the decade following the end of the Cold War was clear. That a 'New Atlanticism' – a reinvigorated commitment to the idea of co-operation based on an ever denser fabric of common values and interest – would be the outcome was much less certain. Yet comparing the words coming out of the US State Department and the German Foreign Office at the dawn of this decade, one could optimistically conclude that this is indeed the case. The increasing investment and information flows attest at any rate to growing interdependence.

Clearly, there remains a broad range of issues that pester the relationship, from American beef with hormones to Europe's small bananas. There are also some big points of contention: EU versus NATO, power-sharing versus burden-sharing, and Europe versus the world. These are, however, challenges that have been with partnership since the days when John Foster Dulles talked of 'agonizing reappraisal'. Despite the annoyances and despite the big questions, it is difficult to argue that relations are any worse than they were during the 1980s or that common challenges have disappeared with the demise of the Soviet threat. Germany and the United States remain extremely important to one another.

Germany and America have accomplished much over the last decade. The European continent has been transformed – and not in the horrific way scenario planners had imagined during the Cold War. Large-scale killing in the Balkans has ended. Belgrade might just be on its way to joining the

Partnership for Peace. These are common achievements, built on the multi-dimensional channels of communication heralded since the beginning of the decade as 'interlocking institutions'.

The common Atlantic vision is reinforced by a transatlantic space profoundly more inter-connected than it was a decade ago. The communications revolution and growing transatlantic commerce have multiplied the volume of ties between Germans and Americans. 'The daily exchange of goods and services between Europe and America', brags Joschka Fischer, 'is now topping the billion dollar mark.'[22] One needs only look to Daimler-Chrysler to realise that globalisation is at its most intense across the Atlantic.

It is these connections that move Karsten Voigt, the German government's official Coordinator for German–American Cooperation to speak of a 'New Atlanticism', a much broader based Atlanticism than the security-dominated arrangement of the Cold War.[23] A host of challenging issues, he maintains, are involved in managing the dense network of transatlantic relationships. Moreover, a growing global agenda necessitates co-operation not only between governments, but also among the multitude of actors comprising international civil society and the global economy. This German–American relationship, greater now in breadth if not in depth than ever before, is thus also more infused with potential points of friction. Reflecting the dialectics of German diplomacy, today's problems are thus not a sign of a weak, but rather of a strong and ever-closer Atlantic relationship.

This broad-based view of an Atlantic community challenged as much by societal issues as security threats is also shared by Clinton's Ambassador to Germany, and long-time German hand at the State Department, John Kornblum. He sees the American presence in Europe as 'destiny', he sees the common challenge as being domestic policy and global democratisation:

> The United States will continue to be a central element in the new Europe we are building together. It is our destiny – but our role will be different. We will no longer be protecting Berlin and Western Europe against threat. We will increasingly become a partner in a joint effort to ensure the health of our societies and to extend the benefits of democracy.[24]

All the same, one should not forget the geostrategic side of the argument. It may not be surprising that Kornblum refers to the United States as a 'European power', reflecting one of his predecessors', Richard Holbrooke's, assertion that the US is an essential, even existential, part of the European system and power structure.[25] It is more surprising that Joschka Fischer explicitly echoes this sentiment:

The US is still present in Europe today, it is a "European power". That has been a tremendous stroke of luck for Europe and especially for Germany.

This is why the American presence in Europe and close ties between our continents will remain so crucial for Germany. Apart from the security gap which would emerge in Europe, an American withdrawal would force Germany into a role in Europe which it neither can nor wants to perform. Even if the European Union develops ever more into a self-confident, independent political player, its inner stability will still rest to a great degree on continued American commitment.[26]

These words clearly illustrate the fundamental continuity in Germany's approach to European order. This sentiment is shared by a very large majority of the commentators and analysts in the Federal Republic. Germans regularly emphasise that American power in Europe remains critical for European stability, and not just to guard against any Russian resurgence. Many Germans would also agree that the American presence is a precondition for any German role in Europe that is commensurate with its economic weight and geopolitical position.

The American presence is, however, contingent on some sort of common vision. Indeed, one could argue that this is the strength of the relationship. Germany and the US share the same conception of Europe and the same strategy on the major contemporary European foreign policy issues. This strategy includes enlarging Western institutions eastwards: enlargement of NATO and the EU is in both American and German interests, especially as Germany wants what it calls 'Western allies to its East'.

There is thus a symbiotic relationship between Germany's Atlantic and European partnerships – at least according to most German observers. They claim that 'Europe as a unitary actor', whether on trade, exchange rates, or security and defence, is a precondition for a stronger Atlantic partnership. Fewer would openly say that it is the US military guarantee that continues to provide the umbrella under which European integration can advance. All the same, Germany's commitment to forsake any kind of national nuclear deterrent – still an important condition of European integration – is dependent on a close (nuclear) relationship with the United States. This "reinforcing" relationship is seen in German policy expositions, which usually speak of relations with the United States in terms of Euro-Atlantic, as opposed to German–American.

CONCERNS AND CONFLICTS

For all the common interests, common values, and common challenges in transatlantic relations, conflict happens. Differences of opinion, perspective and approach are real. Interests of countries, and, more frequently, those of specific constituencies within countries, inevitably clash. Reconciling and re-balancing interests – log-rolling – is thus an important part of the relationship.

Some of this is like big city traffic. There is a lot to keep track of across the Atlantic. Collisions occur. Sometimes it is just about who gains how much from trade. Often it is more. Is Airbus unfairly subsidised? Is AOL/Time Warner too much a monopolist? Is child labour a route to development? These questions bring up what Karsten Voigt calls the 'value versus value-added' clash. He sees different views on standards (social, environmental, safety, fiscal, and so on) as an important new element of transatlantic relations. Consumer protection has gone international.

There are also permanent 'structural' problems that condition conflict resolution and require constant high-level attention. These are the big questions: burden-sharing and power-sharing, Europe versus the World, and force and diplomacy.

The German View

A German discussion of problems between Germany and the United States would probably begin with Germany's interest in a truly multilateral world order. Germany has always been multilateralist in Europe. Now it has global horizons. Germany's internationalism will be felt on the world scene. Its complaint with the United States will remain that US foreign policy is afflicted by an 'America First' tendency that Berlin fears could turn into a more obnoxious form of unilateralism. The Helms–Burton and Iran–Libya Sanctions acts with their extraterritorial aspirations still hurt. There is a host of other areas where the 'unilateralist' problem shows itself: United Nations' debt, the Comprehensive Test Ban Treaty, National Missile Defence, the International Court of Justice, landmines, climate change, and so on.

American universalism, if not exceptionalism, makes Germans wary, to say the least. Germans think more in terms of a 'common' canon of political principles, also seeing this as the glue that holds the Alliance together and as the standard by which new applicants should be measured. 'Common' means that the Germans want to be heard too. They do, after all, pride themselves on philosophy, if not strategy. Recognising that whole societies are increasingly rubbing up against one another, Germans worry about America not being sufficiently accommodating. They are also bothered by the death penalty and high income inequality in the US.

This said, if America can reconcile leadership with co-determination, Germany will appreciate (and accept) American leadership. The main German foreign affairs journal, *Internationale Politik*, devoted an issue to transatlantic relations that carried the titled 'Unequal Partners'. It seems that Germany is willing to accept that unequal partners (Europe and America) can still be strong partners, provided they follow the principles of partnership. Germany would also have a much easier time convincing its 'hereditary friends' (*Erbfreunde*) in France that Atlanticism belongs in twenty-first century Europe if it can show that America can be a part of the continent without riding roughshod over it.

Germans are concerned about America fearing Europe and European integration. They want US support for the project (though not US control of it, for example, on Turkey) and, while recognising that the US should not be surprised by European developments, they also want America to respect European decisions. Now that the monetary union is in place, and for a host of other reasons, extending from Saint Malo to Kosovo, the European Union has put security and defence policy high on its agenda. It has thrown its political weight behind the goal of developing the capacity by 2003 to put a corps of about 50,000–60,000 troops into a crisis zone within 60 days and to sustain them there for a year. Germans very much want this to fit into (though not to be run by) NATO. This means that they also hope the United States will be helpful in defining the modalities by which this can be achieved. The cheaper America can make European 'autonomy', the better. Germany wants the US to lend a helping hand by providing Europeans with the lift capacity, the information assets, and the odd staff officer or crew chief to make the hand-over work. The issue will remain on the agenda for some time to come, no matter how novel the ideas for 'leasing', 'pooling' or otherwise 'sharing' military intervention capacity might be.

Germans are aware of the discussions about the consequences of their failure to raise defence spending, particularly investment spending, which has suffered seriously for the last ten years. The security community in Germany is skilled at using American spokesmen to further (and to legitimise) their goals, as noted above. Nevertheless, no one likes to be berated. Feelings get hurt. Relations can suffer.

The way in which Europe goes global – whether in defence, diplomacy or digitisation – will affect the Atlantic relationship for some time to come. Will Germany only be a trading power, or will it take 'responsibility'? The odds are that Germany's global engagement will grow. What Germany defines as 'responsible' will, however, still be contested. From Russia to China, from Iran to Indonesia, Germany sees these relationships much more in economic than strategic terms. This makes sanctions a problem. This makes questions about when jointly to apply pressure on the rogues of this world an important topic for discussion. Germany will continue to feel awkward about wielding a stick, any kind of stick, even one held firmly by the United States.

The US View

What Germany is 'willing to wield' when it comes to international security and 'responsibility' is at the centre of US concerns about the German–American relationship. The sharing of costs, not only of blood and treasure but also of political risks, is understandably a contentious issue. America has expected Germany to do more. This was part of Washington's argument for giving German unification significant support: the US would gain a stronger ally and forgo the risk of losing a stronger Germany. The US accepted, even expected, that a unified Germany would also be a more assertive Germany, a real partner in leadership. For the United States, more distant from Germany and economically secure, this prospect was easier to contemplate than it was for Germany's European partners.

US support was not enough: Germany has been reluctant to take on a role commensurate with its economic power (which, as noted, has grown more slowly than most expected). In retrospect, the US probably exaggerated the potential of Germany as a leadership partner. Germany has moved some way towards such a role, but not as far as the US thought or hoped. Germany thus remains at the centre of the transatlantic burden-sharing debate, which was stirred up by the Kosovo war, but is very much an enduring feature of the relationship.

Burden-sharing has been about leadership and responsibility, about military spending and the use of force. It has also been about relations with various other important regions of the world. The US is wary of a Germany interested in global commerce, but not in global security. Some in Washington might even see Germany's 'multilateralism' as a guise for maximising deals and minimising defence spending. The German relationship with Iran is seen in the US as a manifestation of this phenomenon. Many in the US view Europeans in general, and Germans in particular, as 'free-riders' when it comes security. Madeleine Albright, US Secretary of State, said to Germany: 'You may feel we pull the sanctions trigger too quickly; we feel you are too quick to go for contracts.' One reason why the US aims to have Germany as a global diplomatic-military power is to overcome this difference by giving it the sense of responsibility for global security that must go along with such a position.

While Iran, China or Russia might sometimes be the subject of different views, Americans have been pleased with Germany's work to bring Turkey closer to the European Union. The United States, wanting to keep Turkey ensconced in the Western camp, had long seen Germany as a big obstacle to a more open treatment of Turkey. By the same token, the US would like to see EU enlargement move more quickly, particularly as a way of exporting stability to the Baltic states and the Balkans. European Union enlargement raises far less concern in Washington than deepening. While, on the whole, the United States has been satisfied with the new trends in German foreign policy, it might have wished that they would progress even further and faster. The overall relationship between the United States and Germany is still strong even if Germany is not – or not yet – a bigger version of the United Kingdom in terms of global military power and capacity.

CONCLUSION

Continuity in the face of change? The two always seem to co-exist; so the relevant question becomes what changes and what does not. For Germany, fundamental views and principles about Germany's role in Europe and the world have endured. Germany has followed a clear line over the past decade: *Westbindung als Staatsräson* (Western integration as a fundamental goal of the state). The integrationist impulse and multilateralism as the most vital interest – Germans have put this goal above qualms about the use of military force. During the Kosovo War, government leaders enjoyed public support, despite briefly leaving the UN (and international law) outside the loop. Putting multilateralism first is still seen as enlightened self-interest. The intrinsic appeal of the Atlantic community of values certainly plays a role in this orientation. Germany's history of devastation and recovery has also served to anchor the norms of individual liberty, social democracy and international co-operation into the national psyche. The twentieth century has provided clear lessons for the Germans in regard to foreign policy.

For Germans, foreign policy means replacing the European balance of power with integration and co-determination. Germans also recognise, and continually hear, that this is best done by keeping America as a European power. Germans also see a need for global politics to move in an integrationist direction, with an Atlantic core. Germans prefer not to think about the possibility of this 'Atlantic core' facing a peer power military threat. They are, however, increasingly focused on the military problems involved in today's proliferation challenge, and on the military means required to fulfil the West's humanitarian impulse.

Germany's challenge has been to reconcile deep-seated principles with the changing international reality. Can multilateralism flourish in Europe without an assertive Germany? Can the commitment to peace be real without the readiness to use force? Can a deeper Europe be achieved when a wider Europe is necessary? Can burden and power be shared equitably between America and Europe? Can the Atlantic and the European be mutually reinforcing? The inherent tensions in Germany's foreign policy have been reshuffled during the last decade as Germany, Europe and the world have undergone fundamental changes. Germany has navigated these tensions with finesse. Its diplomacy has stood the test during the last ten years.

Indeed, in many ways, the biggest foreign policy challenge has been Germany's economic stagnation. Domestic problems, especially in the east, have consumed valuable political capital that could have been used to advance foreign policy objectives. (The defence budget might have benefited as well.) There is no doubt that an EU with a GDP growing at four per cent instead of two per cent would be more open to enlargement and more willing to give the member states' militaries the wherewithal to achieve the EU's aspiration of becoming a more powerful force in the world.

In seeking to reconcile different goals, Germany has moved, certainly in terms of assertiveness, and in a qualitatively significant way on military matters. It seems, however, that these moves have primarily been motivated by a desire to not undermine Germany's ties to the West, that is, Germany's multilateralism.

Germany has become more assertive; Germany has seized the initiative on a number of issues, from NATO enlargement to the EMU Stability Pact; it has pushed through its own sense of the community interest. Economic problems, however, have translated into assertiveness of a more parochial nature. Politicians do sometimes play 'anti-European' themes to the gallery, though they frequently relate to the perception that Europe costs too much, not that Europe is useless. The public discourse does show that talking about German 'interests' and 'influence' has become more legitimate. All the same, both are still very much defined in the European and Atlantic context. Germany will be the West's 'assertive multilaleralist' for some time.

Germany moved significantly on the use of force, though not because of any blood lust in the Bundeswehr, greediness in the arms industry, or aspirations to make Germany a 'global military power'. It was the lesson of Srebrenica and IFOR. It was also a consequence of the fact that the Left was holding the reigns of power and no longer interested in opposing the use of force to oppose the Kohl government. Whether on the ground or in the air, Germany's capability to be there in some future military crisis will increase. There are lessons in the Kosovo experience: if you fly with the best, you can set the terms of the peace; if you run your sector the way the Germans run Prizren, you can be a very valuable partner. If you have a good strategy, if you see all the pieces, you can do a lot to make the world a better place.

Multilateralism is Germany's meta-strategy. Go-it-alone politics are still anathema: Germans do not think unilateralism makes sense in today's world. This is not just the lesson that they have learned from history. Since at least the 1970s, Germans have also been astute observers, commentators and contributors to a variety of theories positing a growing international interdependence. Perceptions of global problems as common problems, of the transnational dynamic as the parallel to multiplying intergovernmental organisations, and of the overwhelming power of information technology to change the scale of interaction and make the world a smaller place (but a bigger market) have served to re-legitimise and redefine Germany's multilateralism. Indeed, the combination of historical need and global imperative has even introduced a certain notion of German 'exceptionalism' when it comes to multilateralism.

Transatlantic relations are much more than Germany and the United States, though these two are at their core. Brussels will grow in importance, but if people are talking about California's foreign policy, they should not be discounting Germany's foreign policy. Berlin will need to be on board both European and Atlantic initiatives. At the same time, it is increasingly clear that you will only get Berlin if you get Europe. Other actors are also very important. Great Britain is certainly number one when it comes to global military action and domestic economic organisation. But when it comes to Europe, Berlin usually wins over both London and Paris. The strong affinity between Germans and Americans that characterised the Bonn Republic has lived on. Berlin and Washington share many objectives, not only traditional ones about power and peace in Europe, but also on a whole host of challenges that have come with globalisation, both in the wider world and in the multiplicity of commercial and civil relationships across the Atlantic. It is hard to imagine what kind of future might make Europe and America go their own separate ways. It is very easy to imagine a multitude of scenarios in which Europe (and thus Germany) and America would have every interest in continuing to co-operate. Their habits and patterns of co-operation are very useful today; they could be of existential importance tomorrow.

NOTES

1. See 'Not By Bombs Alone', *The Economist*, 8 April 1999.
2. See statistics from www.oecd.org and www.bundesfinanzministerium.de/stabipro.pdf.
3. Michael Mertes, 'Die Gegenwart der Vergangenheit. Zur außenpolitischen Relevanz von Geschichtsbildern', *Internationale Politik*, 55/9 (Sept. 2000), pp.1–8.
4. Hans-Peter Schwarz, 'Die Politik der Westbindung oder die Staatsräson der Bundesrepublik.', *Zeitschrift für Politik*, 22 (1975), pp.307–37.
5. Sebastian Harnisch and Hanns W. Maull (eds.), *Germany – Still A Civilian Power? The Foreign Policy of the Berlin Republic* (Manchester: Manchester University Press, forthcoming, 2001), and Hans-Peter Schwarz, 'Die Zentralmacht Europas auf Kontinuitätskurs: Deutschland stabilisiert den Kontinent', Deutschland in Europa, *Internationale Politik*, 54/11 (Nov. 1999).
6. See the various survey results and analysis supporting this picture of Germany and provided for the Bundeswehr by the independent polling firm EMNID at www.bundeswehr.de (demoskopie).
7. 'Essential Aspects of German Security Policy', *German Security Policy and the*

Bundeswehr, http://www.bundeswehr.de/index_.html.

8. Roman Herzog, 'Die Grundkoordinaten deutscher Aussenpolitik', *Internationale Politik*, 50/4 (1995), pp.3–11.
9. 'Essential Aspects of German Security Policy ...' http://www.bundeswehr.de/index_.html.
10. Strobe Talbott, address, 'The New Europe and the New NATO', to the Deutsche Gesellschaft für Auswärtige Politik, Bonn, Germany, 4 Feb. 1999;   remarks/1999/990204 talbott transat.html.
11. Sebastian Harnisch, 'Deutsche Aussenpolitik nach der Wende: Zivilmacht am Ende?' Beitrag für den 21 DVPW-Kongress in Halle, 1–5 Oct. 2000, p.9. Available at: www.deutsche-aussenpolitik.de.
12. In discussion with the author, September 2000.
13. Harnisch, 'Deutsche Aussenpolitik nach der Wende: Zivilmacht am Ende?', p.43.
14. Ibid., p.25.
15. Ibid., p.9.
16. Hanns Maull initiated the discusion of the notion that German (and Japan) represented a new type of power. See Hanns W. Maull, 'Germany and Japan: The New Civilian Powers', *Foreign Affairs*, 69/5 (1990), pp.91–106. This civilian power mode is now said to consist of three central elements: (1) Desire to influence the environment; (2) forsaking autonomy; and (3) seeking to advance norms, even at the expense of interests. See Harnisch, 'Deutsche Aussenpolitik nach der Wende: Zivilmacht am Ende?', p.23.
17. 'Aufbruch und Erneuerung – Deutschlands Weg ins 21. Jahrhundert: Koalitionsvereinbarung zwischen der Sozialdemokratischen Partei Deutschlands und Bündnis 90/Die Grünen', Bonn, 20 Oct. 1998. Available at www.spd.de.
18. Hanns W. Maull, 'Germany and the Use of Force: Still a 'Civilian Power'?' *Survival*, 42/2 (Summer 2000), p.57.
19. 'We particularly commend Minister Scharping for speaking out so strongly for the critical funding needed to field the Bundeswehr of tomorrow ... I would like to add just a personal view, this is not any view of my government or others who serve in the government: truly complete reorientation of the Bundeswehr would involve even further, far more dramatic increases in the Crisis Reaction Force, perhaps doubling or even tripling its size.' Remarks delivered by Secretary of Defense William S. Cohen, Hamburg Congress Center, Hamburg, Germany, Wednesday, 1 Dec. 1999 (http://www.defenselink.mil/speeches/1999/s19991201-secdef1.html).
20. Henry Kissinger, among others, has expressed this concern: 'If ... Europe fails to make a real defense effort, resentments against American dominance will only increase. And if the quest for independence is driven largely by anti-American motives, it will saddle the Alliance with all the compulsive competitiveness that nearly destroyed Europe before the Atlantic Alliance was founded in 1949.' Henry Kissinger, 'The End of NATO as We Know It?' Los Angeles Times Syndicate, *Washington Post*, <www.washingtonpost.com> Sunday, 15 Aug. 1999, p.B07.
21. 'From Confederacy to Federation – Thoughts on the Finality of European Integration', speech by Joschka Fischer at the Humboldt University in Berlin, 12 May 2000, http://www.auswaertiges-amt.de/8_suche/index.htm.
22. Joschka Fischer, Herbert Quandt Lecture des Bundesministers des Auswärtigen vor der Georgetown-Universität Washington DC: 'Towards a New Transatlantic Partnership: The United States, Germany and Europe in an Era of Global Challenges', 11 Sept. 2000; http://auswaertiges-amt.de/2_aktuel/4/index.htm.
23. Karsten Voigt, 'Begründung eines neuen Atlantizismus: Von Partnerschaft zu euroatlantischer Gemeinschaft', Ungleiche Partner: Herausforderungen für die atlantische Gemeinschaft, *Internationale Politik*, 55/3 (March 2000), pp.3–10. Also available on the website www.dgap.org/.
24. John C. Kornblum, 'Ten Years of German Unity: An American View from Berlin', in *10 Years of German Unity* (Jaron Verlag, 2000); http://www.usembassy.de/us-botschaft-cgi/speech.cgi?lfdnr=1131.
25. Richard Holbrooke, 'America: A European Power', *Foreign Affairs* (March/April 1995).
26. Joschka Fischer, Herbert Quandt Lecture.

The European Policy-Making Machinery in the Berlin Republic: Hindrance or Handmaiden?

SIMON BULMER, ANDREAS MAURER AND
WILLIAM PATERSON

A NEW GERMAN EUROPEAN POLICY OR INSTITUTIONALISED CONTINUITY?

The characteristics of any member state's policy towards the European Union are bound up with the three 'I's': interests, institutions and identity. For many theorists of international relations it is the first of this trinity – national interests – which is paramount. Whether defined by the pursuit of security in an anarchic world or by the interplay of domestic preferences, in this view it is national interests which are the key to determining policy. The institutions in which European policy is formed, by contrast, are simply conveyor belts for transmitting domestic preferences to Brussels. The identitive dimension, moreover, is accorded negligible importance.

It is our argument that the relationship between the three 'I's' – at least in the German case – is rather different.[1] We argue that the Federal Republic's early engagement with European integration was at a time when national interests beyond the goal of international rehabilitation were, for historical reasons, suppressed, albeit with the notable exception of the pursuit of national unity. The consequence was that institutions and identity took on a greater role in the articulation of German European policy. External institutional constraints were of key importance to West Germany's semi-sovereignty in the post-war era, but domestic institutional constraints were also notable.[2] An openness to constructing a new international identity was part of the Bonn Republic's response to history.

The machinery created in the 1950s for German European policy-making has evolved incrementally over succeeding decades. It became increasingly complex as the scope of European integration widened. How would it respond to the new circumstances brought about by the end of the

Simon Bulmer, University of Manchester; Andreas Maurer, University of Cologne; William Paterson, University of Birmingham

Cold War and German unification? Would a fundamental reform be triggered? Or would the prevailing pattern of institutional pluralism persist, with implications for efforts to conduct a new German European policy? We argue that a change of interests alone is insufficient for such a new policy. Since 1989 a number of changes have indeed been made to the FRG's European policy-making machinery but it retains its complex and diffuse character. We examine the implications of this character for the prospects for continuity or change in the substance of German European policy.

In order to develop our argument we look back to the framework for European policy-making created with German participation in the three European Communities. We give a brief review of how that framework evolved prior to the seismic changes of 1989/90. What those changes brought about was a clear redefinition of the political and economic environment surrounding the FRG's engagement in integration, with potential consequences for national interests. A brief examination of these changes is undertaken before we turn to the adjustments that were made, during the period from 1989 to the present, to the European policy-making system in Germany. Did the major environmental changes lead to a fundamental reappraisal of the system? Did a fundamental change take place in European policy? We examine the present organisation of Germany's European policy machinery and evaluate its strengths and weaknesses. The latter have been seen as structural and in need of reform.[3] We also examine whether Germany's bilateral relations have been adjusted to reflect a major reappraisal of policy. Finally, we connect up our evaluation of the machinery with the broader question of whether German European policy-making reflects the changes which might be necessary to catch up with the post-1989 and post-Maastricht EU, or whether it remains on the path originally set in the early 1950s.

THE ORIGINS OF THE FRG'S EUROPEAN POLICY-MAKING MACHINERY

The origins of the European policy-making system are important to understanding present-day arrangements. Why? In essence, the ministerial responsibilities agreed at the time of the Treaties of Paris (1951) and Rome (1957) defined the pattern of development over the subsequent decades. Apart from the changes which were made as part of the ratification deal of the Maastricht Treaty, and which were designed to formalise the involvement of the Länder governments, the broad pattern of arrangements can be traced from 1951 up to changes made late in 1998.

The situation which the FRG faced in 1951 was unique. The Bonn Republic's institutions were new. They had been designed to create a diffusion of power. In addition, foreign policy responsibilities were weak owing to semi-sovereignty. The Foreign Office was only established in 1951, and Chancellor Adenauer was responsible for foreign policy in the absence of a foreign minister until 1955. For the Bonn Republic the prize offered by integration was the opportunity to regain some sovereignty over coal and steel as well as a pathway to acceptance in the European and international communities. Institutional design of the decision-making system for European policy was a less important concern. As a result of these specific circumstances the European policy machinery was highly influenced by the prevailing logic of government organisation. This situation, combined with the essentially economic substance of integration, resulted in the Federal Ministry for Economics taking on, *de facto*, the lead role in policy management for the European Coal and Steel Community (ECSC). Initially, this took the form of a sub-division created for ECSC affairs and headed by Hans von der Groeben.[4] An inter-ministerial committee, chaired by the ministry, brought together representatives from other ministries, such as the Foreign Office, the Federal Ministry of Finance or the Ministry for Justice to co-ordinate policy as necessary. The arrangements for the ECSC established the Ministry of Economics in a strong position on matters of functional integration, although there had been no formal agreement on the division of labour with the Foreign Office and the Chancellor's Office.

The creation of the European Economic Community (EEC) and Euratom took place in somewhat changed circumstances. The integration process was taking on a wider remit, for instance with the EEC Treaty's agricultural policy provisions, even if the core activities – the common market – still fell within the responsibilities of the Economics Ministry. Despite the appointment in 1955 of the first Foreign Minister, von Brentano, the close stewardship which Chancellor Adenauer had exercised over foreign policy did not disappear with that development. Indeed, his interest in the political purposes of integration was at odds with Economics Minister Erhard's more market-oriented approach. From the resultant tensions came the need for the definitive agreement on European policy responsibilities, reached in 1958.[5] In effect, Adenauer's policy goals prevailed over Erhard's and the Chancellor continued to use his powers to influence the guidelines of integration policy. However, the Ministry of Economics (BMWi) was entrusted with the task of co-ordinating day-to-day European policy. The Foreign Office, by contrast, was left with responsibility for long-term oriented 'integration' policy, a task in line with that ministry's diplomatic and political functions. These were to be the co-ordinating ministries except on those occasions where the Federal Chancellor wished to use other powers in the conduct of European policy: the Cabinet principle (whereby decisions disputed between individual ministers/ries are resolved in the

Cabinet) or his authority to set policy guidelines (*Richtlinienkompetenz*, whereby he takes a directive role on government policy). Beyond these ministries the others would deal with European policy according to the same division of labour as for domestic policy.

Is this account not just a story of bureaucratic history? Of course, there is an element of that but the resultant distribution of co-ordinating responsibilities has affected the federal government's ability to conduct its policy in Brussels by virtue of the complex division of responsibilities in Bonn. Seen from the outside, such as from a British or French perspective, the lack of a single co-ordinating ministry represents an obstacle to the most effective presentation of German interests within the EU. A more centralised system of European policy-making, such as that prevailing in the UK or in France, could be expected to have two consequences.[6] First, within the federal government, we might expect a shift from its strategy of 'shaping the regional milieu' to a more bottom-line, issue-by-issue, short-term view of German interests.[7] Second, in the subsequent diplomacy of the FRG within the EU, we might expect the presentation of a more co-ordinated German European policy. Diplomats from the Foreign Office (AA) are conscious of these aspirations which lie behind their efforts to improve co-ordination but no major change of approach is evident.[8]

Reform of the institutional pluralism of the current system is hampered by two sets of rather immovable features. The first is simply that the German political system is characterised by power-sharing between coalition partners, the principle of ministerial autonomy (Article 65, Basic Law) and a relatively weak norm of information-sharing between ministries. Closely connected with the weak notions of collective responsibility and cabinet government, this situation can lead to fluctuations in the influence of ministries – typically in line with the political importance of individual ministers. It can result in keynote speeches by ministers on European policy being presented in a personal capacity, with consequent ambiguity for fellow member states as to their status in connection with government policy.[9] Common to all member states, European policy is unlike 'normal' foreign policy, so diplomats' views may be criticised as inadequate. However, Germany's European policy-making machinery reflects the distinctive way in which the wide scope of European policy has been absorbed into the prevailing norms and institutional characteristics of government in the FRG. The second feature is the dead-weight of history: a fundamental reform of the division of labour in the co-ordinating system, as set down in the 1950s, requires a trigger of some kind. As we shall see below, German unification and the end of the Cold War proved insufficient to stimulate such a major reform. It is for that reason that we still need to know the origins of the system.

What happened between the decisions on European policy competencies of 1958 and the seismic political changes of 1989/90? The Economics Ministry's European Division (*Abteilung E*) served as the co-ordinating hub for European policy-making. For example, it co-ordinated issuing instructions to the Permanent Representative regarding positions to be taken in meetings of the Committee of Permanent Representatives. It served as the official location from which information was shared to other domestic players in the European policy machinery, such as the Bundestag and Bundesrat. The Foreign Office, by contrast, was confined to maintaining an overview of integration policy and institutional issues, assisted by a set of departments shadowing European policy activities across the rest of the Bonn government. Over time, the Finance and Agriculture Ministries came to have such important, substantive engagement with European policy-making that, together with the AA and BMWi, they became known as the 'four musketeers'. Other ministries, such as Youth, Family and Health, Research and Technology, or Labour and Social Affairs, were brought into the European policy process when the EC impinged upon their domestic responsibilities. The Federal Ministry of Justice offered legal advice; however, the BMWi took responsibility for defending the FRG before the European Court of Justice. Such developments took place incrementally within the existing framework of co-ordination.

At the political level, co-ordination was rather intermittent. The Chancellor could take initiatives if integration became a policy area which the incumbent chose to emphasise, such as Helmut Schmidt did with the launch of the European Monetary System in the late 1970s or Helmut Kohl did with promoting the Schengen Agreement. A small staff in the Federal Chancellor's Office could support such initiatives, which became a greater option for the Chancellor following the launch of the European Council in 1974. Consultation with other ministers could be undertaken in the Cabinet.[10] It was also open to the Foreign Minister to take similar initiatives, although they would not necessarily carry the same degree of governmental authority. Nevertheless, Hans-Dietrich Genscher's lengthy tenure as Foreign Minister (1974–92) enabled him to play such a role, for example, through the Genscher–Colombo Initiative of 1981. Also a key member of the AA's European policy team was the junior minister responsible for European policy, commencing in 1972 with Hans Apel.[11] With Apel's appointment the co-ordination of the Committee of State Secretaries for European Affairs moved to the AA. However, until the change of government in Autumn 1998, the secretariat of the committee was provided by the BMWi. Other committees – the 'Tuesday Committee' to prepare meetings of the Committee of Permanent Representatives (COREPER I) or an informal group bringing together European specialists in federal ministries for more open-ended discussions (the Group of European Specialists) – were co-ordinated by the BMWi.

The other development in the European policy machinery was the increasing impact of EC business upon the Länder governments, collectively represented in the Bundesrat.[12] Initially handled by informal agreements between the Länder and the federal government, the ratification of the Single European Act and the Maastricht Treaty provided an opportunity for the Länder governments, via the Bundesrat, to require more formalised involvement. With the growth of the EC's legislative output (1951–79 on average 214 legal acts per annum; 1979–86 on average 622 acts per annum) the Länder governments were also increasingly responsible for the transposition and implementation of EC law.

By the end of the 1980s German European policy-making had become impeded by sectorisation and bureaucratisation. The former was typically illustrated by the Agriculture Ministry indirectly blocking the Finance Ministry's wish to reduce German EC budget contributions through increasing the costs of the Common Agricultural Policy. The latter was illustrated by the AA's need to have two representatives from each member state on the committee charged with transforming the Genscher–Colombo initiative into what became the Solemn Declaration on European Union of 1984 because of a lack of agreement in the AA as to which division should provide the German members.[13] This was a clear case of the 'primacy of procedures' rather than the 'primacy of policy'.[14] At the same time, however, Chancellor Kohl or Foreign Minister Genscher demonstrated that they could provide an effective lead to European policy when they chose to invest their efforts in the constitutional policy area. German European policy-making was better on strategy, where the Chancellor could assert authority, than on detailed tactical considerations, where the complexities of co-ordination could hamper clarity.

One further dimension of German European policy-making deserves mention, namely the Franco-German relationship (also see below). The relationship has formed the cornerstone of integration since the ECSC. Thus, where German and French preferences have coincided around a particular initiative, it has stood a strong chance of forming the basis of debate within the wider European arena. This dimension is not just a matter of preferences, however, since it is clear that Franco-German initiatives have become a routine even where preferences are not particularly close.

Although the pattern of European policy-making was somewhat atypical in the FRG, because of the prominence of the BMWi, a smooth adaptation to the integration process (Europeanisation[15]) took place. However, it is worth pointing out that two German institutions did not fit into the pattern in the same way. The Bundesbank defended its autonomy from the federal government and was prepared to pursue its monetary policy goals single-mindedly even when they were at odds with the broad line of policy pursued by Bonn. This situation was most evident in the later years of the European Monetary System. It was a factor in the French government's advocacy of monetary union as a way of achieving the ultimate Europeanisation of the Bundesbank, namely through its absorption into the European Central Bank. The other institution which placed limits on Europeanisation was the Bundesverfassungsgericht (BVG), which firmly defended the primacy of the German legal order, most notably but not exclusively in the Maastricht judgment of 1993. However, the BVG is concerned with the judicial consequences of European policy rather than the making of it.

THE NEW GERMANY IN THE NEW EUROPE: CHANGING CONSTRAINTS AND RESOURCES

German unification and the end of the Cold War represented fundamentally changed circumstances for German European policy. We cannot summarise all the changes but identify a few as a way of highlighting the new opportunities and constraints.[16] Most obviously, German unification brought with it the end of the FRG's 'provisional' status. The shift of the seat of government from Bonn to Berlin is symbolic of this normalisation process. The withdrawal of the majority of military forces from German soil symbolised the ending of semi-sovereignty and the removal of external constraints on the FRG. German vulnerability at the front-line of the Cold War was ended.[17] That Berlin is now the seat of government of the FRG after decades of vulnerability to fluctuating superpower relations is the most obvious illustration. Did these changed circumstances simply serve to liberate the shaping conditions of the FRG's European policy? Could attention now be directed to the increasing challenges posed by globalisation? And were a number of historians correct to look back to the nineteenth century to declare 'Germany is back' and in this way seek to understand Germany's new position in Europe?[18]

The 'new Europe' also imposed some new expectations. In the foreign and security policy arenas expectations about Germany's contribution were raised in certain respects. The limitation of German forces to the NATO area began to look anomalous in the context of American troop withdrawals from Europe. Could Germany remain a civilian power in these circumstances?[19] Central and East European applicants for participation in European integration began to see the FRG as their advocate. This development placed the FRG in some difficulty as it had to weigh up its preferences for political stability on its eastern borders with the indirect costs of enlargement, via the EU budget, upon its strained public finances.

In addition, the expectations on the German economy's traditional role as the powerhouse of the European economy appeared more problematic in the aftermath of unification, as the scale of the challenge of modernising the new Länder became apparent.

The impact of the new circumstances was not simply to strengthen Germany's potential power in Europe. In any case, potential power and its deployment are quite different matters. Would enhanced power lead to a more interest-driven European policy than in the past? In abstract terms we are brought back to the relationship between interests, institutions and identity. It is clear that some German interests have changed. A notable example is the wish to have security from crime and economic migration flows from the east. On the other hand, Chancellor Kohl's commitment to monetary and political union was part of a continuing wish to pursue the same path to European integration:[20] to pursue self-restraint (*Selbsteinbindung*) as a political objective even where, in monetary policy terms, the existing European Monetary System secured German goals rather well. Here Germany's commitment to multilateralism as a goal in its own right seemed to be reconfirmed, thereby raising at the very least major questions about the defining of interests and preferences. For some observers, it suggested that Germany had become institutionally embedded in the EU, and that this embeddedness had become part of the FRG's identity to such an extent that these were factors taking precedence over the definition of interests and preferences.[21]

Thus, the picture emerging from German unification and the end of the Cold War is much more complex than at first sight. Circumstances had changed but would the response be to trigger a fundamental reappraisal of German European policy? To take German unification as an example, one of the FRG's few 'national interests' throughout the period of European integration had been to keep open the possibility of a solution to the German question, such as by means of the Protocol on Interzonal Trade attached to the EEC Treaty. Although sometimes regarded as ritualistic, this diplomacy was in fact vindicated by the events of 1989/90. In consequence, the AA could regard this aspect of policy as well as its whole strategy of integration into the West as vindicated rather than there being a trigger for fundamental reappraisal.

DECISION-MAKING AND CO-ORDINATION: AN OVERVIEW

What have been the changes to the policy-making system in the period since 1989/90? Has there been an effort to develop a decision-making system that can follow a more issue-by-issue, interest-oriented approach on the part of the federal government? Or do continuity and pragmatism find reflection in a continuance of the long-standing institutional framework for European policy?

There have been two major changes in policy-making since 1989/90, mixed with some incremental refinements. Paradoxically, the two major changes have primarily been the product of factors *other than* directly responding to German unification and the end of the Cold War. Thus, the main reform following the Maastricht Treaty was to give the Länder a greater say in European policy-making. The most recent reform of the Schröder government was to transfer to the Federal Finance Ministry from the BMWi the traditional power to issue instructions for COREPER I (see below): a power which the latter had held since the 1950s. However, this reform was chiefly the product of inter-party coalition negotiations: to emphasise to EU partners the political profile of Finance Minister Oskar Lafontaine over the non-party appointment of Werner Müller as Economics Minister. As we shall argue, neither of these moves can be regarded as assisting the presentation of a coherent European policy. But we must not be seduced by these two headline-grabbing changes, because there have been some less obvious administrative reforms that have strengthened the AA's co-ordinating role. We consider first of all the changes since 1989/90, and then give an overview of the system as of 1999.

Five changes in the machinery relating to making European policy can be linked to the Maastricht phase of integration. The most significant of these was the revision of the Basic Law (Article 23) to give the participation of the Länder in European policy-making constitutional recognition, where 'their legislative powers are affected'. This development was important to the Länder but formalised a more decentralised European policy-making machinery.[22] The second development also occurred through constitutional revision (Articles 23 and 45) and related to the Bundestag. The decision to establish a Committee for EU Affairs (EU-Committee) was designed to enhance the Bundestag's effectiveness in participating in the EU policy process. A third development arose from the creation of the third pillar of the EU. The consequence was to create a much bigger impact of integration upon the Federal Interior Ministry and the Federal Justice Ministry. Both ministries had already been engaged in home affairs and justice co-operation prior to the Maastricht Treaty (TREVI network on combating criminality and police co-operation, Schengen Agreement on free movement of persons). However, it was the Maastricht Treaty which brought about a formalised role for both ministries in the federal government's EU policy-making machinery. A fourth development was the decision within the AA to create a European Division. Set up in 1993 the *Europaabteilung* was indeed a reflection of the new European architecture of the post-Cold War era, creating a new European policy purpose within the ministry. Moreover, the fact that the AA became strongly involved in EU policy-making across all three pillars gave it a kind of ascendancy over the BMWi, whose remit remained restricted to the European Community pillar. The mere presence of a Foreign Office division head responsible for European policy – initially Dr Hans-Friedrich von Ploetz, who was then promoted to state secretary – gave a new focus within the 'house'.[23] As will be seen, the AA has sought to improve its position incrementally over the subsequent years. The final development was the creation of a European Division in the Finance Ministry: a development which has subsequently been followed in a number of other ministries.

The second of the two sets of changes came in conjunction with the formation of the SPD/Green coalition of Chancellor Gerhard Schröder. The transfer of the power to issue negotiating instructions from the BMWi to the Finance Ministry was motivated by the share-out of posts in the new coalition and strengthened the power base of SPD chairman Oskar Lafontaine as an alternative pole to that of Gerhard Schröder in the Chancellor's Office. Over the post-war period federal governments had tended to push economic and financial interests within the EU rather than overtly power-political ones. Thus, Lafontaine's responsibilities had the potential for a new, even more active policy in these fields, dwarfing the lightweight European-policy role of recent FDP economics ministers and building upon the important European profile which Theo Waigel had given the ministry during the years of negotiating EMU. The need for a new medium-term budgetary settlement as part of Agenda 2000 offered an opportunity to evaluate whether Lafontaine and the ministry might develop a new assertiveness within the EU and within the federal government and its European policy. Whilst such an assertiveness did develop over the need to balance EMU with employment policy initiatives, it did not become more widespread before Lafontaine resigned from the coalition in March 1999 because of differences with Schröder over the direction of government policy generally. Lafontaine's successor, Hans Eichel, played a lower key role in European policy such that the reorganisation of 1998 now appears simply to have been a 'rearrangement of the furniture' rather than wholesale re-equipment. However, it should be noted that the AA did take the opportunity to strengthen its position in the administrative arrangements (see below) for inter-ministerial policy co-ordination.

Who, therefore, are the key players in European policy-making at the federal level?

The Foreign Office (AA)

The AA has extended its responsibilities for European policy beyond what was provided for under the 1958 Erhard-von Brentano agreement, albeit in an incremental manner. The growth of European Political Co-operation activity into the Common Foreign and Security Policy (CFSP) of the post-

Maastricht era has strengthened its position in the balance between federal ministries in recent times. The creation of the European Division in 1993 certainly had an energising effect. Moreover, the AA extended its responsibilities for co-ordination, for example by playing the lead role on relations with the Central and Eastern European countries to the extent of issuing instructions to the Permanent Representation in Brussels directly. This example illustrates the way in which the BMWi, which had traditionally acted as a conduit for instructions from the federal government, lost control. Two developments are responsible: the sheer growth of EU business to the extent that using a single conduit is no longer possible; and the emergence of a new division of labour for preparing COREPER. The latter arrangement was confirmed at the end of 1998, with the AA responsible for instructions transmitted to COREPER II, and the Finance Ministry responsible for instructions to COREPER I (see also Table 3).[24] The AA has also developed co-ordinating functions for special issues, such as the 1996/97 and 2000 inter-governmental conferences and EU enlargement: supported by designated task forces and the co-ordination of related inter-ministerial meetings.

The ministerial level has also been an important determinant of the AA's importance within federal coalitions. Under Genscher the ministry became an important force within government-wide discussions. However, under his successor, the FDP minister Klaus Kinkel (1992–98), it was less able to do so. Lacking the political weight of Genscher, Kinkel was more akin to a bureaucratic actor, for instance through having the AA's opposition to the 1994 Schäuble/Lamers paper on integration written into the coalition agreement. The European minister in the AA, from 1987 to 1998 also drawn from the FDP (latterly Werner Hoyer), tended to be relatively weak politically within the coalition, although occupying a key EU co-ordinating role through chairing the Committee of State Secretaries for European Affairs. Given Helmut Kohl's assertion of his *Richtlinienkompetenz* in the run-up to Maastricht, there was a tendency amongst observers, as the 1996/97 Inter-Governmental Conference approached, to almost discount the views emanating from the AA and its ministers in the expectation that Kohl would take over at the late stage.

The AA has without doubt strengthened its position in the European policy machinery in the 1990s. But assessments from within the ministry tend to gloss over its relative weakness in comparison with other foreign ministries in the EU.[25] The AA still has to contend with the fact that EU co-ordination on EC pillar matters is conducted by another ministry; that the Länder have a say on matters of integration that affect their responsibilities; and that the Federal Chancellor is able to intervene both in grand initiatives or on very detailed matters. The AA simply does not have pre-eminent status in articulating German policy in Brussels. Finally, the AA has itself at times been somewhat disunited on European policy, as was illustrated in the aftermath of the creation of the European Division. The new division and Political Division 2 could not agree on who should be responsible for the co-ordination of CFSP. The resultant patch-up between the two divisions was scarcely conducive to the clear articulation of national interests in CFSP matters and weakened the purpose of the AA's reforms. A recent reorganisation has integrated European bilateral relations and EU business within the same command structure. However, the competition between the 'diplomats' in the Political Division and the 'co-ordinators' in the European Division has not been eased.

Under the Schröder government the Green Foreign Minister Joschka Fischer has been able to strengthen the AA's voice in European policy, building upon his popularity and articulateness. Fischer has not made massive changes by introducing sympathetic 'party-book' diplomats, but has largely adopted traditional AA positions on Europe. These have included an emphasis on the importance of the Franco-German relationship (balancing the Chancellery-based attempts to promote British–German relations) and constitutional reform in the EU, but with a more distinct political profile than that of his immediate predecessor. He has been an influential figure in the run-up to IGC 2000, and has had no significant counter-line to contend with from the SPD, as the leading coalition partner (unlike his predecessor's experience with the Schäuble/Lamers paper, for instance).[26]

The Federal Ministry of Finance (BMF)

Over the years the Ministry of Finance has also grown in importance as a key player in European policy. Customs duties, Economic and Monetary Union, the EC budget and taxation approximation are amongst the substantive concerns of the BMF that have made it a key player. In addition, the new powers of issuing instructions to COREPER I, transferred in 1998, have raised it to a new importance. Of the federal ministries it is 'number 2' in the Berlin Republic. Apart from the policy responsibilities noted above, its new duties since late 1998 include disseminating documents on EC pillar business, representing the FRG before the ECJ, relations with the Bundesrat, co-ordination of preparations for COREPER I and acting as deputy to the AA on those committees where the latter holds the chair. It is somewhat difficult to reach a definitive judgement on how the ministry will achieve an amalgamation of these diverse tasks. The changes were initiated on the eve of the German presidency, in the run-up to the upheavals of the federal government's move to Berlin, and had to contend with Lafontaine's resignation and the arrival of Hans Eichel as his successor. It is perhaps more appropriate to set out possible scenarios than to reach potentially premature judgements. One scenario would see the ministry's EU responsibilities being principally of bureaucratic importance: the BMF has simply inherited tasks from the BMWi that will be co-located with its traditional concerns about financial probity in the EC budget and the pursuit of sound finances in EMU. That the negotiation of EMU has been completed and the Agenda 2000 reforms agreed during the German presidency would thus give Eichel less opportunity to achieve a significant EU profile than was the case for both Theo Waigel and, briefly, Oskar Lafontaine. Another scenario, however, might see a German finance minister combining political and administrative weight to advocate German economic interests within the EU in a way that foreign ministers have eschewed. Oskar Lafontaine might well have been strong competition for Joschka Fischer in the European diplomatic arena.

Evidence thus far suggests potential for the latter scenario to develop. Eichel's interests do not coincide with Lafontaine's neo-Keynesianism. However, his political position has been strengthened as a result of securing domestic budgetary reform. Unlike his predecessors, he is also less encumbered by contending positions emerging from the Bundesbank, owing to the European Central Bank's importance. Eichel is in a position, therefore, to promote a European policy of financial discipline, articulating German budgetary interests in a more hard-nosed manner.

The Federal Ministry for Food, Agriculture and Forestry (BML)

The BML has been one of the key players in European policy since the 1960s. There is scarcely any part of the ministry that is not subject to European legislation. The importance of the Common Agricultural Policy (CAP) has been instrumental in this development. However, the BML has been one of the bastions of a sectorised European policy over the years because of its resistance to agricultural reform – at least until recent times. Several explanations may be offered for the BML's ability to frustrate the wish expressed by several finance ministers and chancellors to cut back on the EC budget, of which the CAP remains the largest spending programme. One explanation traces the situation to institutional features. The EU is weak at horizontal policy co-ordination, so German agricultural ministers could join their counterparts and defend the status of agriculture without having to confront finance ministers. Weak horizontal co-ordination in the federal government is replicated at EU level. A second explanation revolves around the BML being 'captured' by farmers' interests at administrative and political levels, resulting in a coalition against CAP reform. A final explanation draws attention to the persistence until 1993 of agriculture ministers both from junior coalition parties and from Bavaria, the most agricultural western Land. These ministers were seen as playing an electoral card in seeking to enhance their political profile. Whichever of these arguments is adhered to – and evidence supports elements of all three – the result was that the BML could not always be relied on to be singing from the same hymn-sheet as other ministries. As a result of new agricultural circumstances following German unification, increased horizontal co-ordination at EU level and more coalition-oriented agriculture ministers the BML has come somewhat more into line, as was evidenced during the Agenda 2000 negotiations on CAP reform.

The Federal Ministry of Economics (BMWi)

As has been indicated above, the Economics Ministry was a key player at bureaucratic level until the reform of policy-making in October 1998. Its important co-ordinating responsibilities were a source of occasional bureaucratic friction with the AA. Its ministers tended not to speak out on European policy and had been losing influence within the government over a decade or so. Following the 1998 reform it has also slipped down the hierarchy of ministries in organisational terms because it lost out on co-ordination tasks to the AA and on instructing COREPER I to the BMF. Its involvement is now confined to those policy areas where it holds functional responsibilities. These include many policy issues related to the internal market, trade policy, regional policy, competition policy and so on. The BMWi remains an important player in EU policy-making but its position is being challenged by more recently Europeanised ministries, such as the Federal Ministry of the Interior.

The Federal Ministry of the Interior (BMI)

The BMI entered the inner group of ministries engaged in European policy-making with the Maastricht Treaty. Its substantive responsibilities include asylum and visa policy and policing. With the Amsterdam Treaty making an area of freedom, security and justice a matter of priority, as well as integrating the Schengen Agreement into the realm of the EC and the EU treaties, the BMI has become a key player in European policy-making. For instance, it has been instrumental in pushing for agreements with applicant states to ensure that they do not become transit states for economic migrants heading for Germany from the ex-Soviet Union.[27]

The tasks brought in by the Amsterdam Treaty are handled by three divisions which have had a long-standing engagement in inter-governmental co-operation on such matters. Only on EU co-operation on judicial affairs does the BMI need to share its responsibilities, namely with the Justice Ministry. During the negotiations leading to the Amsterdam Treaty, tensions between the BMI and the Länder (with CSU support from Bavaria) on the

TABLE 1
THE CHANCELLOR'S OFFICE, THE MINISTRIES AND THEIR EUROPEAN AFFAIRS
UNITS (AS AT JANUARY 2000)

Ministries	EU-Related Divisions	EU-Related Sub-Divisions	EU-Related Departments
FOREIGN OFFICE Provides Chair of the Committee of State Secretaries for European Affairs	Division E Political Division (CFSP-COREU)	 2 Sub-divisions	4 Departments each and Task Force (1995–97) on the IGC and (since 1997) on enlargement. In July 1998, the political affairs Division's Departments for bilateral relations with EU Member States moved to E Division. Since 10/1998 the E Division also provides the Secretariat of the Committee of State Secretaries on EC Affairs.
INTERIOR	Division V Division P (Police) Division A (Asylum and Foreign Nationals)	....	Working group V I 4 (EC law), Department V I 5 (EP election law), Department V II 4 (German Internal Affairs unit to the Permanent Representative), Department P 6 (police co-operation), Department A 6 (EU Harmonisation of Treatment of Foreign Nationals)
JUSTICE	Division E	2 Sub-divisions	6 Departments each
FINANCE Provides deputy chairman of the committee of state secretaries on European affairs since 10/1998	Division E (European policy Division IX (international finance/ monetary policy	3 Sub-divisions 1 Sub-division	16 Departments , including the representation of Germany before the European Court of Justice
ECONOMICS	Division I (economic policy Division V (foreign 1 economic and European – formerly Division E)	Sub-division VD European policy	4 Departments (regional economic policy of the EU and cross-border co-operation) 4 Departments
AGRICULTURE	Division 6	2 Sub-divisions	13 Departments and Project Group 33 (BSE)

(cont.)

Ministries	EU-Related Divisions	EU-Related Sub-Divisions	EU-Related Departments
LABOUR AND SOCIAL AFFAIRS	Division VII	1 Sub-division	5 Departments
FAMILY AFFAIRS, SENIOR CITIZENS, WOMEN AND YOUTH	....	....	Departments for European and International Women and Family Affairs, Policy for Senior Citizens, and Youth Policy
HEALTH	....	1 Sub-division	
TRANSPORT	....	....	1 Department (EU, OECD, Council of Europe, ECE and OSCE)
ENVIRONMENT	....	....	1 Department (EU, Council of Europe, OSCE, Bilateral co-op eration with EC Member States)
EDUCATION, SCIENCE AND TECHNOLOGY	....	Sub-division 12 Sub-division 31 Sub-division 42	5 Departments dealing with EC affairs 1 Department on Higher Education and EC affairs 1 Department on European Science co-operation
ECONOMIC CO-OPERATION	Division 4	Sub-division 40	2 Departments
REGIONAL PLANNING, BUILDING AND URBAN DEVELOPMENT	....	....	Department on Harmonization of technical norms and Working Group on European co-operation
CHANCELLOR'S OFFICE	DIVISION 2 DIVISION 4	GROUP 21 (Foreign Affairs) GROUP 41 (Economic affairs)	DEPARTMENT 211 DEPARTMENTS 411 and 412

Note: *Abteilung* is translated as division; *Unterabteilung* as sub-division; and *Referat* as department.

Sources: Organisation plans of the Federal ministries and the Federal Chancellery, various dates.

TABLE 2
DIVISION OF LABOUR BY MINISTRY HOLDING THE PRESIDENCY FOR, AND
ACTING AS REPRESENTATIVE OF, THE FRG IN COUNCIL WORKING GROUPS
DURING GERMAN PRESIDENCIES (1988–99)

Ministry	1988		1994		1999	
	Pres	Spoke	Pres	Spoke	Pres	Spoke
Foreign Affairs	2	1	22 (+20)	22 (+21)	30 (+8)	25 (+3)
Economics	29	48	23 (-6)	49 (-1)	38 (+15)	46 (-3)
Agriculture	18	23	42 (+24)	51 (+28)	63 (+21)	64 (+13)
Finance	13	30	2 (-11)	30 (-)	19 (+17)	48 (18)
Justice	24	25	20 (-4)	22 (-3)	33 (+13)	31 (+9)
Interior	3	3	18 (+15)	21 (+18)	33 (+15)	33 (+12)
Labour	3	4	4 (+1)	5 (+1)	1 (-3)	1 (-4)
Transport	4	4	3 (-1)	8 (+4)	1 (-2)	6 (-2)
Youth, Family, Health	3	13	23 (+20)	28 (+15)	35 (+12)	28 (-)
Education, Science, Technology	1	2	4 (+3)	6 (+4)	2 (-2)	0 (-6)
Environment	2	3	2 (-)	6 (+3)	8 (+6)	8 (+2)
Economic Co-operation	0	5	0 (-)	4 (-1)	1 (+1)	1 (-3)
Regional Planning	2	4	1 (-1)	2 (+2)	1 (-)	2 (-)
Permanent Representation	91	26	96 (+5)	30 (+4)	84 (-8)	49 (+19)
Others	2	3	4 (+2)	13 (+10)	2 (-2)	1 (-12)
Total	197	194	264	297	351	343

Key: Pres = Presidency of the Council; Spoke = Speaker of the German delegation in the Council.
Sources: For 1988 and 1994: Wolfgang Wessels and Dietrich Rometsch, 'German Administrative Interaction and the European Union', in Yves Mény, Pierre Muller and Jean-Louis Quermonne (eds.), *Adjusting to Europe* (London: Routledge, 1996), p.83; for 1999: Draft minutes of the European Delegates meeting of 15 December 1998, Auswärtiges Amt, Bonn, 18 Dec. 1998.

one hand, and Chancellor Kohl and the AA on the other were evident. The latter group was willing to see integration of home affairs go further than the former group. The Ministry of the Interior is to a large degree dependent on decisions of its counterparts at Land level. The latter achieved concessions in this policy area during the ratification of the Amsterdam Treaty.

All federal ministries have now had to set up divisions (*Abteilungen*) or departments (*Referate*) to deal with EU business. An indication of the arrangements at the start of 2000 is given in Table 1. Only the Ministry of Defence is excluded. However, it is anticipated that the commitments of the December 1999 Helsinki European Council – for defence co-operation, a Military Committee and so on – will result in this gap being filled. The institutional changes are likely to take place within the Ministry's departments responsible for WEU. In a number of cases, the federal ministries have to liase with their counterparts in the 16 Länder to arrive at an agreed position to advocate in Brussels. This is typically the case in environmental, education, youth or culture policy, for instance. Table 2 gives a crude indication of the balance of EU-related activities of the federal ministries, and how these activities have developed between the German presidencies of 1994 and 1999. The Red–Green coalition initially upgraded the standing of the Ministry of the Environment (BMU) by giving it permanent membership of the Committee of State Secretaries for European Affairs. However, during the German presidency of the EU (first half of 1999) Environment Minister Trittin was harshly confronted with the principles of policy-making. On the instruction of Chancellor Schröder he was obliged to defer a Council common position regarding the Commission's 1997 proposed directive obliging motor manufacturers to recycle old cars at their own expense. After intense lobbying by the Ferdinand Piech of Volkswagen (and President of both the German and European motor manufacturers' associations), Gerhard Schröder, himself a former VW Supervisory Board member, invoked his *Richtlinienkompetenz* to oblige Trittin to block acceptance of the legislation.[28]

The Federal Chancellor's Office (BKA)

The BKA is an important player in European policy-making but it is neither a functional ministry nor does it fulfil the 'ringmaster' role pursued by the Cabinet Office as in the UK context. In other words, it is not the strategic hub of governmental policy, from which radiates a set of spokes aiming at the close co-ordination of government policy as a whole. The Chancellor's Office plays a much more limited role which is determined by the Chancellor's policy priorities and guidelines. Under Chancellor Kohl, the BKA assumed particular importance in general terms at the time of German unification, as Kohl oversaw the realisation of that process. Kohl's personal engagement for European integration, together with an eventual strengthening of his advisory staff and increased involvement in European affairs on the part of the junior ministerial level, resulted in an upgrading of the BKA's involvement in European policy-making.[29] Although the Chancellor's *Richtlinienkompetenz* suggests that European policy initiatives from the BKA should hold sway, there were tensions with the BMI over Justice and Home Affairs in connection with both the Maastricht and Amsterdam treaties. In addition, in the negotiations associated with Intergovernmental Conferences (IGCs) the AA ultimately has to hand over to the Chancellor and his foreign policy advisers when the negotiating package needs final settlement at a European Council session. Despite the exchange of staff between the AA and BKA there is no guarantee of that hand-over being seamless. Moreover, political tensions could develop if the Chancellor were to adopt a different approach to European policy than his

Foreign Minister. For EU partners that would also raise the issue as to which was 'the' European policy of the federal government. During the work of the Reflection Group prior to the 1996/97 IGC some member governments perceived that Elmar Brok, the CDU MEP and one of two representatives of the European Parliament on the Group, was intimate with the policy preferences of Chancellor Kohl. This was a cause of frustration for AA Minister of State, Werner Hoyer, the federal government's real representative, and for the Foreign Office. In this case the policy differences between the AA and the Chancellor were of less significance than the perceptions of other member governments that Chancellor Kohl rather than the AA would be the key player in German European policy at the IGC.

At the bureaucratic level there are two divisions within the BKA that are concerned with European policy. Division 2 is responsible for foreign and integration policy, whereas Division 4 is responsible for overseeing how policy is conducted on a more routine level, including the EU's 'third pillar'. The BKA has slender resources and cannot, in consequence, expect to be able to challenge the expertise in the individual ministries. Hence the BKA's real significance is five-fold. First, it plays a key role in bilateral relations with EU counterparts, which form an important context to EU policy-making. Second, it is of great importance in preparing the Chancellor for meetings of the European Council. Third, it is at the service of the Chancellor to assist with any European policy initiatives he may pursue, such as Kohl's support for Schengen and the TREVI police co-operation network ahead of Maastricht. Schröder's use of the BKA has been characterised thus far by developing bilateral relations (see below), and by the important tasks he faced during the German presidency, including the Agenda 2000 negotiations where he had to balance German budgetary austerity with the need for an agreement to reached. We need a rather longer time-frame than this to be certain of whether Schröder will pursue an active European policy strategy supported by the BKA; or whether his involvement will be one of intervening in the affairs of technical ministries (for example, on the recycling of cars). Fourth, the Chancellor has the task of settling political disputes over European policy within the Cabinet. Disputes can arise at a multitude of levels; their resolution is the purpose of the co-ordination arrangements. Finally, the Chancellor is in a position to develop a European policy 'vision', depending on priorities.

Co-ordination Arrangements

The standing co-ordination arrangements are set out in Table 3. The basic principle for all committees is that ministries attend as necessary but those most affected by the EU are present regularly. Co-ordination of positions is sought at the lowest level but is passed upwards to the next level if

TABLE 3

INTERMINISTERIAL CO-ORDINATION BODIES FOR EUROPEAN POLICY

Body	Level	Frequency	Chair	Nature of issues
Cabinet	Ministerial	Agenda items as needed	Chancellor/BKA	Important political matters
Committee of State Secretaries for European Affairs	State (Permanent) Secretaries	Approx. monthly	Minister of State for Europe, AA; deputy – BMF	Political
Group of European Specialists	European Specialists (officials)	Approx 1-2 months	AA	Exchanges on policy by officials
Preparation of COREPER I	Section heads	Weekly	BMF	Instructions to COREPER I
Preparation of COREPER II	Section heads	Weekly	AA[45]	Instructions to COREPER II

Note: There are exceptions: COREPER II meetings with regard to the Councils on ECOFIN,
Budget, Finance and Tax policy are co-ordinated by the Ministry of Finance.

agreement cannot be reached. A striking feature is that preparations for COREPER follow two different routines depending on which of its formations is to be prepared. Here we see the AA and the BMF demarcating terrain where each holds co-ordination responsibility. The Länder governments have been involved for relevant agenda items following the new Article 23 Basic Law. The substance of preparations in the two committees is overwhelmingly technical and relates to agenda issues in the two formations of COREPER and the many working parties hierarchically subordinate to them. The meetings to prepare COREPER I and II do not tend to resolve differences in the positions of individual ministries.

The Group of European Specialists, established in 1971, brings together the European specialists (at head of department level) and the Deputy Permanent Representative to deal with planning and routine matters rather than political issues. It meets about every two months, but more frequently in the run-up to a German presidency of the EU. It is not really a body for resolving policy differences, which are left to the Committee of State Secretaries for European Affairs, established in 1963. In the post-Maastricht period this body became larger in membership and more unwieldy. Efforts have been made to slim it down but the new importance of co-operation on home affairs, for example, makes this goal difficult to achieve. The Permanent Representative also attends. The top level of policy-resolution is in the Cabinet. Owing to entrenched ministerial autonomy and coalition politics, this arena is more frequently used to settle matters than is the case in the UK for instance.

The Permanent Representation

The Permanent Representation (StV) is a key link between Berlin and Brussels. Comprised of officials from across federal ministries, it is responsible for articulating the government's policy in committees which are within the Council hierarchy and where home-based officials or ministers are not in attendance. What is distinctive about the StV in Germany? First, ministerial autonomy is such that officials in the StV may act as if they are representatives of their ministry rather than of the collective government line. This situation is exacerbated by the fact that inter-ministerial disputes may not be resolved until they reach Cabinet level. By contrast with the British approach to co-ordination, where the principle is to reach an agreed policy early, Germany tends to do this at a late stage. Hence the StV may have the task of representing in Brussels a policy which is unresolved domestically. Second, this autonomy is scarcely helped by the fact that the StV receives instructions from two different federal ministries. Third, to add to this situation, the StV is the representation of the federal government, but there may be significant Länder interests to be taken into account. These circumstances lead to the StV having to pursue a rather difficult task. Especially where home-based officials are attending, officials from different German ministries may advocate quite different positions in Council working groups. This situation may make it difficult for negotiating alliances to be developed on more routine matters because of ambiguity about the German policy line. The Permanent Representative is also less 'plugged into' inter-ministerial co-ordination and preparation within the federal government than some of his counterparts. As a consequence of these circumstances, the StV has to conduct a diplomacy of improvisation which contrasts especially strongly with the more choreographed diplomacy of its British counterpart.[30]

PRIMACY OF POLICY OR PRIMACY OF PROCEDURES?

How may we characterise the resultant system of EU policy-making? It is slow, decentralised, complex and yet a system with a significant degree of flexibility at the later stages of bargaining.[31] Ministries do not always sing from the same European-policy hymn-sheet. Information is not readily shared between ministries, and policy is agreed late, often resulting in an incoherent German negotiating position in the intervening period. When inter-ministerial co-ordination occurs, it is sometimes a matter of damage-limitation, while discussion of an overall strategy is lacking.[32]

In addition, the difficulties of co-ordinating day-to-day policy with the Länder have intensified following the new arrangements in Article 23. The FRG has tended to be seen as good at European strategy but less good on tactics.[33] But this balance is challenged by the need to consult the Länder during preparations for IGCs, subjecting European-policy initiatives to additional party-political considerations and further bureaucratic constraints. For Janning and Meyer it is necessary to strengthen the primacy of policy over the primacy of procedures.[34]

Weighed against these criticisms we must bear in mind two overriding factors. First, can we judge Germany's European policy machinery from this one perspective? Vincent Wright reminds us that observing the machinery alone is insufficient: 'the effectiveness of a country's domestic EU co-ordinating capacity must be judged according to the issue, the policy type, the policy requirements and the policy objectives. Merely to examine the machinery of co-ordination is to confuse the means and the outcomes'.[35] The United Kingdom may have a well co-ordinated machinery but that has offered no assurance of a reliable European policy! In other words, we must recall the important shaping role that the FRG has had on the integration project as a whole. If the picture were simply one of bureaucratic confusion and institutional pluralism, German influence in the EU would not have been so great.[36] It was not just the domestic institutional resources open to Kohl's European strategy, but the fact that he was able politically to devote such energy to this policy area that was critical in this regard. Thus, it would be more indicative of a new German European policy if Germany abandoned its European strategy rather than if it continued to be hampered in its day-to-day policy by the factors outlined above. In that sense the *objectives* of European policy in the post-Kohl era must be examined as much as the policy machinery. Second, the weaknesses in the system of European policy-making are not confined to that policy area. The need for consensus and co-operative federalism are norms of the German political system. They are endemic to the domestic public finance system and to a host of other policy areas. That European policy has been absorbed into these norms reflects its character as 'domestic policy'. Fundamental reform of European policy-making would necessitate domestic constitutional change.

BILATERAL RELATIONS AND EUROPEAN POLICY-MAKING: HELP OR *HINDERNIS*?

Our critical evaluation of EU policy-making would be incomplete without giving due attention to the bilateral dimension, which is so important in the EU. In what follows we explain how bilateral relations can interact with the arrangements outlined already to further complicate Germany's European policy. Moreover, any effort to move towards a new German European policy has inevitable consequences for 'multiple bilateralism', illustrated here by the strongly established Franco-German partnership but also by the more fragile German–British relationship.

A crucial point is that German initiatives in the EU have tended to be developed in concert with the French. The Franco-German relationship was part of the founding myth of European integration and is at the heart of the view of the EU as a community of values and peace. That this relationship has become highly institutionalised is reflected in Boyer's calculation that there were 115 meetings between the German Chancellor and the French President between 1982 and 1992.[37] Links between the AA and its French counterpart are also particularly developed but they have extended to links between the technical ministries. In this way German initiatives in European policy are normally presented in Franco-German form. However, even at the level of day-to-day policy institutionalised relations with French counterparts may enter calculations. In the latter case the impact of bilateralism can be asymmetrical. The more tightly co-ordinated French system enables it to use bilateralism as an opportunity for a defined French position to be expressed to German counterparts. A clearly defined German position is much less likely to be available at an early stage of negotiations. Moreover, in the more loosely co-ordinated German system the consequence of bilateralism may be to reinforce sectorisation.

A specific illustration may be given by agricultural policy, where a French government might pursue a more protectionist policy as a matter of national interest. That French position might chime with the BML's interests. But the BML's position might not have been reconciled into the overall federal government position in Berlin/Bonn. The efforts which were made in Bonn to try to retain a joint position with the French during the Uruguay Round negotiations – despite apparently divergent interests – are indicative of this scenario.[38] But, as the Berlin European Council on Agenda 2000 showed, when President Chirac weakened the CAP reforms somewhat, institutionalised bilateralism may temper French interests much less than it does German ones. It is striking, then, that Paris secured this deal, closely corresponding to its original goals, whereas the Schröder government conceded on its wish for co-financing the CAP, a policy which would have reduced German contributions to the EC budget very substantially.

Eastern enlargement is an issue which raises tensions in the Franco-German relationship. France is concerned that enlargement will re-balance the EU in Germany's favour. Foreign Minister Fischer's endorsement of reinforced co-operation may provide a solution to such tensions by facilitating enlargement while enabling closer Franco-German co-operation at the centre of a 'pioneer group' in certain policy areas.[39]

The federal government's continuing commitment to the Franco-German relationship reinforces continuity in the FRG's European policy. Despite the fact that France is willing to sacrifice bilateralism where it clashes with its national interests, the German elite has tended to see the relationship more as transcending such considerations. A new European policy would necessitate the taking of a different German approach to the Franco-German relationship, such as a more instrumental use of it alongside other bilateral relationships. Suggestions of a move from continuity arose with a debate in late 1997 that was concerned with the issue of whether German policy was becoming more 'British', sparked by an article in the *Frankfurter Allgemeine Zeitung*: 'Wird die deutsche Europapolitik britischer'?[40] This was a reference to a possibly more hard-nosed policy, but the evidence of this actually taking place is unclear. The debate was certainly prompted by the then federal government's attempt to shape the agenda regarding German budgetary contributions ahead of the Agenda 2000 negotiations. However, the rhetoric was not really matched by the nature of the deal which the subsequent government accepted in Berlin.

The election of a Red–Green coalition under Schröder caused some consternation in Paris and keen anticipation in London, as the prospect of a *ménage à trois* seemed possible. In reality, the outcome was a qualified form of continuity. The move on 1 January 1999 to the first stage of EMU left the United Kingdom on the sidelines. Moreover, Joschka Fischer restated the classic goals of AA foreign policy, including the primacy of the Franco-German relationship. Emphasising the potential of Franco-German relations to reinforce sectorisation, Oskar Lafontaine pursued close co-operation with the French Finance Minister, Dominique Strauss-Kahn, on counter-balancing the financial austerity written into the EMU rules. This line was at odds with the Bundesbank's view and Lafontaine's broad economic and financial strategy collapsed because of disagreement with Chancellor Schröder.

But if these developments seem to suggest continuity, it is arguably with Chancellor Schröder himself that the choices rest concerning the future of bilateral relations. While the British government was disappointed by the lack of headway in improving Anglo-German relations in the early months of the Red–Green coalition, progress was improved from January 1999. The Schröder/Blair paper bringing together 'die neue Mitte' and 'the third way' was clearly about embracing globalisation as a way of handling European competitiveness.[41] Were this policy to achieve results it would be a departure from Germany's previous position of defending the European (Rhineland) social model rather than embracing globalisation. There is an economic logic to this position, and it reflects the economic strategies of German companies like Daimler/Chrysler and Deutsche Bank, for whom corporate strategy is perceived in transatlantic and global terms rather than across the Rhine. That logic is at odds with France's more protectionist approach to the World Trade Organisation (WTO). Forthcoming WTO negotiations on agriculture could expose Franco-German differences to a marked degree.

There is, of course, a large element of speculation in these observations. However, they reveal that while the Franco-German relationship is a massive and institutionalised force for continuity, global changes may place it under pressure in the coming years. Such a development would have important implications for the patterns of European policy-making. It would also open up the possibility for a new German European policy based on greater pragmatism. But the asymmetrical character of bilateral relations with more co-ordinated governments like France and the UK is also revealed. Paradoxically, a more instrumental use of bilateral relations might result in an even more discordant German European policy.

CONCLUSION: NEW EUROPEAN POLICY OR INSTITUTIONALISED EMBEDDEDNESS

So has German European policy taken a new direction since the end of the Cold War? Or have entrenched institutional arrangements for policy-making constrained adaptation? In reality, the outcome has inclined towards continuity. In order to spell out our conclusions, we need to look first at the broader context.

An initial point to make is that the consequences of German unification and the end of the Cold War were not merely geo-political in nature. To assume in the aftermath of 1989 that 'Germany is back' was to fail to take into account the economic dimension of these events.[42] The costs of German unification were enormous and placed serious financial constraints on European policy. Only now is the dust settling. And this is happening at a time when European integration is experiencing some problems of acceptance in the FRG, notably because of the weakness of the Euro but also because of concerns about possible consequences of eastward enlargement. In addition, the Schröder government – including the Chancellor himself – has been preoccupied with the domestic reform agenda rather than EU issues: something of a legacy of inattention by Kohl to the former in favour of the latter.

The general pattern emerging in our analysis supports a scenario of continuity. There have been some improvements to the AA's powers and its capacity for action in Brussels ('Europafähigkeit'). But they have been offset by increased involvement by the Länder and the Interior and Finance ministries. What is quite clear is that the events of 1989/90 did not serve to trigger a fundamental shift in the institutional structure towards a more interest-driven policy. The absence of such a trigger for a centralising reform is not especially surprising. The end of the Cold War and German unification represented *a success* for the foreign and European policies of successive Bonn governments. Change of policy was not needed; nor was a change of the machinery. The later, post-Maastricht changes moved in the opposite direction: towards further decentralisation. And those of 1998 were largely about reshuffling responsibilities rather than creating a more efficient machinery. Moreover, at political level Joschka Fischer's policy has been to emphasise continuity of approach, including the Franco-German relationship, albeit with a willingness to give serious consideration to reinforced co-operation amongst a smaller group of states. Also supporting this interpretation is the government's wish to have the pre-existing commitment to EMU take effect rather than to pursue new policy directions. Chancellor Schröder's own European policy has not yet displayed a consistency: shifting between the language of national interests and 'die neue Mitte' forged through Anglo-German links.[43] The failure to secure the desired extent of CAP reform in the Agenda 2000 negotiations also harked back to past failures of German governments to make financial interests 'stick' in the EU. All these developments display elements of continuity.

But there is some scope for policy change. Thus, an alternative scenario sees the Finance Ministry in the ascendant in Berlin, as Eichel's prestige grows as a result of domestic reform achievements. At the time of the Berlin European Council (March 1999) he was still grappling with his brief in the immediate aftermath of Lafontaine's resignation, and Chancellor Schröder had to pull back from his instincts due to the need, during Germany's EU presidency, to broker a reform package on Agenda 2000. This second scenario might see Eichel exploiting the BMF's new responsibilities to pursue a European policy more strongly emphasising financial interests along the lines of Schröder's early rhetoric. Moreover, the Chancellor may himself have to respond to two related developments: the declining public enthusiasm for integration; and the more populist European policy of the CDU leader, Angela Merkel. Should the CDU/CSU seek to play up the issues of organised crime and immigration as possible consequences of enlargement ahead of the next *Bundestagswahl*, Schröder might have to take on a more hard-nosed approach himself to secure a further term of government. Should these developments come about – and we enter the realms of speculation here – then it will be as a result of the intersection of a set of factors rather than as a simple consequence of unification. These factors include the wider political and economic ramifications of both unification and enlargement; and the declining political consensus on European policy between the main parties. European business might become polarised along the Left–Right spectrum. In this regard, the ongoing party-group dynamics in the 1999–2004 European Parliament could spill back into the German arena, thus giving the electorate a more visible basis for selecting the next Parliament. In any event, the AA would be a strong force for continuity, and its position is relatively strong under Foreign Minister Fischer

NOTES

This is a revised version of the authors' article 'Das Entscheidungs- und Koordinationssystem deutscher Europapolitik: Hindernis für eine neue Politik?', in Mathias Jopp, Uwe Schmalz and Heinrich Schneider (eds.), *Neue deutsche Europapolitik. Kontinuität und Wandel nach 1990* (Bonn: Europa Union Verlag, 2001 forthcoming). We are grateful to the editors for permission to re-work this article here. We also acknowledge the support of the ASKO Europa-Stiftung in facilitating our work within that project.

1. For theoretical discussion, see Peter Katzenstein, 'United Germany in an Integrating Europe', in Peter Katzenstein (ed.), *Tamed Power: Germany in Europe* (Ithaca, NY: Cornell University Press, 1998), pp.1–48.
2. William E. Paterson, 'Beyond Semi-Sovereignty: The New Germany in the New Europe', *German Politics*, 5/2 (1996), pp.167–84.
3. See for instance Josef Janning and Patrick Meyer, 'Deutsche Europapolitk – Vorschläge zur Effektivierung', in Werner Weidenfeld (ed.), *Deutsche Europapolitik: Optionen wirksamer Interessenvertretung* (Bonn: Europa Union Verlag, 1998), pp.267–86.
4. Joachim-Jens Hesse and Klaus Goetz, 'Early Administrative Adjustment to the European Communities: The Case of the Federal Republic of Germany', in E. Heyen (ed.), *Jahrbuch der Europäischen Verwaltungsgeschichte*, No.4 (Baden-Baden: Nomos, 1992), pp.181–205.
5. Organisationserlaß des Bundeskanzlers, in *Bulletin des Presse- und Informationsamtes der Bundesregierung*, No.203, 30 Oct. 1957, p.1864. For analysis, see D. Koerfer, 'Zankapfel Europapolitik. Der Kompetenzstreit zwischen Auswärtigem Amt und Bundeswirtschaftsministerium 1957/58', *Politische Vierteljahresschrift*, 29/4 (1988), pp.553–68; Hesse and Goetz, 'Early Administrative Adjustment to the European Communities: The Case of the Federal Republic of Germany'.
6. See, for instance, Simon Bulmer and Martin Burch, 'Organizing for Europe: Whitehall, the British State and the European Union', *Public Administration*, 76/4 (1998), pp.601–28. On France, see Christian Lequesne, *Paris-Bruxelles: Comment se fait la politique européenne de la France* (Paris: Presses de la Fondation Nationale des Sciences Politiques, 1993).
7. On shaping the regional milieu, see Simon Bulmer, Charlie Jeffery and William E. Paterson, *Germany's European Diplomacy: Shaping the Regional Milieu* (Manchester: Manchester University Press, 2000).
8. It is worth pointing out that the European Council is seeking to encourage efficient domestic systems of European policy-making in order that the Council of Ministers can function effectively after eastward enlargement. See European Council of Helsinki, 10/11.12.1999, Conclusions of the Presidency, Annex III: An Effective Council for an

Enlarged Union, Guidelines for Reform and operational Recommendations, Point I.14. No major reform of machinery had emerged in Germany by early 2000.

9. An example of such personal views was Joschka Fischer's keynote speech in May 2000 at the Humboldt-Universität Berlin: see J. Fischer, 'Vom Staatenverbund zur Föderation – Gedanken über die Finalität der europäischen Integration', *Integration*, 3 (2000), pp.149–56. Fischer's views were subsequently endorsed by Chancellor Schröder.

10. A Cabinet Committee for European Policy existed for some years but was rarely used and has subsequently been abolished.

11. During the period 1969–72 Katherine Focke had been junior minister with this responsibility, but based in the Bundeskanzleramt.

12. See, for instance, Michèle Knodt, 'Auswärtiges Handeln der deutschen Länder', in Wolf-Dieter Eberwein and Karl Kaiser (eds.), *Deutschlands neue Außenpolitik: Band 4 Institutionen und Ressourcen* (München: R. Oldenbourg Verlag, 1998), pp.153–66.

13. Elfriede Regelsberger and Wolfgang Wessels, 'National Paper on the Federal Republic of Germany', in Colm O Nuallain (ed.), *The Presidency of the European Council of Ministers* (Beckenham: Croom Helm, 1985), p.80.

14. The terms are from the critique of EU policy making by Janning and Meyer, 'Deutsche Europapolitk – Vorschläge zur Effektivierung', p.275.

15. On the concept of Europeanisation of domestic politics and institutions see Andreas Maurer and Wolfgang Wessels, 'The EU Matters: Structuring Self-Made Offers and Demands', in Wolfgang Wessels, Andreas Maurer and Jürgen Mittag (eds.), *Fifteen into One? The European Union and its Member States* (Manchester: Manchester University Press, 2001 forthcoming); Robert Ladrech, 'Europeanization of Domestic Politics and Institutions. The Case of France', *Journal of Common Market Studies*, 32/1 (1994), p.68; Klaus Goetz, 'National Governance and European Integration. Intergovernmental Relations in Germany', *Journal of Common Market Studies*, 33/1 (1995), pp.91–116; Wolfgang Wessels, 'Institutions of the EU System: Models of Explanation', in Dietrich Rometsch and Wolfgang Wessels (eds.), *The European Union and Member States* (Manchester: Manchester University Press, 1996), pp.20–36; Caitríona Carter and Andrew Scott, 'Legitimacy and Governance beyond the European Nation State: Conceptualizing Governance in the European Union', *European Law Review*, 4/4 (1998), pp.437–45; Simon Bulmer and Martin Burch, 'The Europeanisation of British Central Government', in Rod Rhodes (ed.), *Transforming British Government Vol. 1 – Changing Institutions* (London: Macmillan, 2000), pp.46–62.

16. For more on the changed circumstances, see Simon Bulmer and William E. Paterson, 'Germany in the European Union: Gentle Giant or Emergent Leader?', *International Affairs*, 72/1 (1996), pp.9–32.

18. Gregor Schöllgen, 'National Interest and International Responsibility; Germany's Role in World Affairs', in Arnulf Baring (ed.), *Germany's New Position in Europe* (Oxford: Berg, 1994), p.35. Also see other contributors to Baring.

17. Paterson, 'Beyond Semi-Sovereignty: The New Germany in the New Europe'.

19. On civilian power, see Hanns Maull, 'German Foreign Policy, Post-Kosovo: Still a "Civilian Power"?', *German Politics*, 9/2 (2000), pp.1–24.

20. We allude here to the argument of Paul Pierson in 'The Path to European Integration: A Historical-Institutionalist Analysis', in Wayne Sandholtz and Alec Stone Sweet (eds.), *European Integration and Supranational Governance* (Oxford: Oxford University Press, 1998), pp.27–58.

21. See, for instance, several contributions to Katzenstein, *Tamed Power*. For an explicitly identity-based interpretation of this problematique, see Stephen Wood, *Germany, Europe and the Persistence of Nations: Transformation, Interests and Identity* (Aldershot: Ashgate, 1998).

22. For more on the involvement of the Länder in EU policy-making, see Knodt, 'Auswärtiges Handeln der deutschen Länder'. Our chapter is only interested in the impact of the Länder on German European policy-making from a wider perspective.

23. Dr von Ploetz is now the FRG's Ambassador to the UK.
24. Draft minutes of the European Delegates meeting of 15 Dec. 1998, Auswärtiges Amt, Bonn, 18 Dec. 1998. COREPER II consists of ambassadors, that is, the head of the member state's Brussels Permanent Representation. It prepares meetings of the General Affairs, Development, Economics and Finance (Ecofin) formations of the Council of Ministers. COREPER I is made up of deputies and prepares the other Council formations. For fuller details on COREPER, see Fiona Hayes-Renshaw and Helen Wallace, *The Council of Ministers* (Basingstoke: Macmillan, 1997), pp.72–84.
25. For an internal assessment, see for instance the essay by Werner Hoyer, the then FDP Minister of State for European policy in the AA. Werner Hoyer, 'Nationale Entscheidungsstrukturen deutscher Europapolitik', in Eberwein, and Kaiser (eds.), *Deutschlands neue Außenpolitik: Band 4 Institutionen und Ressourcen*, pp.75–86.
26. Indicative of his impact on the debates during the IGC round was his Berlin speech, 'Vom Staatenverbund zur Föderation – Gedanken über die Finalität der europäischen Integration'.
27. See Heather Grabbe, 'The Sharp Edges of Europe: Extending Schengen Eastwards', *International Affairs*, 76/3 (2000), pp.519–36.
28. For a slightly fuller account, see Bulmer, Maurer and Paterson, 'Das Entscheidungs- und Koordinationssystem deutscher Europapolitik: Hindernis für eine neue Politik?'.
29. E. Gaddum, *Die deutsche Europapolitk in den 80er Jahren* (Paderborn: Verlag Ferdinand Schöningh, 1994), pp.73–4.
30. See Andreas Maurer and Wolfgang Wessels, 'Die Ständige Vertretung Deutschlands bei der EU – Scharnier im administrativen Mehrebenensystem', in Michèle Knodt and Beate Kohler-Koch (eds.), *Deutschland zwischen Europäisierung und Selbstbehauptung* (Frankfurt: Campus Verlag, 2000), pp.293–324.
31. See Dietrich Rometsch, 'The Federal Republic of Germany', in Dietrich Rometsch and Wolfgang Wessels (eds.), *The European Union and member States* (Manchester: Manchester University Press, 1996), p.102; Andreas Maurer, 'Germany – Fragmented Systems of a Congruent State', in Wessels *et al.* (eds.), *Fifteen into One*.
32. See Janning and Meyer, 'Deutsche Europapolitk – Vorschläge zur Effektivierung', p.274.
33. Hans-Ulrich Derlien, 'German EU Policy Coordination – "Failing Successfully"', in Hussein Kassim, Guy Peters and Vincent Wright (eds.), *The National Co-ordination of EU Policy. The Domestic Level* (Oxford: Oxford University Press, 2000), pp.54–78.
34. Janning and Meyer, 'Deutsche Europapolitk – Vorschläge zur Effektivierung', p.275.
35. Vincent Wright, 'The National Co-ordination of European Policy-Making: Negotiating the Quagmire', in Jeremy Richardson (ed.), *European Union: Power and Policy-Making* (London: Routledge, 1996), p.165.
36. For a review, see Simon Bulmer, 'Shaping the Rules? The Constitutive Politics of the European Union and German Power', in Katzenstein (ed.), *Tamed Power*, pp.49–79.
37. Y. Boyer, 'France and Germany', in B. Heurlin, *Germany in Europe in the Nineties* (Basingstoke: Macmillan, 1996), p.243.
38. On the Uruguay Round negotiations, see Alice Landau, 'Bargaining over Power and Policy. The CAP Reform and Agricultural Negotiations in the Uruguay Round', *International Negotiation*, 3/3 (1998), pp.453–79.
39. See J. Fischer, 'Vom Staatenverbund zur Föderation – Gedanken über die Finalität der europäischen Integration'. Note in this respect, however, that Fischer is not willing to exclude Italy as a traditional German partner with regard to joint initiatives on the European Union's 'finalité politique'. The joint German–Italian paper on closer co-operation, presented to the Nice IGC on 6 Oct. 2000 (CONFER 4783/00) clearly reflects the idea of Fischer to shape any kind of 'pioneering' group together with the founding Six.
40. See Peter Hort, 'Die deutsche Europa-Politik wird "britischer". Bonn stellt das Integrationsmodell in Frage und orientiert sich mehr an Kosten und Nutzen', *Frankfurter Allgemeine Zeitung*, 30 Oct. 1997, p.16.

41. See 'Der Weg nach vorne für Europas Sozialdemokraten. Ein Vorschlag von Gerhard Schröder und Tony Blair', Bonn, 1999.
42. Schöllgen, 'National Interest and International Responsibility: Germany's Role in World Affairs'.
43. On his rhetoric of national interests, see Bulmer *et al.*, *Germany's European Diplomacy*, pp.109–11.

Abstracts

Introduction: German European and Foreign Policy Before and After Unification, *by Douglas Webber*

The pre-unification European and foreign policy of the 'old' Federal Republic was marked by four principal traits: an emphatically Western orientation, a strong commitment to multilateralism underpinned by close bilateral relations with France and the US, its civilian character, and Euro-centrism. Although it took place in radically different circumstances and under radically different conditions to the first, the second German unification nonetheless gave rise to fears among the political leaders of many other states in Western, Central and Eastern Europe – and among the proponents of some international relations theories – that it would herald sweeping changes in Germany's foreign policy orientation and profoundly destabilise inter-state relations in Europe. The contributions to this volume show that, in the decade following the second unification, there has been more continuity than change in German European and foreign policy. The most important change concerns attitudes and behaviour in respect of the use of military force. Under the pressure of its Western allies and events in the Balkans which have forced it to choose between opposition to war and opposition to genocide, Germany has shed much of its earlier inhibitions concerning the use of military force and become much more like a 'normal' big power in Europe. However, because this trend has been explicitly encouraged and welcomed by Germany's allies and partners and because it has taken place exclusively within the multilateral frameworks of NATO and the EU, it does not presage the return of a political 'Frankenstein monster' or the revival of the pre-Second World War patterns of European inter-state rivalry. The second German unification will assuredly not turn out to be a re-run of the first.

Germany and the Kosovo War: Still a Civilian Power? *by Adrian Hyde-Price*

This article assesses the motives, significance and implications of Germany's participation in the 1999 Kosovo War. This was all the more remarkable, because it took place under a Red–Green government and was not legitimised by a UN mandate. Events in Kosovo forced the new government to choose between two foreign policy articles of faith of the German Left: 'nie wieder Krieg' ('never again war') and 'nie wieder Auschwitz' ('never again Auschwitz'). The government tried to ease this dilemma by flanking its participation in the war with intensive efforts to secure a negotiated settlement of the crisis involving Russia. Despite its participation in the war, Germany remains a 'civilian power', as it is committed to deploying military force strictly multilaterally. Kosovo shows that it has become a normal 'civilian power', comparable to other mature democracies in the Euro-Atlantic community.

Change and Continuity in Post-Unification German Foreign Policy, *by Sebastian Harnisch*

Ten years after unification, Germany still maintains its post-Second World War foreign policy course based on transatlantic multilateralism and European integration despite changes in Germany's international and domestic contexts. This study argues that neither realist nor institutionalist explanations can explain the post-unification pattern of German foreign policy. Instead, continuity and change in this policy can be understood best through a role-theoretical approach based on the civilian power ideal-type. Two causal pathways are developed which account for continuity in foreign policy orientation (goals) and strategies while explaining change in the choice of foreign policy instruments. First, the apparent success of Germany's traditional foreign policy role concept during and after unification helped to reify a broad foreign policy consensus around the goals and strategies of an ideal-type civilian power. Second, major foreign policy crises, such as the Yugoslavian wars, stirred the long held hierarchy between the core values of reticence *vis-à-vis* the use of force (never again German militarism) and the special German responsibility to prevent genocide (never again Auschwitz). The interaction between domestic and foreign expectations provides a promising source for explaining change and continuity in Germany's foreign policy role concept and behaviour.

Germany and the Use of Military Force: 'Total War', the 'Culture of Restraint' and the Quest for Normality, *by Rainer Baumann and Gunther Hellmann*

For most of the past century, Germany's attitudes towards and practices of war have deviated from those of other Western countries. After the conduct of war had been pushed to new extremes during the Third Reich, following the Second World War Germans turned into zealous proponents of anti-militarism. Since the late 1980s, the discrepancy between Germany and its Western partners has, however, been shrinking, as Germany has shown a growing readiness to contribute to international military operations. This study examines these changes, paying particular attention to the interplay of public attitudes, political discourse and concrete foreign policy behaviour. Many observers maintain that the development of Germany's foreign policy behaviour on this issue has largely been a response to both (mostly international) structural incentives and (mostly domestic) structural constraints. In contrast, others view it as driven by a deliberate strategy of re-militarisation adopted by a small group of decision-makers. We argue that neither the structure- nor the actor-centred perspective is sufficient alone to understand the development of the German position on the use of military force. Thus, we assume a third perspective, stressing the co-constitutive effects of public and elite discourse, public attitudes and foreign policy behaviour. We substantiate our argument by examining the interplay of these three factors since the 1980s, paying special attention to the two most important conflicts of the 1990s, the Gulf War and the Kosovo War.

Recasting the Security Bargains: Germany, European Security Policy and the Transatlantic Relationship, *by Alister John Miskimmon*

This article analyses recent developments in European Union (EU) security policy and their implications for Germany's bilateral relations with France, the United Kingdom and the United States of America. It contends that the development of a greater EU security capability has significantly affected Germany's bilateral relations with the USA and Germany's main European partners. This has resulted in a recasting of the previous transatlantic security bargains of the Cold War period. Greater expectations on behalf of France and the UK concerning German involvement in military security within the Common European Security and Defence Policy (CESDP) have also affected Germany's approach to security policy-making.

Germany in Europe: Return of the Nightmare or Towards an Engaged Germany in a New Europe? *by Wolfgang Wessels*

Especially since (re-)unification, perceptions of Germany alternate between the fear of the return of the German hegemon and – at the same time – the diametrically opposed call for more German leadership based on Germany's outstanding pro-European engagement. Nonetheless, Germany's foreign policy has changed little since 1989: it is still cautious rather than assertive. Due to Germany's experience with the two world wars, German foreign policy places great value on the enlargement as well as the deepening of the EU. In sum, Germany can best be characterised as a normal and engaged European state.

Germany's Power and the Weakening of States in a Globalised World : Deconstructing a Paradox, *by Anne-Marie Le Gloannec*

It is somewhat ironical to ponder Germany's power at a time when radical changes due to globalisation vastly limit the efficiency of state actions world-wide. Certainly, Germany's resources increased with reunification – though the country also has to bear its costs. An enumeration of the – possible – resources of German power provides us, however, with little understanding of the nature of German power, embedded as the country is in a European system from which it derives its strength. Hence, only an analysis of this system fully renders the picture, contrary to what neo-realists and liberals might assume. While Germany did exercise a semi-hegemony over Western Europe in the monetary area up to EMU, the further integration of the EU has altered the European structure and diffused Germany's power. A particular configuration allowed Germany to devise one-sidedly the rules of EMU. This configuration does not exist in other issue-areas, such as, for example, defence and enlargement. This does not mean that power is absent from Germany's tool-box: political credit in particular is abundant. Yet in a larger Europe, where coalitions are more issue-oriented and hence more volatile than formerly, Germany's power will turn out to be more limited than its demands for recognition may lead us to believe.

Germany, *Quo Vadis*? A View from the Diplomatic World, *by Philippe De Schoutheete*

Viewed from the heart of the EU in Brussels, German European policy has not been significantly altered by unification. A major reason for this policy continuity is the stability of the composition of German's foreign policy 'establishment' in the federal bureaucracy as well as in the political parties. For a combination of reasons, including the economic conjuncture, the enhanced European policy role of the Länder governments, and the lack of socialisation of east Germans into the European project after the Second World War, the political climate has, however, grown more hostile to closer integration. This may prove though to be a conjunctural phenomenon, which will change with an upturn of the German economy. There will be no 'Britishisation' of German European policy.

Germany, *Quo Vadis*? A View from Poland, *by Jerzy Kranz*

The transformation of Polish–German relations since the end of the Cold War has been a success story. The two countries are linked by a community of interests founded on common values and goals. Although Germany, in its policies towards Central and Eastern Europe, occasionally attaches too much weight to trying to mollify Russia, the united Germany has supported the Eastern enlargement of the EU and, ultimately, of the NATO. It genuinely wants 'Western' neighbours to its east. German foreign policy will continue to be characterised by continuity, with a strong emphasis on multilateralism. There is a danger, however, that Germany's European engagement and support for closer integration will be weakened by its preoccupation with its domestic economic and social problems.

German Foreign Policy and Transatlantic Relations since Unification, *by Andrew Denison*

Looking at German foreign policy and transatlantic relations since unification, this article argues that fundamental views and principles about Germany's role in Europe and the world have endured. The integrationist impulse remains strong. As shown by Kosovo, Germans have put this multilateralism above qualms about the use of military force. This has also left Berlin and Washington continuing to share many objectives, not only traditional ones about power and peace in Europe, but also on a whole host of challenges that have come with globalisation, both in the wider world and in the multiplicity of commercial and civil relationships across the Atlantic.

The European Policy-Making Machinery in the Berlin Republic: Hindrance or Handmaiden? *by Simon Bulmer, Andreas Maurer and William Paterson*

This article examines European policy-making in the Berlin Republic. The basic puzzle explored is whether the policy machinery is able to facilitate the projection of a 'new European policy', characterised by greater emphasis upon national interests. In order to suggest answers, the article reviews the origins of the policy machinery and the changes made in the pre-unification period. It then explores the current situation in the Berlin Republic. It argues that the legacies of the past – institutional pluralism and the post-war adoption of a European identity – are not easily cast off. Although the machinery has been reorganised since 1990, notably under the Schröder/Fischer coalition, and there have been some adjustments to bilateral relations, a new European policy has not yet emerged, although it is a possible future scenario.

Notes on Contributors

Rainer Baumann is Lecturer in International Relations at the Institute for Comparative Politics and International Relations, Johann Wolfgang Goethe University of Frankfurt. His main interests include German foreign policy, European security and international relations theory.

Simon Bulmer is Jean Monnet Professor of European Politics at the University of Manchester. His research interests include Germany and the EU, and European Union governance and new institutionalism. Recent publications include *Germany's European Diplomacy: Shaping the Regional Milieu* (with Charlie Jeffery and Willie Paterson, 2000), and *The Governance of the Single European Market* (with Kenneth Armstrong, 1998). He has also worked on European policy and policy-making in Britain. His current research projects are concerned with the EU as a medium of policy transfer and European policy-making in a devolved Britain.

Andrew Denison is director of Transatlantic Networks, a research consultancy focusing on foreign and defence policy, in Königswinter, Germany. He co-operates in Transatlantic Networks with a variety of organisations and institutions in Europe and the United States, lectures regularly to various publics in Germany, and serves as a commentator on German radio and television. He was a faculty associate at the Department of Political Science, University of Bonn from 1997 to 2000.

Sebastian Harnisch is currently Associate Professor of International Relations at the University of Trier. With Wolfgang Brauner he directs the online project on German foreign policy. His recent publications include *Foreign Policy Learning* (2000, in German), *Nuclear Weapons in North Korea* (with Hanns W. Maull, 2000, in German) and, co-edited with Hanns Maull, *Germany – Still a Civilian Power?* (forthcoming, 2001). He is currently researching Germany's foreign and security policy process.

Gunther Hellmann is Professor of Political Science at the Institute for Comparative Politics and International Relations, Johann Wolfgang Goethe University of Frankfurt and Head of the Research Group on International Organisation of the Peace Research Institute Frankfurt (HSFK). His research interests are in the fields of international relations theory, German foreign policy and European foreign and security policy.

Adrian Hyde-Price is Senior Lecturer in the International Politics of Central Europe at the Institute for German Studies, University of Birmingham. His current research interests include German relations with East-Central Europe and the implications for European order of the dual enlargement of NATO and the EU. He has published numerous articles in books and journals, and his most recent books are *Germany and European Order: Enlarging NATO and the EU* (2000), and *Security and Identity in Europe: Exploring the New Agenda* (edited with Lisbeth Aggestam, 2000).

Jerzy Kranz is Polish Ambassador to the Federal Republic of Germany. He studied at the universities of Poznañ and Warsaw. After having worked for 15 years at the Institute for Legal Sciences at the Polish Academy of Sciences, he joined the Polish foreign service. From 1990 to 1995, he worked at the Polish Embassy in Germany, for the last three years as envoy. From 1995 to 1997 he was deputy director of the Centre for International Relations at the Institute of Public Affairs in Warsaw. Before becoming Poland's Ambassador to Germany in 2001, he was Deputy State Secretary in the Polish Ministry of Foreign Affairs.

Anne-Marie Le Gloannec is currently Deputy Director of the Centre Marc Bloch in Berlin and a research associate at CERI (Centre d'Etudes et des Recherches Internationales), Paris. She has taught in Paris, Berlin and Bologna. Her research focuses on the role of Germany in Europe, the German state and the state in Europe.

Andreas Maurer is a Research Fellow attached to the Jean Monnet Chair for Political Science, University of Cologne, and Deputy Secretary General of the Trans-European Policy Studies Association, Brussels. Research and teaching focus on European Union–member state relations, the analysis of institutional developments in the EU's policy-making arenas and the theory and practice of European parliamentarism. Recent publications include *Fifteen into One? The European Union and its Member States* (ed. with Wolfgang Wessels and Jürgen Mittag, 2001), *Le pouvoir renforcé du Parlement Européen après Amsterdam* (2000), and *What Next for the European Parliament?* (1999).

Alister Miskimmon is a doctoral candidate at the Institute for German Studies, University of Birmingham. He studied previously at the University of Stirling, Scotland and the University of Trier, Germany. His thesis deals with Germany's role in the development of the EU's common foreign and security policy in the 1990s.

William E. Paterson is Professor of German Politics and the Director of the Institute for German Studies at the University of Birmingham. In 1999, he was awarded the Officer's Cross (Bundesverdienstkreuz) of the Federal Republic of Germany and the OBE by Queen Elizabeth II for scholarship in German studies. Professor Paterson is on the Advisory Board of the Centre for British Studies at Humboldt University Berlin, and is the Vice Chairman of the German–British Forum. His latest books include *Germany's European Diplomacy* (with Simon Bulmer and Charlie Jeffery, 2000), *The Future of the German Economy* (co-edited with Rebecca Harding, 2000) and *The Kohl Chancellorship* (co-edited with Clay Clemens, 1998).

Philippe de Schoutheete, a retired Belgian diplomat, has been involved for a long time in European affairs. He was political director at the Belgian Foreign Ministry from 1985 to 1987 and then served for ten years, until 1997, as Permanent Representative to the European Union. He was one of the negotiators of the treaties of Maastricht and Amsterdam. He now teaches at the Institut d'Etudes Européennes at the University of Louvain and serves as special adviser to European Commissioner Michel Barnier. His latest book, *Une Europe pour Tous* (1997), is published in English under the title, *The Case for Europe* (2000).

Douglas Webber is Associate Professor of Political Science at INSEAD (European Institute of Business Administration), currently based at the institute's Asian campus in Singapore. He worked at INSEAD's campus at Fontainebleau, France from 1991 to 1999. From 1995 to 1997, he was a Jean Monnet Fellow at the European University Institute, Florence. He has published numerous articles and co-authored two books on German and European politics. Most recently he edited *The Franco-German Relationship in the European Union* (1999). Apart from German domestic politics and foreign policy, his research interests include the theory and practice of European integration, EU agricultural and trade politics, the Franco-German relationship, regional integration in East Asia and Asia-Pacific and democratisation and marketisation processes in post-Communist Europe.

Wolfgang Wessels holds the Jean Monnet Chair at the Institute of Political Science and European Affairs, University of Cologne, and has recently been a visiting professor at the Institut d'Etudes Politiques in Paris and at the Robert Schuman Centre for Advanced Studies at the European University Institute, Florence. He is chairman of the board of the Institut für Europäische Politik, Bonn and of the Trans-European Policy Studies Association (TEPSA), Burssels. Recent publications include *Die Öffnung* *des Staates. Modelle und Wirklichkeit grenzüberschreitender Verwaltungspraxis 1960–1995* (2000); *Fifteen into One? The European Union and its member states* (with Andreas Maurer and Jürgen Mittag, 2000); and 'The Amsterdam Treaty in Theoretical Perspectives' (with Jörg Monar), in *The Treaty of Amsterdam: Analysis and Prospects* (2000).

Index